History of the Principal Events of the Reign of Frederic William Ii., King of Prussia
by Louis-Philippe Comte De Ségur

Copyright © 2019 by HardPress

Address:
HardPress
8345 NW 66TH ST #2561
MIAMI FL 33166-2626
USA
Email: info@hardpress.net

H 758.01.1

Bought of
Little & Brown,
with the
Library Fund
subscribed in 1842.
Rec'd March 10,
1843

HISTORY
OF
THE PRINCIPAL EVENTS
OF
THE REIGN
OF
FREDERIC WILLIAM II.
KING OF PRUSSIA;
AND
A POLITICAL PICTURE OF EUROPE,
FROM 1786 TO 1796.
CONTAINING A SUMMARY OF THE
REVOLUTIONS
OF
BRABANT, HOLLAND, POLAND, AND FRANCE.
IN THREE VOLUMES.

By L. P. SEGUR, the Elder,
FORMERLY AMBASSADOR OF LOUIS XVI. AT ST. PETERSBURG, BERLIN, AND VIENNA.

" Quod verum atque decens curo et rogo, et omnis in hoc fum."
HOR.

TRANSLATED FROM THE FRENCH.

VOL. III.

LONDON:
PRINTED FOR T. N. LONGMAN AND O. REES, PATER-NOSTER-ROW;
BY H. BALDWIN AND SON, NEW BRIDGE-STREET.
1801.

14552.3
I.1160
H758.01.4

CONTENTS.

CHAP. X.

Division in the Convention between the Girond and the Mountain.—Trial and Death of Louis XVI.—Conquest of Nice, Savoy, Mentz and Frankfort.—Siege of Lisle.—Battle of Jemappe.—Invasion of Brabant.—Preparations of all Europe against France.—Rupture of France with England, Holland and Spain.—Dumouriez enters Holland. The Austrians raise the Siege of Maestricht.—They retake Brabant.—Battle of Nerwind.—Defection of Dumouriez.—Manifesto of the Prince de Cobourg.—Revolution of the 31st May . . . . Page 1

CHAP. XI.

New constitution of 1793.—It's duplicity.—The Dictatorial power is intrusted to the committees of public safety and of general safety.—Their tyranny.—Debasement of the Convention.—Proscription of the most energetic members.—Revolt of Lyons.—Insurrection of several departments.—Death of Marat.—Division among the tyrants.—Portrait of Robespierre.—Death of Custine; of Biron; of the Duke d'Orleans.—Toulon delivered up to the English.—Progress of Cobourg.—Success of the royalists in La Vendée.—Fury of the Jacobins, the Cordeliers and the Commune of Paris.—General armament in France.—Emission of assignats.—The King of Prussia takes Mentz.—The Prussians and Austrians force the lines of Weissemberg, invest Landau and menace Strasbourg.—Cobourg advances towards Landrecy.—Errors of the coalition and the royalists.—Cruelty of the French government.—Death of the Queen and Madame Elizabeth.—Toulon is retaken.—Lyons is subdued and destroyed.—The Spaniards driven from Roussillon.—La Vendée depopulated and sacked.—The Duke of Brunswick and the Austrians are defeated and driven from Alsace.—The English are put to flight near Dunkirk.—Priests, nobles and persons of property are every where imprisoned and massacred. Terror reaches all classes and sexes.—Death of Danton.—Division among the coalesced powers.—The King of Prussia thinks of withdrawing from the coalition.—He invades Great Poland.—Battle of Fleurus.—Successes of Jourdan and Pichegru.—Second conquest of Brabant.—Fury and delirium of the Decemvirs.—Division among them.—Revolution of the 9th Thermidor, and Death of Robespierre . . . . . . Page 48.

CHAP. XII.

Revolution of Poland.—Perfidiousness of the courts of Petersburg and Berlin.—Contradictory declarations of Frederic William.—His troops enter Poland.—Diet of Grodno.—Violence exerted over the Diet.—Treaty extorted.—Insurrection of the Poles.—Character and conduct of Kosciosko.—He takes Cracow, and defeats the Prussians.—Revolution at Warsaw.—The Russians are driven from that city.—Advantages of the Poles at Vilna, and in several other actions. Frederic William besieges Warsaw.—Insurrection in Great Poland.—Frederic William raises the siege of Warsaw

CONTENTS.

Warsaw and retreats.—Suvaroff enters Poland. Kosciosko betrayed, loses a battle fought against Fersen.—He is wounded and taken prisoner.—Suvaroff besieges Warsaw; takes by assault the suburb of Prague.—Horrible massacre.—Warsaw surrenders.—Dispersion of the Polish troops.—Stanislaus Angustus quits his capital, and goes first to Grodno, and afterwards to Petersburg.—Total partition and enslavement of the Poles, ... Page 124

CHAP. XIII.

Influence of the revolution of Poland on the minds of the French.—Their ardour against the coalition.—Conquest of Holland.—Flight of the Stadtholder.—Revolution in Holland.—Abolition of the Stadtholderate.—Conspiracy of the Jacobins.—Accusation and transportation of the Colleagues of Robespierre.—Revolution of Prairial.—Fortitude of Boissy-d'Anglas.—Errors of the Convention.—Reaction in the south.—New Constitution.—Events of the 13th Vendemaire.—Negociations of Barthelemy.—Treaty of peace between the Republic, the King of Prussia, the Landgrave of Hesse, and the King of Spain.—Neutrality of the north of the Empire.—Dissolution of the coalition.—Campaign on the Rhine.—The French forced to repass it.—Inaction of the King of Prussia.—End of the reign of Frederic William II.—His death, hopes conceived of his successor.—A slight view of the events which passed in the last two years of his reign.—Campaigns of Bonaparte and Moreau.—Conclusion of this History. . . . . Page 163.

APPENDIX.

Extract from Mr. Pitt's speech in the House of Commons, on the 9th Feb. 1790 . . . . Page 231.

Letter

CONTENTS.

Letter from the King of Prussia to the Count de Goltz .. 232.

Declaration of the Ministers of Russia and Prussia, to the confederation of Poland .... 233.

Answer of the King of Prussia, to the King of Poland, dated Berlin, 8th June 1792 .... 238.

Declaration of the King of Prussia, on the affairs of Poland .... 241.

Answer of the King of Poland to the notes of the courts of Berlin and Petersburg .... 249.

Letter from the Duke of Brunswick to the King of Prussia, 250.

Treaty of peace between the French Republic and his Majesty the King of Prussia .... 254.

Convention between the French Republic and his Majesty the King of Prussia .... 259.

Treaty of peace between the French Republic and his Majesty the King of Spain .... 264.

Treaty of peace between the French Republic and the Landgrave of Hesse-Cassel .... 271.

Summary narrative of the circumstances which attended the detention of Latour Maubourg, Bureau de Puzy, la Fayette, and his family .... 275.

Note respecting Poland .... 289.

HISTORY
OF
THE REIGN
OF
FREDERIC WILLIAM II.

KING OF PRUSSIA;

AND

A POLITICAL PICTURE OF EUROPE.

CHAP. X.

Division in the Convention between the Gironde and the Mountain.—Trial and Death of Louis XVI.—Conquest of Nice, Savoy, Mentz and Frankfort.—Siege of Lisle.—Battle of Jemappe.—Invasion of Brabant.—Preparations of all Europe against France.—Rupture of France with England, Holland and Spain.—Dumouriez enters Holland. The Austrians raise the Siege of Maestricht.—They retake Brabant.—Battle of Nerwind.—Defection of Dumouriez.—Manifesto of the Prince de Cobourg.—Revolution of the 31st May.

1792.] THE invasion of the Prussians had lost Louis XVI. his crown and liberty, and their retreat did not save his life. Frederic William had committed

committed an obvious error, by exasperating a part of the French people, in reducing to despair the revolutionary party by threats which doubled their activity and strength, and by exciting the popular distrust against all those who wished to support the throne, and defend the constitution; but this error could only be retrieved by some triumph; it was, on the contrary, aggravated by retiring. The existence of the French monarch appeared too dangerous to the men who had just imprisoned him; lest a tardy moderation might disarm a hatred, of which fear was the principle and the sustenance; and as a blind imprudence had exposed the King's life: victory alone could save it.

It was no longer a time to depend on the principles of justice and the sentiments of humanity; to these, political fanaticism and religious fanaticism, are equally foreign. Those bold men, who without consulting the will of the nation, had violently changed a monarchy into a republic, were placed on a precipice; the opposition of the majority of the people, the resistance of the constitutionalists, the hatred of the friends of order, and the vengeance of the laws, surrounded them with danger; and, to prevent their perishing in this abyss, they resolved to fill it up with the wrecks of the throne,

throne, of the aristocracy and the wealthy. Fear always produces tyrants; and from the moment that a government knows it is hated, it feels the necessity of being dreaded, and endeavours to dispel its own terrors, by those which itself inspires.

The coalition, by its rash attack, its irritating manifestoes, the pillage and disorders committed by its troops, completely seconded the views of the revolutionists of the 10th of August.

The people and the army, who would perhaps have condemned that revolution, sanctioned it by their silence, because a foreign invasion had attracted to the frontiers the whole activity and energy of the nation. All the parties which were divided united together against this common danger; and the interest in favour of the throne was weakened by the hatred which was felt against the Kings who called themselves its allies. Every thing then combined to complete the triumph not only of the republicans, but even that of the anarchists.

The deluded people thought the court perjured, when they saw foreigners conquering and ravaging France in its name; they conceived all the nobles to be traitors, when they saw their kindred ranged under the standards of the enemy; all the rich, enlightened, and moderate

rate became suspected by them, because these wished the maintenance of order and justice. The retreat of the Prussians, the success of Custine, the triumphs of Dumouriez filled up the measure of popular intoxication ; the constitutionalists had contended without means and without success ; their misfortune was regarded as a crime ; the revolutionists were victorious, and every thing they had done was considered as necessary ; the pretext of the public safety excused their crimes, which fortune covered over with a brilliant but perfidious gloss ; and the dazzled multitude enthusiastically followed those factious men who flattered their passions, promising places to ignorance, and riches to the poor.

The King's life was then become the only object of fear in the conquering party ; every moment the misfortunes of this Prince might excite pity, awaken justice, and revive monarchy. Robespierre, Danton, Marat, and their adherents resolved on his death, and the destruction of those by whom it should be opposed. It was an easy matter for them to sacrifice him privately ; but a legal condemnation and a public death seemed to them more beneficial ; they hoped, by taking advantage of the fanaticism excited by the coalition, the terror produced by by the massacres of September, and the intoxication inspired by the flight of the Prussians, that they might constrain the nation to permit that attempt, to sanction their revolution, and to bind themselves to their system. Their hope was gratified.

A great number of deputies on the most violent side of the legislative body had been returned members of the convention. Brissot, Petion, Vergniaux, and their friends, almost all remarkable for their talents and their eloquence, formed what was called the party of the *Gironde*. Republicans in opinion, they had by their intrigues contributed to weaken the constitutional throne, but had not at all taken a share in the conspiracy which overturned it. The 20th of June was their work, and their aim at that time appeared to be to govern France by ministers of their own choice. The revolution of the 10th of August had been conducted by Danton, Robespiere, Chabot, Barbaroux, Fabre d'Eglantine, Collot d'Herbois, and the members of the new *Commune* of Paris. These terrible revolutionists, the formidable mass of whom assumed the Name of the *Mountain*, aspired at reaping the fruit of their boldness, and governing the republic which they had created. The Girondists wished to dispute with them the honour and the advantages of this revolution, though they falsely boasted of, and slowly concurred in it. They were at first supported in their plans by the public wish, and by the majority of their colleagues who detested the tyrannical system, and the sanguinary designs of their adversaries. Thus from the commencement of the sittings of the convention, it was divided into two parties, whose violent struggle evidently announced new storms.

Though, for several months the Girondists appeared to have a decided advantage over their rivals, it was easy to foresee that in this contest they must succumb.

Compelled to excuse crimes, to sanction the violation of the laws, to maintain the code of spoliation which had destroyed the morals of the people, it was in vain they endeavoured to stop the revolution, whose impetus they had accelerated; they had promulgated too many iniquitous decrees to be able to restore justice, inflamed too many resentments to regenerate moderation, and too much favoured anarchy to re-establish order.

Their latter intentions were laudable; but the change of their language rendered them suspected by the multitude, to whom the party of the Mountain appeared more patriotic and more

in

in earneſt. They forgot that thoſe who begin revolutions never finiſhed them; and that they loſe the right and the power of repreſſing factions, when they have themſelves been factious.

The Girondiſts in ſuperſeding the conſtitutionaliſts ought to have foreſeen their own fate. They wiſhed to oppoſe principles to paſſions, reaſon to intoxication, juſtice to cupidity; they were only orators, whilſt their enemies were conſpirators; and in civil broils, fortune is always in favour of the perſon who ſtrikes againſt him who ſpeaks.

The trial of the King was the firſt important conteſt between the two parties; and his death the firſt defeat of the Gironde; for, though ſeveral of this party had ſtained themſelves by his condemnation, it appeared that their intention was to ſave him; and in this reſpect they were equally deficient in conduct and in courage. The King had been accuſed of crimes antecedent to his acceptance of the conſtitution; and of the general amneſty that had effaced every thing; which was truly abſurd. He was reproached with not having accepted the conſtitution with ſincerity; with having favoured the emigrants, and with having been in connivance with foreign enemies. None of theſe accuſations were accompanied by proofs. But even ſuppoſing it had

had been proved that he wished to change the constitution, his ministers only were responsible; and it was not they, who had so lately destroyed the constitution, that could make it a crime in him not to have loved it. Besides, the republic had been decreed; Louis XVI. was no longer King; his deposition, the only punishment that could be inflicted by the constitution, was in fact pronounced; and he could no longer, according to the rules of justice, be proceeded against but for subsequent crimes. Policy as much as equity opposed his death, since his execution might render the war more cruel and more general. Lastly, humanity ought to shudder at the bare idea of taking away the life of an enemy vanquished and disarmed. But the passions neither listen to justice, policy, nor humanity; and, unfortunately, the party who wished to defend the King were as weak and divided, as those who were determined on his death, were strong and united.

The infallible means to save Louis XVI. was to oppose his sentence. It was on so serious an occasion the most advantageous ground on which they could place themselves for the contest; in fact the convention was not competent, the Prince was not amenable. If it were desirous to accuse the King of not having been faithful

to

to the constitution, it was the constitution only that ought to be consulted; this had declared the monarch to be inviolable: and if he had been guilty of any crimes, that same constitution which had foreseen them had decided, *that the ministers alone were responsible.* Unfortunately, five deputies excepted, no one saw clearly enough, or had sufficient courage to maintain this principle. The terror which the revolution of the 10th of August had inspired, and the apprehension of declaring themselves against it, misled those who were the most determined to save the King; all the Girondists who had declared in favour of this revolution, thought they condemned themselves if they condemned it. Thus the whole party who voted against the death of the King, had the fatal folly to begin by declaring him culpable and amenable. This first error must necessarily have given a great advantage to the Mountain. When a tribunal is acknowledged competent, and has declared the innocent to be guilty, the possibility of saving them is nearly lost. In contempt of that constitution which no longer existed, but which they still dared to quote, and without regard to all the principles of probity, to all the maxims of jurisprudence, and to all rules of morality, men who had violated all laws pretended to avenge them; and impudently

impudently dared to act at once as legiflators, magiftrates, denunciators, witneffes, accufers and judges.

The fpeeches which were delivered during this celebrated trial, evinced that the party determined to take away the King's life, had come to that determination from different motives. Some gloomy and cruel politicians thought, by his death, to fecure their own exiftence, and that of the republic; others, from a blind fanaticifm, thought himfelf each a Brutus, and regarded Louis as a tyrant. The greateft number obeyed only from terror, and profcribed from fear of being profcribed.

1793.] The unfortunate monarch appeared before this affembly, whofe jurifdiction he ought not to have acknowledged, and in which he found only divided friends, and implacable enemies; he carried thither the firmnefs of virtue, the coolnefs of courage, and the fimplicity of innocence. His anfwers were as precife as the queftions were infidious; and this dignified defence, without art and without preparation, would have fufficed to give a triumph to truth, if it had been heard by juftice and not by paffion.

Louis XVI. had for defenders Deféze and Tronchet, whofe talents and probity were efteemed, and who from their courage will live in the minds of posterity. Malesherbes, whom they had pointed out to him, braving the rage of proscribers, also undertook his defence. We cannot pronounce this name without respect, nor without shedding tears of sorrow and admiration.

Virtuous without pride, learned without pedantry, a minister without ambition, this illustrious magistrate, the friend of men, of the laws, of letters, and of the arts, distinguished in every way, and never deviating from true glory, was ever the supporter of the people, whilst the King was powerful in his palace; he never became a courtier till the moment the Prince was in prison. The supporter of national liberty against the abuses of the monarchy, and the defender of the monarch against popular tyranny, his probity remained uncontaminated in the midst of the general corruption; his courage unshaken when fear was universal. He perished whilst crime reigned; the most heroic death crowned the most noble life, and the infamous scaffold, which he ascended without emotion, was the last point from which his pure soul rushed towards immortality.

The defence, drawn up by these three experienced advocates, and digested by Deféze, was correct, noble and convincing; it opposed truth to calumnies,

calumnies, facts to suppositions, and reason to opprobrium. It left no doubt uncleared, no reproach un-refuted. This luminous speech dissipated, by its perspicuity, all the shades which party spirit endeavoured to extend over the minds of a fanatical multitude.

If the question had been only to carry conviction into all minds, this speech would have completely attained its aim; but it was necessary to contend with the passions, and perhaps the assistance of a pathetic eloquence would have been necessary to be added to the most acute deductions of logic.

Never had a subject more noble and more affecting presented itself to the talents of an orator. A powerful monarch precipitated from the height of his throne into a dungeon; a King, unarmed, pursued by enemies without pity; the humane legislator who had abolished torture; the protector of America, the liberator of the slaves of Jura; the voluntary restorer of French liberty, fettered by the people whom he wished to make free; the feeling and pacific man, persecuted by implacable proscribers whose blood he had spared, and who were desirous to shed his; the contest of kindness against hatred, virtue against crime, and courage against destiny; the picture of all the misfortunes his death would

would occasion; the vengeance this attempt would excite; the frightful description of the remorse which must eternally goad his judges; all these means so well calculated to re-animate courage, to awaken sensibility, and to terrify hatred were forbidden by Louis XVI. to his defenders; and when Deféze presented to him the affecting peroration which was to terminate his speech, this Prince desired him to suppress it, and said to him: *I will not appeal to the passions.*

The deputies who spoke against his death, in vain displayed the arguments of an enlightened reason, a political foresight, and a generous humanity; their terrible adversaries, so much more vehement as their cause was more unjust, at last obtained, in spite of the firmness of their opponents, a fatal triumph. The death of Louis XVI. was decided by a majority of five voices. It was in vain that Malesherbes and his colleagues protested against the illegality of this decree; the criminal code required the majority of two thirds towards the condemnation of every one who was accused: but the predominant party was determined to regard no law; and the ferocious Danton audaciously answered: "*That when the Convention decided on the destiny of an empire by a simple majority of voices,*

it

it was absurd to be stopt by vain forms, when the question was to judge a tyrant."

The members who wished to save the King in vain voted for an appeal to the people; they then strove without success to obtain a suspension of the sentence till a peace. Their wishes were rejected; the decree was carried to the monarch, who supported this terrible trial with the dignity of his rank and the composure of virtue.

On the 21st of January 1793 he was decapitated; he died pardoning his enemies, and *praying Heaven to avert the misfortunes with which he saw France threatened by his death.*

The Parisians, dismayed, deplored without daring to defend him; foreign enemies shewed themselves more disposed to avenge than to succour him. Otcaritz, the envoy from Spain, alone made one noble attempt to prolong his life; and the terror which chilled all souls in that fatal instant recalls to our remembrance what Tacitus says, speaking of the death of Galba

" *Isque habitus animorum fuit, ut pessimum*
" *facinus auderent pauci, plures vellent, omnes*
" *paterentur.**

---

* Such was the state of the public mind, that if an act the most atrocious were to be committed, some would be found who would dare to do it, many would be inclined to do it, and all would be disposed to suffer it to be done.

The

The confequences of this event were terrible. The party of the convention who had decreed the death of Louis XVI. from that inftant dreaded being expofed to the refentment of all thofe members who had voted otherwife, and of an immenfe majority of the French nation, terrified by this decree; as well as of the enemies of France, the number and hatred of which this tragical event increafed. Virtue only can be the principle of a republican government; and the Mountain, founding its power on an injuftice fo ftriking, was by its own act condemned to the neceffity of exercifing a tyrannical power.

Men deftitute of morality were the only patriots on whom they thought they could depend; every man of probity appeared to them a formidable judge; and from one fatal error the words juftice and counter-revolution with them became fynonimous.

This refult of an iniquitous and cruel fentence was not at firft felt in its full force: a part of the convention that had voted from weaknefs for fome time, again rallied round the party of the Gironde, who wifhed to govern the republic with wifdom and moderation. The triumphs of the armies, by removing danger to a diftance, diminifhed fear. But when, a few months afterwards,

wards, fortune feemed to abandon the French ftandards, terror gave predominancy to the Mountain, and fubjected all France to the moft atrocious tyranny that had ever polluted the annals of hiftory.

It is certain that the fuccefs of the republican armies was owing to the enthufiafm of the French for independence, to the fudden spring which equality had given to general ambition, and to the errors of the coalefced powers. But by an unfortunate chance, reverfes took place at the time when the government was moderate; and victories returned when it became cruel. Frederic William and feveral Princes who had threatened the conftitutionalifts, negotiated with the jacobins; and the infatuated multitude, not only in France, but in many other countries for a long time thought that barbarifm was ability, moderation perfidy, and juftice weaknefs.

The French foldiers were as much intimidated by the firft difafters, as they had been intoxicated by their firft fuccefs. The retreat of Frederic William effected a complete revolution in the national fpirit; and the fame people, who were in fear of not being able to defend themfelves againft one king, afterwards thought themfelves ftrong enough to fubdue all Europe. Opinion does every thing; and by efcaping, at the moment

ment they leaſt expected, ſo preſſing a danger, each French warrior thought himſelf a hero, and became ſuch.

Monteſquiou rapidly penetrated into the dominions of the King of Sardinia, and conquered Savoy without reſiſtance. General Anſelme took poſſeſſion of Nice. Biron was not attacked in Alſace. Cuſtine made himſelf maſter of Worms, Spire, and Mentz; raiſed contributions on Heſſe, and captured Frankfort. Kellerman entered the electorate of Trèves. The Auſtrians, who had conceived the preſumptuous folly of endeavouring to take Liſle with twenty-four thouſand men, raiſed the ſiege after having bombarded it in vain. Dumouriez, releaſed from the Pruſſians by diſeaſe, famine, and negociations, had marched into Flanders at the head of an army of thirty thouſand men; that of the Auſtrians was ſtrongly entrenched at Jemappe: he reſolved to try the event of a battle, and he obtained a complete victory, which opened to him the Gates of Mons. This unexpected and brilliant triumph of ardour over experience, of undiſciplined valour over methodical tactics, raiſed to the higheſt pitch the aſtoniſhment of politicians, the enthuſiaſm of the French, and the conſternation of their enemies.

Dumouriez took advantages of his victory with

with more activity than prudence. He rapidly possessed himself of all the Low-Countries; and whilst Beurnonville advanced against Trèves and Coblentz, and Valence seized on Namur, he made himself master of Ghent, Brussels and Antwerp; dispatched Lamorliere into Prussian Gueldres, laid siege to Maestricht, and prepared to invade Holland. We shall soon see what a change of fortune was occasioned by this too extensive plan, and this display of forces, which weakened his means by dividing them. The people of Brabant, and the people of Savoy, under the influence of French cannon, desired or rather appeared to desire, their union with France; and the National Convention made a decree by which the French republic promised its assistance to all nations who would rise in insurrection for the purpose of obtaining liberty.

These rapid conquests, at the moment when politicians were employed only in the dismemberment of France, struck terror into all the cabinets of Europe; and menaced with seeing every where extended, that torrent they had thought to repel so easily to its source; they then began to feel, a little too late, that Mirabeau was right, when Burke wrote, *that France was only a chasm in the mass of Europe,* in answering, *that chasm is a Volcano.*

After

After the first moments of surprise, the coalition thought only of multiplying their forces, and avenging their defeats. The Emperor and the King of Prussia formed closer connections; Frederic William ordered numerous levies of soldiers, and forced into the field even fathers of families. The Landgrave of Hesse joined a part of his troops to those of Prussia, and took up arms in defence of his dominions. All the Hanoverian troops were put in motion; the Elector of Saxony furnished his contingent; the Emperor sent fresh forces to the Rhine and the Meuse under the command of Coburg. The King of Spain, who had endeavoured to soften matters in favour of Louis XVI. by his neutrality, acceded to the coalition; and England at length, though she did not actually declare war, rejected peace, shewed such dispositions and made such preparations, as quickly determined the Convention to attack her.

At this epoch there were in England three parties: that of the Tories devoted to the court, and preponderating by their riches and their power; the republican party, few in number, but active and turbulent; lastly, that of the Whigs, attached to the constitution, but jealous of liberty, and hostile to all extension of the royal prerogative. This last party were desirous of parliamentary reform: Mr. Pitt formerly entertained the same sentiments; but had changed his opinion either from ambition as a minister, or from prudence as a politician. The spirit of equality had excited so much fermentation, that it did not at that moment appear to him adviseable to make an experiment of modifications, which might degenerate into revolution.

The first efforts of the French to obtain their freedom had been too much applauded in England by the Whigs and the republicans, for the government openly to disapprove of them; and when Burke wrote a bitter Phillippic against the constituent assembly, Mr. Pitt, in February 1790, delivered a speech* in which he unequivocally expressed his wish for the solid establishment of liberty in France. Time has too strongly evinced his animosity against that country to warrant the sincerity of his language; but it proves what then was the public opinion in England; and how much address, and how many events should concur, to enable the British cabinet, without losing their popularity, to prevail on a free people to become accomplices in the destruction of Polish liberty; to make them

* See *Appendix* for an extract from this speech.

embrace

embrace the quarrel of abfolute governments againſt a reprefentative government, and to determine proteſtant troops to ſhed their blood in the cauſe of the Pope and the Catholic religion.

The Engliſh miniſtry probably flattered themſelves that the conteſt of liberty againſt royalty weakening the French nation by internal feuds, would for a long time releaſe them from the political and commercial rivality of that power; they manifeſted, like all the governments of Europe, their hatred againſt the democratical principles which had deſtroyed the nobleſſe; but they did not feel the ſame fear as the others; and the love of the French for abfolute equality, making them forefee anarchy which is generally its confequence, fecured them againſt the dread of true and folid liberty, which would give too much wealth and power to France.

In this perfuafion, Mr. Pitt diverted the King of England from taking an active part in the war which was kindled between the French and the Germanic courts. It has been even afſerted that he adviſed the King of Pruſſia to avoid it, becauſe he perhaps foreſaw that it might rally the parties in France againſt a common danger. The revolution of the 10th of Auguſt, and the atrocities by which it was followed, afflicted only the Whigs; the Tories beheld in these disorders the juftification of their harangues againft the French revolution, and the accomplifhment of their predictions; and the republican party, elevated by these events, flattered themfelves that the eftablifhment of a great republic was on the point of realizing all their hopes.

The firft defeat of the French, and the rapid march of the Pruffians might make the Britifh cabinet, like all Europe, believe, that the counter-revolution was at hand; and that Louis XVI. reftored to a reduced throne, would be obliged to pay his protectors by the dismemberment of his kingdom.

But the maffacres of September, the abolition of royalty, the refiftance of the republican troops, the unexpected retreat of Frederic William, the explofion of the martial ardour of the French, the impetuous energy of the Convention, the fuccefs of Dumouriez, the fplendid victory of Jemappe; the conqueft of Brabant, the propagation of democracy in Holland, and in the Low-Countries; totally changed the plan of the Englifh miniftry, and they came to a refolution to re-animate the coalition, and to deftroy that republic whofe principles menaced focial order, and which fhewed in its cradle fo much audacity, power, ambition, and inhumanity.

After

After the 10th of Auguſt, the miniſtry had recalled from Paris their ambaſſador Lord Gower, and refuſed to acknowledge Chauvelin who was accredited by the proviſional executive council. A more generous policy would doubtleſs have adviſed, inſtead of ſuſpending the negotiations, to redouble their activity in order to ſave the unfortunate French monarch, by making a ſincere offer of peace, if his life were ſpared, and of war if his death ſhould be reſolved. But whether they ſaw with pleaſure that France by the execution of Louis XVI. would participate in the reproaches of cruelty that the condemnation of Charles I. had drawn on England; or whether they wiſhed that the enemy they were preparing to combat might excite more hatred; they did not take any ſtep in favour of the King, whoſe fate they ſo loudly deplored: he periſhed, and they thought themſelves obliged to make greater exertions after this cataſtrophe, as they had uſed no efforts to prevent it.

Though the French were at the height of anarchy, their ſtandard bore the name of Liberty; and this word, ſacred to the Engliſh, impoſed on the miniſtry great precautions, if they wiſhed to render the war national and popular.

The navigation of the Scheldt, which the Convention

Convention proposed to restore to the Belgians, was not a sufficient motive; for in 1786 Sir Joseph Yorke, the English ambassador, had himself pressed the Emperor to reclaim the liberty of that navigation.

The invasion of Brabant could not authorise the rupture; for England being neutral could not forbid the French, whose territory the Emperor had invaded, from carrying their arms against him.

The abolition of royalty was an internal alteration with which they had no right to intermeddle. The massacres of September and the death of the King might inspire horror; but these events were foreign to the interests of England, and France had not made war on Cromwell to avenge Charles I.

The dangers with which they said Holland was threatened were not evident; and when Lord Auckland offered to the States-General the succours stipulated by treaties, they answered him, that they did not believe France had any intention to attack them.

In order to give weight to these different motives, it was necessary for the English administration to rally round their system all people of property, by exciting their alarms; and the delirium of the English and French jacobins

bins furnished in this respect all the pretexts they could desire.

Thomas Payne had published a book against the English constitution, which would probably have been little read if the government had less rigorously prohibited its circulation. For a long time there existed a correspondence between the clubs of London and Paris. The English constitutional society had, it was said, just sent a patriotic donation of a thousand pair of shoes to the French armies; the republican party had excited some commotions at Leith and at Yarmouth; many of the Whigs had signed addresses for the purpose of obtaining a parliamentary reform; the French clubists, elevated by these slight events, had published with their usual folly and arrogance, that the French revolution would make the tour of Europe. At last that which was undoubtedly the most striking circumstance, the National Convention, intoxicated with its first triumphs, and as infatuated as Anacharsis Clootz, one of its members, who called himself *the orator of the human race*, had in the month of November published a decree, by which the republic promised assistance to all nations who would rise in insurrection for the establishment of liberty and equality. It is too true that such a decree,

decree, whilst it subsisted, placed France in a state of hostility with all established governments.

The British cabinet, taking advantage of these united events, and of the terror which jacobinism inspired in kings, princes, nobles, priests and the rich, pretended to feel the most lively alarms. They warned the English people by proclamations of the dangers which threatened them; they in an extraordinary manner convened the Parliament, assembled the militia, and invested themselves with an authority which nothing but a most formidable crisis could render necessary.

In contempt of the clauses in the treaty of commerce, they prohibited the circulation of assignats, and interdicted the French from the purchase of corn in the British ports; they equipped strong fleets; negotiated with the coalition; compelled the Stadtholder to accede to it; and ineffectually endeavoured to prevail on the King of Denmark and the Grand Duke of Tuscany to dismiss from their dominions the French ministers.

The Gironde at that time had the majority in the Convention; and the executive council, subject to its influence, in vain redoubled its exertions to avert the war. Chauvelin unsuccesssuccessfully offered, reparation for the grievances of which the court of London complained; he could not obtain any satisfactory answer. Maret, an enlightened, spirited, judicious and moderate negotiator, twice ineffectually attempted to bring about an accommodation; which English policy rendered impossible. It constantly appeared, that France offered to leave it to the Belgians to discuss the subject of the navigation of the Scheldt, without attempting to interfere in it; that she promised her troops should not approach the frontiers of Holland. Lastly, after having endeavoured to give to the decree of the convention a construction which would have annulled it, they consented to its repeal. It has been even asserted, that in his second mission, Maret being invested with more extensive powers, was authorised to offer concessions still more advantageous both to England and Holland. He was not listened to; and on the 24th of January, Chauvelin received an order to quit England within eight days. The National Convention irritated by these affronts, and too impetuous to act with policy, then no longer preserved any measures; and taking on itself, as Mr. Pitt desired, the appearance of aggression, it formally declared war against Holland and England,

England which the latter had, in fact, already commenced.

France, in her declaration, recapitulated all the infractions by the English of the treaty of commerce; the recall of Lord Gower, the intrigues of the British cabinet with the coalition, the interdiction against circulating assignats, the prohibition against the purchase of corn, the menacing equipment of some English squadrons, the hostile counsels given, and the succours promised to the Stadtholder, the refusal of any proposed explanations, and the insulting dismissal of the French envoy.

The King of England on his side, in his manifesto, after having made a merit of his desire to preserve peace, proved by his neutrality, painted in glowing colours the ambition of the French revolutionists; the invasion of Brabant and Savoy; the danger of the principles of the jacobins; the activity of their attempts to stir up all nations to rebellion; the audacity of their decrees, which tended to overturn all governments, and to overthrow social order; the dangers with which Holland was threatened, and the plots contrived by the French in order to excite troubles in England.

All that can be concluded from these opposite declamations, is, that the Convention, without

out finances and without a navy, dreading to have one enemy more, sincerely desired to preserve peace with England; though her principles, her actions, and her orators were in permanent hostility with all governments; and that on the other side, the English administration, who ought less to have dreaded than any other the propagation of jacobinism in a country where the laws are just, the people happy, and the government strong; having remained indifferent spectators of the revolution whilst it enfeebled France, was determined to fight her as soon as they perceived she had acquired sufficient energy to obtain conquests.

Manifestoes are the veils of politicians; but by removing them it is evidently to be seen that the conquest of Brabant, was the true cause of the war, and the possession of it is still an obstacle which the jealousy of England opposes to peace.

War being thus declared between England and France, Spain and nearly all the powers of Europe followed the example of the British cabinet. The Convention informed of the intentions of the King of Spain, declared war against him as well as the Stadtholder of Holland; and the French nation, without money and without credit, torn by a thousand factions, tyrannised

tyrannised in the interior by sanguinary men, and threatened from abroad by the armies of all Kings, did not seem capable, without a miracle, to extricate herself from so terrible a crisis

Her enemies, in consternation from the first successes of the republican soldiers, passed suddenly from the excess of a panick fear, to that of an unbounded confidence; and the indignation inspired in them by the death of Louis XVI. the massacres of September, and the threats of the Convention, giving to their ardour the violence of hatred, all hope of accommodation vanished; every sentiment of moderation gave place to the passion of vengeance; and on both sides, they no longer fought to conquer, but to destroy.

In this bloody contest between a government that is popular and those which are absolute, the French had a very remarkable advantage; each warrior of their armies thought he was fighting his own individual cause; whilst the soldiers of the coalition, indifferent to the interests of their chiefs, fought only from obedience; and did not feel that enthusiasm, which alone has formed in all ages, either martyrs or heroes.

This difference, which escaped the attention
of

of passionate or ignorant minds, was alone sufficient to counterpoise the superiority of power and riches; and to render France triumphant over all Europe, in defiance of the efforts of her enemies, and the ferocious folly of several of her rulers.

Dumouriez, profiting by the terror which his victories had inspired, and of the support promised him by the Batavian patriots, had rapidly entered into Holland, had taken Breda by force, captured Gertruidenberg, besieged Klurdert, and Williamstadt, and blockaded Bergen-op-Zoom. By a very extraordinary solecism in politics, the British ministry, who never had been willing to treat with French envoys, consented to permit Lord Aukland to negotiate with Dumouriez, whose forehead had been recently ornamented with the *bonnet rouge*; and who, in order to flatter or deceive the anarchists, audaciously assumed in his letters, the title of *Sans-Culottes*; but the splendour of Dumouriez's successes was doomed to be as short as it was brilliant, and his fall was as sudden as his elevation had been rapid.

Maestricht, besieged by Miranda, defended itself with obstinacy. D'Autichamp, and several emigrants distinguished themselves by vigorous sorties. The Prince de Cobourg and General Clairfait

Clairfait, arriving unexpectedly at the head of a strong army, surprised the dispersed French cantonments, and possessed themselves of Liege, which was unsuccessfully defended by General Valence, killed four thousand of his men and took twenty pieces of cannon. Miranda found himself obliged to raise the siege of Maestricht; Dumouriez, compelled to quit Holland, could scarcely rally in the Netherlands the troops which were pursued by the Austrians. The Dutch, secure after this departure and supported by the Prussians, obliged the French troops to shut themselves up in Breda. Dumouriez, wishing to attempt a last effort to stop the enemy, who had advanced as far as St Tron, fought, and lost the battle of Nerwind. In this action the French disputed with fury the victory of their enemies. Their right wing had long the advantage, but it was not seconded by the left. The son of the Duke d'Orleans fought with intrepidity; General Valence also, who commanded the cavalry, after several charges precipitated himself into the midst of the enemy's ranks, and returned covered with wounds.

General Miranda, who was reproached by Dumouriez for the loss of the battle, in his turn accused his general of having betrayed France on that

that day. These two improbable accusations were not supported by any proofs: it appeared that in this affair the deficiency of troops and of discipline, alone obliged French valour to yield to Austrian tactics. After this battle, Dumouriez arrested the pursuit of the Austrians, and repulsed them in a bloody action which took place near Louvain; he afterwards agreed to a suspension of hostilities with the Prince de Cobourg; Clairfait, not being informed of this convention, attacked the French posts, and in another quarter the Austrans retook Namur. Dumouriez, to save the wreck of his army, which he could not expose to the faith of a convention concluded without the knowledge of the French government, abandoned all his conquests, re-entered France, and retired into the camp of Maulde.

It appeared, that from this moment, knowing the disposition of the Convention, and foreseeing the fate which the suspicious republicans prepared for a vanquished general, he resolved to change his side, to betray that which he served, to make his peace with the coalition, and to march with his troops against Paris, there to effect a revolution and re-establish monarchy.

His connections made it believed that he had formed a design of placing the Duke d'Orleans on the throne: this was even then the moft accredited opinion; but what renders it altogether improbable is the concert that prevailed between the Auftrians and him. Such was the underftanding between them, that they efcorted rather than purfued him in his retreat to Mons. They even permitted the troops he had left in Holland to rejoin him at Courtray: and every thing induces a belief, that his plan, if he could have preferved his influence over the army, was to reftore the crown to the Dauphin, and by this revolution to avert the vengeance of the republicans, whofe violence and inflexibility he well knew.

However this may be, the event completely difappointed his hopes. If the French government was hated by the nation, foreigners were ftill more fo; the ardour for the republic was too recent to be fo eafily extinguifhed; and Dumouriez foon experienced, that treachery was more odious to the French than tyranny. He might perhaps have drawn them into a civil war; but his underftanding with the enemies of the nation excited their well-founded diftruft, and occafioned him to be entirely abandoned by the army, who honourably preferred the danger of inteftine troubles, and the perils of an unfortunate war, to the difgrace of fubjugation to a foreign yoke. The

The news of this event spread consternation through France, and roused the fury of the Jacobins. The Girondists, preserving an apparent majority, made a feeble struggle for some months after against the Mountain. This violent faction, who could never pardon them for having wished to save the life of Louis XVI. had attempted, in the month of march, to excite an insurrection in the capital, to renew the scenes of September, and to massacre in the midst of the Convention the deputies whose moderation paralised their fury. Beurnonville, distinguished in the field for his valour and his spirit, was then minister of war; he denounced the project of the Jacobins, prevented its effect, and proposed to the Girondists to have this formidable party exterminated by a numerous body of officers and soldiers, whom he had successively drawn to Paris. But the Gironde, formerly factious against the court, seemed to have at once assumed its place and its weakness.

Marat, impeached by them, but acquitted by the influence of the *Commune*, daily insulted the Convention by his triumph. In vain had Louvet, in denouncing Robespierre, unveiled his tyrannical plans. The *Commune* being ordered to deliver in their accounts, enjoyed with impunity their crimes and dilapidations; and the orators of the Gironde contented themselves with opposing to the conspiracies of the Mountain eloquent harangues, the only effect of which was to retard the progress of the Conspirators, whilst they ought to have disarmed their strength and prevented their attacks.

Whatever may be the weakness of a government, it preserves its authority whilst its operations are crowned by victory; but no sooner is it defeated than its misfortunes become crimes.

The Girondists had constantly supported Dumouriez against the declamations of Marat, and the accusations of the Jacobins; as soon as that general was defeated, the Mountain, whose cry was repeated by all the clubs throughout France, awakened among the people the most violent suspicions respecting his intentions and those of his protectors; and when information was received by the denunciation of three emissaries who had been sent to him, that he had an understanding with the enemy, and was preparing to make war on the Convention, in vain did the terrified Girondists join the Jacobin party in order to take measures for opposing his treason and punishing his revolt; they were not the less considered, by the deluded multitude, as accomplices in his plans, and from that moment their ruin was inevitable.

Camus,

Camus, Bancal, Quinette, and Lamarque, all four deputies, departed with the minister of war, Beurnonville, to secure the attachment of the army, and the person of the General. Dumouriez, who saw with uneasiness their arrival in the camp, received them with coldness, surrounded by an overawing retinue. The commissioners could not elude his vigilance. On the other hand it was impossible for him to shake the fidelity of Beurnonville, and allure him into his projects; and after a long and acrimonious conversation, erecting openly the standard of revolt, he ordered the minister and the deputies to be arrested, and delivered them up to the Prince de Cobourg, as hostages for the safety of the persons of the royal family, whom the Convention had imprisoned.

Hitherto the soldiers, ignorant of their General's views, had, notwithstanding their calamities, preserved for him an enthusiastic regard. They were discontented with the Convention and the government whom Dumouriez had accused of being the cause of all their misfortunes. Hence, in the first instance, the arrestation of the commissioners was approved by the army, who with indignation saw them dare to come into the centre of the camp, to arrest a general covered with so many laurels.

Dumouriez,

Dumouriez, depending on the attachment of his troops, then thought himſelf certain of ſucceeding in his plan. However, Liſle and Condé, which he had promiſed to deliver to the Auſtrians, as places of ſecurity, refuſed to receive the detachments he ſent thither. A corps of troops, alarmed at the reports which were ſpread, had juſt cut off the communication between the General and the camp at Maulde: and this reſiſtance muſt have warned him of obſtacles which would arreſt his progreſs.

But the criſis having arrived for his proclaiming aloud his projects, and paſſing the Rubicon, he repaired to the Prince de Cobourg, and drew up in concert with him two manifeſtoes. The Prince de Cobourg, in his manifeſto, made a brilliant eulogium of Dumouriez, and, renouncing all idea of conqueſt, he promiſed to ſecond the efforts of the French army to deſtroy the tyranny of the Convention, and terminate the misfortunes of France, by re-eſtabliſhing the monarchy and the conſtitution of 1791.

After this tranſaction, Dumouriez, with an Auſtrian eſcort, rejoined his camp, and delivered an harangue to his army, in which he circulated the manifeſto he had juſt compoſed,
endeavouring

endeavouring to enflame the minds of the soldiers by a picture of the evils of anarchy, the crimes of the Convention, the fatuity of the government, and the misfortunes of the royal family. He called on them to acquire immortal glory by restoring the throne, and to secure their liberty, by re-establishing a constitution which had been sanctioned by the national will, and overturned by a conspiracy.

He was at first encouraged by the acclamations of those who surrounded him, and the silence of an undetermined multitude, who did not dare to manifest its sentiments in a circumstance so unexpected; but afterwards, learning that the artillery had quitted the camp for the purpose of retiring to Valenciennes, all the troops animated by their officers, who were indignant at the defection of the General, and the presence of the enemy, universally expressing a murmur of dissatisfaction, which soon breaking out into complaints, reproaches and threats, completely dispelled his illusion, and left him no other resource for his safety but in a precipitate flight. He set out, leaving on the frontier his dreams of glory, and carrying with him only the shame of a project so rashly conceived, and which so suddenly miscarried.

Seven or eight hundred soldiers only consented

sented to accompany him, and defend him in his flight. Thus did this man, who incited the enthusiasm of all the troops, become in an instant the object of their detestation. He expected to give an army to the coalition, and he could only bring with him a few proscribed individuals.

The *ci-devant* Duke de Chartres, General Valence, and some officers, who had not joined in the revolt of Dumouriez, but who were too much connected with him not to be suspected during the reign of passion, learning that they were pursued by decrees and mandates of arrest, found themselves compelled to fly their country. The General, enflamed with rage, advised the Prince de Cobourg, to take advantage of the disorder then prevalent in the French army. Cobourg accordingly advanced rapidly, thinking he should have to fight only with some dispersed troops, without courage, without plans, and without commanders. He was deceived, and the unexpected and persevering resistance of France at this conjuncture ought to have opened the eyes of the Kings of Europe, and convinced them, that the French nation, whatever calamities it might experience, was determined to perish rather than renounce its independence.

The

The ministers of the King of Prussia and the Emperor, assembled at this period with Lord Auckland, the Prince of Orange and the envoys of Naples and Spain. This congress decided the fate of Europe. It might probably have re-established general tranquillity, by offering peace to France, in her state of alarm. If they would have acknowledged the the republic, the Convention would then have been easily brought to renounce their projects of aggrandisement, and set the royal Family at liberty. But they were too much bent on conquest to be contented with peace, and too violent in their resentments to listen to prudence.

Every thing conspired to redouble the infatuation of the coalesced powers and reanimate their hopes. Holland was delivered; the Netherlands re-conquered; Frederic William at the head of the Prussians and Hessians, had defeated Custine, retaken Frankfort, blockaded Mentz, and penetrated nearly to Landau. Another corps of Prussians and Austrians had got possession of the electorate of Treves. The French fleet, in the Mediterranean, had unsuccessfully attempted an expedition against Sardinia. The royalists having erected the standard of revolt, had incited to insurrection the
people

people of la Vendée, and a great part of Brittany. The Spaniards were attacking the southern provinces, the French colonies in America were exposed, without defence, to the invasion of the English, who were at the same time preparing a formidable attack on Provence. The French government, divided into two violent factions, appeared on the eve of destruction, by an intestine war. The concurrence of all these circumstances satisfied the coalition, that France, encompassed by so many enemies, and rent by such cruel convulsions, would offer to them only a prey which they could easily share. They resolved, therefore, to push the operations with vigour. Condé was besieged, and the English combined with the Imperialists resolved to possess themselves of Valenciennes.

General Dampierre, rallying all the different armies, was placed at their head. After several bloody engagements he fell heroically in the battle of Famars, fighting till his last breath, and making the enemy dearly purchase a victory which they did not expect could have been disputed with them.

The troops which defended the entrenched camp of Famars still for some time opposed a vigorous resistance to the Austrians, but they were at length compelled to yield to numbers, and

and to disperse to different places, in expectation that fresh reinforcements might put them in a situation to fight. Their retreat relieving the Prince de Cobourg from every obstacle, he invested Valenciennes, which he was not able to take, till after a long and murderous siege.

General Custine soon after took the command of the wreck of the army, but his unsuccessful effort to succour Mentz had already rendered him suspected of treachery by the Convention; and having imprudently dispatched a memorial, in which he developed the dangers of the disorganising system of the jacobins, and the necessity of having recourse to a species of dictatorship, for the purpose of restoring order, his ruin was determined; his fidelity was the cause of his death; he could never have foreseen a fate he did not merit. He came and gave himself up without suspicion to the tyrants, who hurried him to the scaffold. Montesquiou escaped the same destiny, by flying into Switzerland, at the moment when commissioners were come to arrest him in his camp. A decree of impeachment also passed against General Anselme, but his infirmities and want of importance saved him from proscription.

The defeats of the armies, the success of the

King

King of Prussia, and the invasion of the Austrians, dismayed the enlightened, and excited the blind populace to fury. It is impossible for the multitude to reflect sufficiently, to attribute their misfortunes to their real cause; it is more easy for them to attribute every thing to treachery: and all those demagogues who tell them that they are deceived, are certain of being listened to from their credulity, of pleasing their passions and directing their resentment.

Robespierre, Marat, Danton, Collot d'Herbois, and all the leaders of the Mountain perfectly understood this secret, which has on all occasions promoted the success of the factious: they every where spread the poison of calumny, and the Girondists, who no longer preserved any influence except in the Convention, soon experienced that the power was not in the assembly, and that the strength of the clubs was paramount to all the constituted authorities.

The *Commune* of Paris, the sections, the popular societies, resounded with complaints, threats and imprecations against the party in the Convention which retained some sentiments of humanity, some love of order, and some regard for justice. The Girondists, apprised of their danger by the triumph of Marat, by by the seditious clamour of the tribunes, and the factious harangues which they could not avoid hearing throughout the suburbs of Paris, induced them to employ a departemental guard, and to transfer the fittings of the Convention to Bruges. All these plans, without execution, redoubled the fury of their enemies, and determined them to attempt a new revolution.

Most of the departments, in spite of the efforts of the agitators, supported the majority of the Convention. The Mountain had only in its favour the jacobin club and the dregs of the people of Paris; but it knew that the triumphant party in that immense city was certain to command, from terror or obedience, throughout the whole extent of the republic; and whilst the Girondists were reasoning, deliberating and menacing, it conspired, struck and reigned.

On the 31st of May the tocsin was sounded; the barriers were shut. Heuriot, commandant of the National guard, devoted to Robespierre, in each section kept under arms the citizens who might thwart his views. Round the Tuilleries he posted only three thousand men, on whom he could depend. The Convention, surrounded by a ferocious mob, impatient to overthrow the last barrier opposed to anarchy, saw arrive at its bar a central committee, composed of revolutionary committees from each section; a fatal institution which was suffered by the weakness of the Girondists, and was their ruin. This committee denounced twenty-two deputies to the Convention, accused them of being accomplices with Dumouriez and the coalition, attributed to them the intention of breaking the unity of the republic, and dividing it into federal republics; they accused them also of belonging to the Orleans' faction. All these absurd and contradictory accusations mutually destroyed each other; but when there is a wish to inflame the multitude, the number of complaints has more force than their probability.

At length this factious committee, supported by the *Commune*, by the suburbs, and even by the departemental administration itself, demanded the imprisonment and trial of the denounced deputies, in spite of the clamours of the tribunes, the cries of the seditious, and the vociferations of the Mountain. The majority of the Convention still, that day, opposed some resistance to the conspirators. It had not the strength to punish them, but it did not sacrifice to them the victims they required.

This effort to defend them was the last which
it

it attempted. Terror seized quickly all minds, and the National Convention having, two days afterwards, in vain endeavoured to break the chain that surrounded it, and awe the people by its presence, shamefully passed all the decrees demanded of it, committed to prison the accused, who allowed themselves to be arrested, proscribed those who by flight escaped the scaffold, sent to all the departments commissioners charged to inspire obedience by terror, and, without reserve, subjected itself as well as all France, to the most odious and bloody tyranny.

CHAP.

CHAP. XI.

New constitution of 1793.—Its duplicity.—The Dictatorial power is intrusted to the committees of public safety and of general safety.—Their tyranny.—Debasement of the Convention.—Proscription of the most energetic members.—Revolt of Lyons.—Insurrection of several departments.—Death of Marat.—Division among the tyrants.—Portrait of Robespierre.—Death of Custine; of Biron; of the Duke d'Orleans.—Toulon delivered up to the English.—Progress of Cobourg.—Success of the royalists in La Vendée.—Fury of the Jacobins, the Cordeliers and the Commune *of Paris.—General armament in France.—Emission of assignats.—The King of Prussia takes Mentz.—The Prussians and Austrians force the lines of Weissemberg, invest Landau and menace Strasbourg.—Cobourg advances towards Landrecy.—Errors of the coalition and the royalists.—Cruelty of the French government.—Death of the Queen and Madame Elizabeth.—Toulon is retaken.—Lyons is subdued and destroyed.—The Spaniards driven from Roussillon.—La Vendée depopulated and sacked.—The Duke of Brunswick and the Austrians are defeated and driven from Alsace.—The English are put to flight near Dunkirk.—Priests, nobles and persons of property are every where imprisoned and massacred.—Terror reaches all classes and sexes.—Death of Danton.—Division among the coalesced powers.—The King of Prussia thinks of withdrawing from the coalition.—He invades Great Poland.—Battle of Fleurus.—Successes of Jourdan and Pichegru.—Second conquest of Brabant.—Fury and delirium of the Decemvirs.—Division among them.—Revolution of the 9th Thermidor, and Death of Robespierre.*

IN 1788, the disturbances in France had for their object a reform of abuses: the evil was evident, the remedy necessary; and all France, with the exception of a few courtiers, had but one wish, and one opinion; and indeed, justice dictated all the publications, and directed all the measures. In 1789, the faults of the court, and the love of liberty effected a great revolution. Fear and the passions banished prudence; and enthusiasm, over-leaping the bounds of policy and reason, produced too many errors, sanctioned too many follies, and excused too many deviations; but the court and the two first orders alone suffered by this movement, and the great body of the nation who thought they gained by it, still in their hearts supported the revolutionists.

In 1792, distrust and ambition misled the people's minds, and the love of equality succeeded to that of liberty. They forgot that in politics, as in architecture, symmetry is indispensable; that, without alluding to the hereditary hierarchy, there must be different gradations in a building, and that in every structure to equalize is to demolish.

Equality of rights was no longer sufficient for men eager to assume a character. They overturned all the antient institutions and all the new laws; they destroyed even the academies: nor ought this to occasion surprise; a government so absurd and barbarous, necessarily dreaded and hated reason and knowledge. The ambitious, the poor, the intriguing, followed them with ardour; the peaceable, and all those who from their principles or their interest were attached to order, combated them unsuccessfully; and in this new revolution the dominant party, being no longer supported by the general opinion, was obliged to substitute force for persuasion, and terrour for justice.

In vain did the Girondists, after the death of the King, wish to fix the Republic on its true basis, that of virtue; in vain did all France, unable to recal the past, rally round those men who announced their intention of governing with moderation. The Mountain braving the public will, and marching audaciously to tyranny under the standard of licentiousness, immolated those repentant factions, those undeterminate politicians, on the wreck of the throne which they had all combined to overturn.

These sanguinary and ferocious tyrants thought, that if the system of the Girondists were realised, they should be ruined; and that the day justice regained her sway would be the day of their fall, perhaps of their destruction.

They

They knew that they never could enjoy the esteem of the virtuous, the approbation of the enlightened, or the confidence of the wealthy; and that they could never disarm the hatred of the aristocrats, after having massacred their families and broken their idols; nor appease the resentment of the founders of liberty, whose principles they had prostituted, and destroyed her work.

In this persuasion, they formed the most enormous plan of atrocity of which history affords an example; and they attempted a third revolution, whose object was to make all property change its owners, and to exterminate all that part of the nation which possessed any knowledge, wealth, talents, or virtue.

To ruin the morals of the poor, by giving them the property of the rich; to destroy every species of religion, in order to stifle all remorse; to impeach all the ex-nobles, all the men of understanding, and all the friends of order, of being accomplices with foreign nations; and to massacre them in order to free themselves from every sort of opposition; to ruin commerce, in order to intoxicate the multitude by the transient enjoyments of plunder; to proscribe all genius, in order that knowledge might not enlighten the people; to sacrifice all the treasure of the nation, in order to send youthful energy to battle, and fascinate by victories the minds appalled by such a multiplicity of crimes; such were the intentions and the means of these terrible conspirators, who, reigning for above a year on heaps of carcasses, will astonish posterity at once by the ferocity of their characters, the patience of their victims, the madness of their policy, the splendour of their triumphs, and by the terror which, long after their fall, the wrecks of their party inspired in men who made all Europe tremble.

It is not however to be thought that all the deputies who rallied round this formidable Mountain, penetrated into the projects and partook the crimes of those who sat on its summit. The most of those who increased this party were chained to it by the terror it incited in all minds, the invasion of foreigners, and dread of the fate with which the imprudent fanaticism of the royalists then threatened the republicans. When fear seizes the soul, the most violent party is that which ever inspires greatest confidence in the weak; in this horrible conjuncture it required great courage to remain attached to the moderate party, which was at the same time exposed to the proscriptions of revolutionists, and the vengeance of the enemies of the revolution.

A very

A very great majority of the Convention hated the Mountain and its principles; they did not submit to it, but at a moment when they were compelled by the violence of an unruly multitude; afterwards terror condemned them to a long silence and a forced obedience; but no sooner did a division take place among the tyrants, than they seized with transport the opportunity of throwing off the yoke, breaking their chains, expiating a part of the crimes committed, and sacrificing or banishing the insolent demagogues who had so long humiliated, oppressed, sullied, and decimated them.

When hypocrisy lays aside its veil, and audacious criminality reigns without shame, violence takes place of all other merit; power pertains necessarily to the most wicked.

Accordingly Robespierre, Danton, Marat, Collot d'Herbois, Billaud and Couthon by this right became the rulers of France. They associated with themselves some ferocious individuals whose talents were necessary to the administration, and who consented to serve them, some through fear, some from ambition, and some from policy. Their first act was to send every where commissioners, to calm the discontent which the fall of the Girondine party was likely to inspire, and to induce the nation to obedience by by calumny, corruption and terror. They wifhed at the fame time to deceive the people whom they enflaved. They haftily drew up a celebrated conftitution, under the title of the conftitution of 1793, none ever exifted more abfurd, or more favourable to anarchy. Legiflation was confined to a fingle council, the members of which were elected without any qualification of property; the executive power was divided among twenty-four minifters, appointed by the affembly and difmiffed at their pleafure; the permanence of partial infurrections was decreed by the conftitutional eftablifhment of the Jacobins and all the affiliated clubs, by the power granted to the *Communes*, by the frequency of the affemblage of the fections, and by forcing down all laws by popular interference.

This conftitution, which was afterwards fo often the ftandard of the factions, was only prefented to cover tyranny with a democratic mantle; its perfidious authors, fporting with their own works, fhut it up in an ark, audacioufly declaring that this conftitution fhould not be in force until the period the country was out of danger; and that till then France fhould be fubject to a revolutionary government.

This government, the moft abfolute and the moft

most ferocious of which there has ever been an example, was confided to two sections consisting of twelve deputies. The one was called the *committee of public safety*, and the other the *committee of general safety*. They were to be renewed every month; but by one of the incalculable effects of fear, which blinds those whom it governs, the Convention, divesting itself of it's inviolability, intrusted the committees with the formidable right of imprisoning its members, and thus rendered the power of the government as solid as it was extensive. Every deputy who should propose to change the committees would find himself proscribed; and from this moment tyranny was unrestrained, and slavery unbounded.

In the mean time several of the Girondist deputies, who escaped the proscription, published their protest and excited insurrection. Several departments indicated a disposition to avenge themselves, and resist oppression; some of them took up arms. Lyons erected the standard of revolt, and France became then both ravaged by foreign powers, who advanced into Roussillon, Flanders and Alsace, and rent by the civil war kindled by the Royalists in La Vendée, and by the Girondists in the centre of the republic.

E 4   History

History, whose impartiality ought to resist even the horror inspired by ferocity, is obliged in describing the most odious governments, no more to dissemble their talents than their enormities.

In the midst of this violent crisis, which was likely to deliver exhausted France to the resentments of her enemies, and perhaps efface her name from the list of nations, the revolutionary government displayed an energy, which triumphed over all obstacles, found resources which it was impossible to foresee, and employed forces which carried dismay to the very extremities of Europe.

The means were terrible, but the effects were prodigious. Four hundred thousand disciplined troops prepared to conquer the Republic. In the west, forty thousand royalists had just defeated the unskilful generals who opposed them; Cobourg overran Flanders, took Condé and Valenciennes, and afterwards advanced to Landrecy. Puisaye and Wimpffen, with an army of malcontents, were within twenty leagues of Paris. Bourdeaux armed several battalions to avenge her proscribed representatives. Lyons, in a state of revolt, assembled within her walls a crowd of rebels who braved the decrees of the Convention, and presented a formidable

formidable focus of insurrection. The King of Prussia, after having driven the French from Frankfort, had made himself master of Mentz. The Prussians and Austrians, combined with the Prince de Condé, had forced the lines of Weissemburg, killed fifteen thousand French, and produced the emigration of fifty thousand of the Alsatians. Landau was blockaded, Strasburg threatened, and lastly the English and Spaniards having jointly obtained possession of Toulon, expected, for the moment, to become masters of all the southern departments.

The reader must not expect to find here a methodical and detailed history of military events: all the facts we have just mentioned, in order to present a political picture, belong to the same period, although separated from each other by slight intervals. But it was necessary to collect them into one view, in order to shew the perilous condition of the French, the brilliant situation of the coalesced powers, and the efforts and prodigies required by an infant republic to resist so many enemies, and survive so many disasters. The only advantage of the then existing tyrannical government, was to adventure every thing, to have absolute power, to be interrupted by no opposition, by no principle, by no pity; and, at its pleasure, to dispose of of the lands, the industry, the labour, the gold, and the blood of twenty-four millions of persons subject to its disposition. This shocking government, founding its power on the terror inspired by a revolutionary tribunal, extorted from the weakness of the Girondists who became its first victim, in an instant covered the surface of France with revolutionary committees, revolutionary armies, bastilles and executioners.

Creating an immense quantity of assignats, it compelled the people to receive them, and in order to give them an apparent value, it seized all the property of the rich, whom it accused of conspiracy, and whose death it resolved. All the property of the Bourbons remaining in France was already sequestrated; they were detained as hostages, when Dumouriez delivered up to the Emperor the deputies he had arrested. The servile compliance of the Duke d'Orleans with the Jacobins did not soften them towards him; he was imprisoned at Marseilles, as well as his relations; and the virtues of his ill-fated wife, who was universally respected and beloved, did not prevent these monsters from keeping her in close confinement, and incessantly threatening her life, which however they did not venture to take. The nobleman was then imprisoned as a traitor; the banker

banker as a counter-revolutionist; the merchant as a monopolist. The populace, paid to attend the sections, expected to reign, and rushed into slavery with a sort of fanaticism for men who gratified all their constant propensities, idleness, envy and cupidity.

The tyrants having filled the emigrant lists with the names of all their enemies, seized all deposits in the hands of the notaries, confiscated all the specie which they could discover, put into requisition all the provisions, and all the arms necessary for the support of their troops, cashiered all the officers whose resistance they dreaded; and multiplied without bounds the fictitious paper money, quickly dispersed the forces of the malcontents, by gaining over the multitude by largesses, and terrifying the leaders by punishments; corruption extended every where, the ruin of morals was general, and terror universal. In every quarter crime had accomplices; tyranny, spies; virtue, enemies; and innocence, executioners.

The son denounced his father; the poor impeached his benefactor; the servant betrayed his master; the brother imprisoned his brother; the indignant honest man durst not breathe his resentment; the affectionate wife concealed her tears; an individual scarcely dared to think: nothing

nothing escaped the tyrants; no retreat could screen their victims; no succour protect them from danger; no consolation accompany them in their dungeons; and a stupid and infatuated mob, with a ferocious joy, insulted them at their execution.

A general resistance being then impossible, few partial efforts were attempted to throw off this odious yoke.

Charlotte Corday, celebrated for her courage, alone gave an example of intrepidity; which found no imitators: she plunged a dagger in the bosom of Marat; and as it is observed by Madam Rolland, who was then in confinement, and suffered a few days afterwards; *this blow, though well struck was ill directed.* Marat, the apostle of the banditti, was more contemptible than formidable; an absurd declaimer, bare-faced anarchist, preaching openly a war of the poor against the rich, a calumniator of all talents, an orator for a mob, his faction treated him as a madman, and considered him merely as an instrument. Besides he was dying; and his assassination, instead of weakening tyranny, strengthened it, by justifying in the eyes of the multitude its distrust and cruelty.

A rampart more difficult to be overthrown,
still

still however impeded in its progress the most violent party of the new masters of France. Danton, who was then styled one of the pillars of the revolution, and who from his athletic form and Stentorian voice, seemed to be its Colossus, did not entirely concur in the anarchical and absurd system of his fanatic colleagues. This ambitious advocate, successively paid by all parties, had followed the standard of liberty only to attain power, acquire wealth, and unreservedly abandon himself to voluptuousness.

Followed at first by the constitutionalists, and gained afterwards over alternately by the court and by them, still he betrayed them, and overturned the throne, which he saw too weak to be maintained.

A proscriber in the month of September, in order to dismay and govern his enemies, he said to one of the first founders of the constitution of 1791, that if he saw no means of saving Louis XVI. he would be one of the first to condemn him; and he kept his word. After the death of the King, and the fall of the Girondists, he wished to terminate the revolution, and place the crown on the head of the Duke d'Orleans, who had neither spirit enough to accept it, nor virtue enough to refuse it.

No proscription alarmed him, when he thought it useful; but to him it seemed absurd to prolong these violent and dangerous measures, and to inspire fear with the energy of despair.

Danton, therefore wished to put a period to the bloody anarchy to which he had given birth; and he would have been assisted in this design by the majority of the Convention; but his indiscreet luxury had diminished his popularity; his schemes were discovered; and Robespierre, who already meditated his destruction, spread suspicions against him, which forced him to quit the committee of public safety, and attend to his own security. Robespierre freed from his rivalship, postponed his death, and suddenly acquired such a preponderance, that he was universally considered as the head of the tyranny.

Posterity will with difficulty comprehend how this man, who possessed nothing great, could dominate so long over a country so vast, a nation so energetic, and repress factions so fierce.

Robespierre, in reality an advocate without reputation, an orator without eloquence, a politician without judgment, a legislator without knowledge, and factious without courage, had not any of those qualities which shed a lustre over ambitious characters in popular tempests;

tempests;—his stature was low, his visage ignoble, his complexion livid, his unsteadfast look indicated fear and inspired distrust; he possessed neither the bravery which dazzles by its audacity, nor the opulence which attracts partizans by gifts, nor the amenity which conciliates friends, nor the benevolence which attaches adherents. Dreaded by all men, he loved none. At the very time when liberty was the standard of the French, he fettered actions, and stifled thought; an enemy of philosophers in a philosophical age; preaching virtue, and protecting every crime; always talking about humanity, and deluging France with his victims; it is inconceivable what were the means of his fortune, the causes of his popularity, and the foundation of his power, without attentively considering the disposition of minds, the progress of the passions, and the corruption of manners at this fatal epoch.

The French revolution, prepared by the lights of philosophy, had changed its direction. Instead of tending to elevate, as was the wish of superior minds, it had no other object but to abase, according to the desire of those of inferior intellect. Fear and envy were become the ruling passions, and those who felt the most lively impressions, and spoke the most energetic language,

language, were neceffarily the men moft heard and beft underftood. But fear and envy compofed the whole of Robefpierre's character, and gave him a perfect moral refemblance to the populace, then exclufively called the people.

Sufpicious like the multitude, and, like it, always believing in plots, hating like it all that was raifed above the common level by wealth or talent ; in a word, irafcible and fanguinary like it, they were fo perfectly analogous, that in his fears, in his fury, in his fpeeches, in his actions, it recognifed all the impreffions which it experienced, all the ideas by which it was governed, and all the defires which it cherifhed.

Robefpierre was the faithful interpreter of its fentiments, the energetic organ of its will;— their caufe appeared to be a common one ; and this it never denied, when he pretended that his enemies were thofe of the people, that to attack him was to attack the people, and that his power and the power of the people were one.

The fimplicity of his manners, his frugality, his continuing to live with the family of a joiner, his determined poverty confolidated the affection which the indigent had conceived for him ; it became a fpecies of fanaticifm, and invefted him with that inconceivable power,
which

which fo long aftonifhed policy, confounded reafon, and afflicted humanity.

Robefpierre, inftructed by fear, had learnt from experience, that thofe will be crufhed by the revolutionary chariot who attempt to arreft its career.

Necker, Lally, Mounier, were the firft examples; La Fayette, Lameth, Barnave, who fucceeded them, had been overwhelmed while endeavouring to ftem the democratic torrent.

The Girondifts, who imagined they had fufficient force to fupprefs crimes and to reftrain anarchy, became their victims; laftly, Danton himfelf notwithftanding his energy, his influence, and his intrepidity, had loft his power by ceafing to be terrible.

Robefpierre was threatened with the fame fate by his colleagues, and particularly by the *Commune* of Paris, and by the club of cordeliers, whofe violence and ferocity daily increafed. He therefore refolved, in order to avoid being profcribed, to be always the moft dreadful of profcribers, and conftantly to place himfelf at the head of the revolutionary column, however accelerated it's fall might be into the abyfs of anarchy.

Always accufing, left he fhould be accufed, he propofed no laws, but he inceffantly complained

plained of their inefficacy; he nominated no generals, but he rendered them responsible for every misfortune; he mixed with no party, but he accused them all successively of intrigues, of royalism, or of corruption; escaping censure because he produced nothing; always commiserating the people, whom he said the rich betrayed by their avarice, the legislators by their pusillanimity, and the tribunals by their tardiness. He exculpated himself from all the public calamities by executions, and by his rigour made all success be attributed to himself.

The revolutionary tribunal, consisting of men devoted to tyrants, through fanaticism and wickedness, condemned without examination all the victims marked out to it. The proscribed deputies of the Gironde, and all the members of the constituent assembly whom they could seize on, the eloquent Barnave, the virtuous Bailly, the brave Custine, Biron and Beauharnois beloved by the people and the army, were sent to the scaffold: the greater progress the enemy made, the more the government thought itself obliged to multiply proscriptions, in order to prevent revolt by terror.

Seventy-three deputies, whose moderation was suspected, were imprisoned, and lived twelve months under the cruel apprehension of death, with

with which they were inceſſantly threatened. The Queen, Marie Antoinette, over whom the French had no authority, and whom the people hated without a motive, periſhed under the revolutionary axe. She could only be reproached with her birth, the pride of the houſe of Auſtria, and the natural levity of her ſex. But her misfortunes ought to have excited pity in the moſt ferocious breaſts, and the unworthy treatment ſhe experienced, and the abſurd and infamous accuſations with which ſhe was loaded, were perhaps more atrocious than her execution. If her political life was not entirely exempt from the imputation of intrigue, her fortitude in priſon, her noble dignity in preſence of her deſpicable judges, and her conſtancy when going to death, inſpired equal admiration of her character, as of horror for her executioners.

Soon after the Duke of Orleans, who hoped to eſcape deſtruction by ſacrificing his honour to his fears, mounted the ſcaffold to which he had condemned his Sovereign, and bore with firmneſs the general and humiliating exultation which his death excited among the people.

To the very laſt moment he truſted that his partizans would obtain his acquittal. It has even been aſſerted that Robeſpierre remained for some time undetermined whether to crown or to sacrifice him; but finding his name too dangerous for the Republic, and his character too feeble for the throne, he decreed his death.

Robespierre and his colleagues justified in the opinion of a great part of the people the atrocity of their rigours, by the imminence of the dangers which threatened them, and in which the people believed they participated.

Success, which always dazzles, shed for fifteen months a fatal splendour over their atrocities. Four hundred thousand foreign enemies vanquished or driven from their frontiers, Lyons subjected, Toulon delivered, and la Vendée subjugated, excited some admiration of a government which ought only to have inspired a just horror. Its means were immense; the terror which it spread insured the execution of its most tyrannical orders.

It commanded a levy in mass; twelve hundred thousand soldiers marched against the enemy: it wanted money, a forced loan placed all men's fortunes at its disposal.

Some solid security was necessary for it to give currency to a *Milliard* of assignats which he put in circulation; all the property of foreigners, of priests, and of aristocrats was seized. It

It will be easily conceived, that wealth was then deemed a crime; and that every opulent man was pointed out as a counter-revolutionist or monopolizer. The resistance of the ex-nobles occasioned some inquietude, they were disarmed. The mass of debts might become troublesome; the creditors of the emigrants, disappointed of their property, were paid in paper without value.

Cattle, grain, clothes and muskets were wanted to feed, equip and arm the numerous battalions which were created; every thing in the possession of the substantial citizens was put in requisition; all the towns were filled with founderies, and metamorphosed into arsenals. Humanity might encourage disobedience by saving some victims; denunciators were paid; accusation became a patriotic virtue, infidelity a merit; civic crowns were decreed to ingratitude; the courageous pity which gave an asylum to misfortune, was doomed to infamy and condemned to the scaffold; in a word, if the father supported his emigrant son, if the daughter wrote to her mother from her dungeon, the law of tyranny doomed them to death for having listened to the dictates of nature.

Heaven always terrifies those who attempt to oppress mankind; thus the *Decemvirs*, (for so they

they were named after the execution of their two colleagues, Herault and Simon) wished to destroy all idea of religion, in order to choke up the avenue of conscience which resisted their unjust decrees. They had proscribed the priesthood, they doomed religion to contempt, and profaned with ignominy all it's emblems and all it's ornaments. The greater part of the priests who sat in the convention publicly abjured their creed, and shamefully avowed that they had deceived the world.

It was attempted to substitute for the Christian religion a sort of paganism, whose metaphysical deities sanctioned all the interpretations which policy required. Reason and liberty were their new Gods; under whose names frenzy and slavery predominated, and whose altars flowed with the blood of human victims shed without motive, without measure, and without pity.

Perhaps there never existed a country desolated at the same time by so many scourges; it might have been said that Hell was unchained on purpose to consume it by all her fires, and to infect it by all her poisons. Virtue every where found death, innocence a snare, weakness danger, and vice encouragement. Accusation, divorce, debauchery, sacrilege, assassination and plunder were incessantly held out as the

means

means of protection to the timid, wealth to the poor, and elevation to the ambitious.

All the candidates who offered themselves to the clubs and revolutionary committees were unblushingly asked, *what crimes they had committed, what punishment they had merited, in case of a counter-revolution?* Such were the requisite qualifications; this, in the language of these barbarians, was what they called *giving pledges to the revolution.*

Thus in these dreadful times, when tranquillity was not the lot even of humble obscurity, probity and energy occupied only two places, the prisons and the camps; these were their only refuge. But while France deplores this cruel epoch, she may yet justly boast of the courage of her victims, and the heroism of her warriors.

These warriors soon astonished the coalition by their number, their strength, and their rapidity. The generals sacrificed on the scaffold were succeeded by men whose birth exposed them to less hatred, and who soon rendered their names illustrious by prodigies of valour.

Carnot, a member of the government, charged exclusively with the military department, then produced a great revolution in tactics. Soaring above the system of circumscribed manœuvres in narrow countries, he considered vast frontiers

as

as so many fields of battle; and combining the movements of different armies in this immense space as it had formerly been the custom to calculate on the revolutions of a few regiments on a plain, he disconcerted the policy of the cabinets, and the experience of the generals of the enemy. Jourdan, Pichegru, Moreau, Kleber, and so many others whom this war will immortalize, executed with skill the designs which had been planned by genius; and these ambitious powers, who, for the second time, imagined they could seize and divide an easy prey, saw at the end of the year their hopes destroyed, their troops vanquished, and their frontiers threatened. It is true the Kings leagued against the Republic had no steadiness in their system, no measure in their ambition, no expedition in their enterprizes, and no concord in their operations.

When the Prince de Cobourg was joined by Dumouriez, he announced in his manifesto that the Court of Vienna relinquished all idea of conquest, and that it's purpose was to assist the party who wished to destroy tyranny, to deliver the royal family, and to restore the constitutional throne of 1791.

This manifesto, which might have produced division, was disavowed a few days afterwards; and

and the allies no longer diſſembled their projects of re-eſtabliſhing abſolute monarchy, and of puniſhing as rebels all the partizans of liberty.

In vain did ſeveral politicians repreſent to the heads of the coalition, that the conſtitutional party in France was ſtill very numerous, and that united with the moderate party of Republicans, it compoſed an immenſe majority of the French nation; in vain were they urged to obſerve, that the revolts of Bourdeaux, Lyons and Marſeilles would receive a very rapid increaſe, if their progreſs were not reſtrained by the dread of counter-revolutionary vengeance. Far from conſenting to diſſipate this dread by releaſing la Fayette and the conſtituent deputies who had been arreſted, their ſufferings were augmented;* and the coaleſced powers, as well as the emigrants, remained obſtinately perſuaded that the frenzy of the Jacobins was more favourable to their views than the principles of the moderates, and that good could only ſpring from the exceſs of evil. Strange ſyſtem! as falſe in policy as cruel in morals, and of which unhappily experience has not yet cured all Europe.

The Auſtrians, the Engliſh and the Pruſſians

* See the Appendix, Narrative of the Captivity of la Fayette, Maubourg, and Bureau-de-Puzy, extracted from their notes.

having

having taken the violent resolution of not to conciliate any party, to accommodate no opinion; but to restore the antient system in France, ought at least, in order to pursue this plan with success, to have openly and vigorously assisted the rebels in la Vendée who had raised the royal standard; they ought to have furnished them with ships, arms, soldiers, and above all, to have sent the French Princes, who any where else could only fight as foreigners; but who in these provinces, being in the bosom of their country, might have collected more partizans, and might perhaps have even seen themselves surrounded by all those who detested the decemviral tyranny. On the contrary, they prevented those Princes from carrying their arms thither, and acquiring the eclat necessary to excite enthusiasm, and to recover their rank in the public opinion; they led them in their train without leaving them either the power of making themselves feared, or the means of making themselves beloved.

They thus accustomed the people to confound them with their enemies. They supplied the Vendéans with some money and warlike stores, but so parsimoniously, that the cabinet of St. James's may be supposed, (as it has been accused), to have rather aimed to prolong the troubles

troubles of France than to terminate the revolution.

Not having in this respect adopted the shortest and most direct road, they ought at least in making conquests to have unequivocally displayed their good faith, by giving up the places which they reduced to the princes whose rights they pretended to support; but Valenciennes was taken in the name of the Emperor; England wished to seize on Dunkirk; by a secret convention, it is said, Alsace was to be ceded to the court of Vienna. Toulon alone, whose navy was destroyed, was from respect to Spain conquered in the name of Louis XVII. and when the English afterwards made themselves masters of Corsica, it was considered as a colony of Great Britain, and a Viceroy appointed.

At the same time, in the other extremity of Europe, the same ambition appeared undisguised. The Empress of Russia, who seemed to arm only for the re-establishment of the Polish emigrants in their privileges, and to restore to that republic its antient constitution, dismembered this unhappy country: notwithstanding the protestations of the deluded emigrants, she had arranged this partition with Frederic William, formerly the support of the Polish revolution,

volution, and who then took possession of Dantzic and Thorn, and of a part of Great Poland, whilst accusing the Poles of jacobinism, because they had changed a republic into a monarchy.

However unjust, however dishonourable might be this policy of Kings, the coalesced powers might have succeeded in their ambitious views against France, had they availed themselves of the terror inspired by their first victories, of the internal weakness produced by anarchy, and of the dispersion of the French after the battle of Famars. But Austria pretended to take possession of the strong places; England was desirous of making war on the coasts and destroying the ports; the King of Prussia, who had nothing to gain in France, attended more to the affairs of Poland than to the interests of his allies. Thus the wise plans proposed by General Mack were rejected; instead of acting in concert, each pursued a separate plan; and losing an invaluable opportunity, time was allowed to the French government to recover from its panic, to suppress internal factions, to recruit, equip and arm a million of warriors, who soon repulsed from all parts the hostile phalanxes, and threatened Europe with a universal revolution.

Prince

Prince de Cobourg, after having taken Valenciennes and Condé, summoned Cambray unsuccessfully, and remained afterwards in a state of inaction perfectly inexplicable, at a time when France had no obstacle to oppose him.

The English threatened at once Dunkirk, Bergues, Gravelines, and Calais. They relied on the understanding which subsisted betwixt them and the town of Dunkirk; but the officer who communicated with them was arrested, and the commandant who succeeded him was equally inaccessible to fear and to seduction. The artillery expected by the Duke of York was sent too late. Houchard, with thirty thousand French, attacked and completely defeated him, taking all his artillery and warlike stores, and was afterwards sent to the scaffold by the decemvirs, for not having entirely destroyed the English army.

The Duke of York was pursued as far as Nieuport, which made a vigorous resistance against the French. England, instead of directing all her forces to one point, scattered them, attempted too many enterprizes at the same time, and struck feebly every where. She seised on Miquelon and Saint Pierre, failed at Martinico, afforded but little aid to la Vendée, and

and notwithstanding the troubles in Saint Domingo could only conquer a part of that colony, whither she had been invited by the treachery of some mulattoes, and the despair of a great number of proprietors put to flight by the sanguinary fury of the revolted negroes.

Admiral Hood, after having unsuccessfully endeavoured to revive royalty at Marseilles, took possession of Toulon at the head of the English and Spanish fleets; but he landed an army of only fourteen thousand men, consisting of Neapolitans, Spanish, English, German and Piedmontese, too weak from their number and from their heterogeneous mixture to extend their conquests, and join the insurgents of Lyons.

The French government, diffusing money and terror, directed against Lyons numerous columns, who triumphed after a dreadful carnage and an obstinate resistance of the malcontents; and this unhappy city, victim of the fury of Collot d'Herbois, one of the decemvirs, beheld in a few moments her glory eclipsed, her wealth pillaged, her manufactures destroyed, her houses demolished, and her inhabitants massacred by order of tyrants, who censured the executioners as being too humane, and the executions as too slow. They wished to exterminate

minate the very name of Lyons; but it will be immortal as the infamy of it's diftroyers.

After the capture of Lyons, the Republican army marched rapidly towards the fouth, defeated the Royalifts at Olioulles, took O'Hara the general of the coalefed troops prifoner, and after a very fhort fiege retook Toulon. On their evacuation of it, the Englifh burnt the magazines and fhips, and with an inhumanity equally odious and impolitic, abandoned moft of the French whom they had induced to revolt to the refentment of their enemies. The decemviral government acted as cruelly at Toulon as at Lyons, and avenged itfelf by feveral thoufand affaffinations for the imprifonment of two deputies, and for the rebellion of the Toulonefe.

In the following year the Convention, by a decree as ridiculous as barbarous, declared Mr. Pitt the enemy of the human race, and by a more atrocious law, ordered all the Englifh who fhould be taken in battle to be maffacred. This law, worthy of cannibals, was not obeyed by any of their armies.

Whilft the committee of public fafety thought to fecure it's power by outraging humanity, the coalition, hurried on by it's paffions, openly violated the law of nations. Marat and Semonville,

ville, French ambassadors, were arrested by the Austrians in a neutral territory, and put in irons. The English, disregarding the neutrality of the Genoese, seized a French frigate in the port of Genoa. Such is the misfortune of wars for opinions, whether religious or political; each fancying virtue on his side and crime on that of his enemy, deems all means legitimate by which he can accomplish his purpose, and infringes without scruple the rules of morality and justice.

The Vendéans being neither assisted by the English, nor supported by the presence of their Princes, and not occupying any strong place which might serve them as a rallying point, exerted under the brave Charrette, all the efforts that could be expected from political and religious fanaticism united.

After several alternate victories and defeats, the garrison of Mentz, which the King of Prussia had impoliticly allowed to return into France, having arrived and increased the force of the troops which attacked them, the royalists were completely beaten, and compelled to disperse in the neighbouring departments. From that moment la Vendée and Brittany were delivered up to the vengeance of an atrocious proconsul named Carriere, who in ferocity surpassed all the

the monsters of his own times and all those of antiquity.

Women, children, old men, nothing escaped the resentment of this barbarian; he shot unarmed men, murdered the infant at the breast of it's mother; and with the irony of a Nero, united in his dreadful chains, under the title of *republican marriages*, lovers and their spouses were crowded in vessels which were funk by his orders in the midst of the stream. In a word, this monster, burning, pillaging, depopulating all countries, shocked foreigners with the sight of the bloody waves which the Loire every day rolled to the ocean.

All the inhabitants of France were indignant at these horrors. But, although they were the victims, they knew that foreigners would render them responsible, and that the French would be the most dishonoured of nations by it's crimes, unless it should become the most illustrious by it's triumphs. They wished to deliver themselves from their enemies, before they punished their butchers. Should they be vanquished, they would be considered as their accomplices; if they were victorious, they might be their judges; they therefore swore to conquer, and they accomplished their oath.

Placed betwixt the scaffold of their tyrants and

and the cannon of their enemies, they despised external danger, triumphed over internal perils, and to their courage France was indebted at the same time for her safety and her glory.

The Austrians, pressed by numerous battalions, were defeated near Maubeuge, and compelled to entrench themselves in the forest of Mormale.

On the Rhine, their success was still more rapid and decisive. The Prussians and the Imperialists were possessed of the lines of Lautern, Weissenburg and Fort Louis; they had invested Landau, and repulsed the French as far as Haguenau. But there existed but little concert betwixt the allies; and though policy concealed the causes of this diffension, which soon after determined Frederic William to quit the coalition, it appears, according to the opinion circulated in Prussia by persons of consideration, that there existed betwixt the King of Prussia and the Emperor a convention, which the latter had not fulfilled. The Prussians had guaranteed the possession of Landau and Strasburg to the Court of Vienna, and the Emperor was to cede to the King of Prussia three bailiwicks in Silesia. It is affirmed, that Baron de Thugut deeming the cession of these bailiwicks dangerous, and the acquisitions on the Rhine more solid,

solid, had persuaded the Emperor to extricate himself from the embarrassment in which he was thrown by this agreement, and commanded the Austrian Generals to change the offensive war on the Rhine into a defensive one, and to evacuate Alsace without allowing the Allies to penetrate into their instructions.

In consequence of this change, the Duke of Brunswick, who pushed his operations with vigour, was faintly seconded, or rather thwarted, in his plans by the Austrians.

General Hoche, who had defeated a corps of the Prussian army near Saarbruck, joined General Pichegru at the end of November. They carried all the redoubts of the allies near Haguenau at the point of the bayonet.

The Duke of Brunswick, sword in hand, in vain rallied the Austrians, who abandoned the Prussian troops; the distinguished valour which he displayed in this conjuncture, had no other effect but that of preventing the retreat from becoming a complete rout. The Republicans availed themselves of their advantage, pursued the enemy, and retook Weissemburg. The Prince de Hohenloe raised the siege of Landau; General Wurmser repassed the Rhine, and the Duke of Brunswick retired to Mentz.

Soon after, the latter Prince resigned the command

mand of the army, and published a letter he had written to the King of Pruſſia; in which he complained bitterly of the want of concord among the allies.*

Thus ended the campaign of 1793; which had revived ſuch brilliant hopes, and terminated in the defeat of theſe formidable armies, whoſe maſters appeared, ſome months before, to be ſolely employed in the diviſion of their conqueſts.

Hiſtory exhibits all coalitions conſtantly committing the ſame errors, and loſing the advantage of the junction of their forces, by the diſunion of their chiefs, and the diverſity of their intereſts. The unſucceſsful operations of the army of the league in 1793 occaſioned a coolneſs betwixt the Courts of Vienna and Berlin, which kindled into animoſity, and ſoon burſt forth in reproaches.

The Duke of Brunſwick, on quitting the army, loudly complained of the Auſtrians, who wiſhed to avoid the hazard of a battle, and whoſe tardineſs paralized his efforts. The Emperor deprived General Wurmſer of the command of his troops; but he diſcovered the diſtruſt with which he was inſpired by the conduct of

* See the Appendix, Letter of the Duke of Brunſwick to the King of Pruſſia.

the

the King of Pruſſia. A report was ſpread in Germany of a ſecret agreement betwixt Frederic William and the French Republic, and of a plan of ſecularization which was to aggrandiſe the Pruſſian dominions at the expenſe of the empire. On the other ſide, the Pruſſian cabinet ſuſpected Auſtria and England of being diſpoſed to treat with the French Government, and it had reaſon to believe, that the Emperor ſaw with uneaſineſs the Pruſſian troops maſters of Dantzick, Thorn, and a part of Great Poland.

The latter ſuſpicion was better founded than the former; for the conduct of the tyrants of France rendered the negociation improbable, and England, knowing the weakneſs of the French navy, relied too much on eaſy conqueſts to be willing to terminate the war.

The Emperor then, repreſenting to all the ſtates of the empire the dangers incurred by Germany, and the efforts which he had exerted againſt an enemy, who every where wiſhed to deſtroy royalty, nobility, religion, and property, invited all the circles to riſe in a maſs, and required that the ſtates which had not yet contributed to the common defence, ſhould furniſh and pay the triple contingent.

This demand was not well received; the impoſſibility

possibility of obtaining peace was not credited in the empire, and the ambition of the great powers, who interfered in the internal affairs of France for the purpose of dismembering it, was not approved of by the weaker powers, to whom war presented much danger without any hope of indemnity. Frederic William embraced this occasion to refute the rumours which had been circulated by the Austrians respecting his fidelity: *He hoped,* he said, *nobody would believe such calumnies; he was influenced by no interested motive; he had no other aim but the safety of the empire, and the maintenance of the Germanic Constitution; his treasure had been exhausted for the common cause, and it was impossible that he could continue efforts so ruinous at his own expense.* He openly opposed the proposition of raising the people of the frontier in mass. According to his opinion, *this was to ruin agriculture; previous to their acting, there would not be sufficient time to instruct and discipline so great a number of recruits; and the agitation excited in men's minds by French opinions rendered the arming of the multitude dangerous.*

On this point Frederic William reasoned justly, and the Austrian cabinet committed a great imprudence, by imploring the succour of the people in the midst of a war declared by a people

people against Nobles and Kings. The result of these discussions was, that the levy in mass did not take place, and that the contingents were badly and slowly furnished.

1794.] In the course of the winter, Frederic William proved by his conduct that the reproaches of his allies were not so unjust as he pretended.

All these suspicions were awakened by a conference which General Karlskreuth had with the French commissioners for the exchange of prisoners, at Frankfort. These commissioners arrived with great pomp in one of Louis XVI's. carriages, on which the cap of liberty usurped the place of the crown and the *fleurs-de-lys*. They were very amicably received by the General; and after this conference, the French Government, contrary to its custom, displayed great attention towards the court of Berlin.

Soon after Frederic William, exaggerating his past sacrifices and his present embarrassments, wrote to the Elector of Mentz, that he could no longer support the cost of a war so expensive, —that the Empire owed him indemnities, that the circles must be charged with the maintenance of his forces; because, in case they did not consent, he should be compelled to recall his troops, and to employ them only in the defence of his own dominions.

On the refusal of the circles, in the month of March, the King declared that he would contribute no more than his contingent as Elector of Brandenburg. And, in fact, having ordered General Mollendorf, who had succeeded the Duke of Brunswick, to retire with his army towards Cologne, he left near Mentz only twenty thousand men under the command of General Karlskreuth, the same person who had received the French commissioners at Frankfort.

The motives for this change in the system of Frederic William, were his aversion to a harassing war, the object of which appeared to him to have failed; the exhaustion of his treasury, which his campaigns and his reverses had ruined; the repugnance which the Prussians constantly manifested to the alliance with Austria; the dread of seeing the revolutionary spirit of the French spread among his troops, and in his country; the desire of employing himself without interruption in the affairs of Poland, and of restraining in that country the rival ambition of Catherine; the discontent of the Poles, and the secret opposition of the Austrians; lastly, his love of pleasure, which was
thwarted

thwarted by the war; and above all, that verfatility of character, which during ten years tormented his fubjects, aftonifhed his enemies, haraffed his allies, defolated his family, deranged his finances, and deprived him of all the refpect which he ought to have derived from his fituation and power.

This defection of the King of Pruffia encouraged the neutral powers to refent the threats of England, who wifhed to force them to take a part in the war.

The Britifh cabinet, which entered laft into the coalition, has fince played the principal part; and, if it's military operations had been as active as its political intrigues, it might have attained its purpofe—the deftruction of France.

But it was more prodigal of money than of men; and loft by it's tardinefs many opportunities which fortune prefented. The French royalifts, for want of aid, were defeated at Noirmontiers, and forced to furrender at difcretion.

The rebels of La Vendée failed in their attack on Granville, becaufe the Englifh forces commanded by Lord Moira, which ought to have affifted them, did not arrive in time; and from that inftant the royalifts in France were no longer in a condition to refift their enemies.

According to the report of Carriere at this time,

time, Charrette had no more than three thousand men, and Stofflet eight hundred; the rest were dispersed in the woods; but they would have been very soon re-assembled, had they been supported by troops, protected by ships, and animated by the presence of a French Prince.

It has always been extremely difficult to calculate the forces of this party. At the attack of Saumur, it had thirty thousand men in arms; at the same time sixteen districts were in open revolt; the armed line was forty square leagues: Carriere and the republican Generals estimated the number of fighting royalists at one hundred and fifty thousand. As soon as their leaders projected an expedition, the sails of the wind-mills served as a signal; they immediately assembled, and, when the expedition finished, each hid his arms, and returned to his own field; so that the troops who advanced to combat the rebel battalions, found only peaceable and scattered cultivators.

This rebellion lasted several years in this district, because the nature of the country, intersected and covered with wood, afforded the peasants impenetrable retreats. It did not extend to the towns; because it was impossible to conceal themselves there, and because the royalists,

royalists, not being supported there by regular armies, must have been exposed without resource to the vengeance of the republicans.

England, having missed the favourable occasion of ruining her enemy by a civil war, resolved to seise on the French West-India colonies; and, in order that the republic should not oppose her enterprise, endeavoured by every means to repair the loss which the coalition sustained by the defection of the King of Prussia, and to render the war on the continent more active.

She made a treaty with the King of Sardinia, lent money to the Emperor, and concluded a treaty of subsidy with Frederic William, which, knowing the dispositions of this monarch, occasioned much surprize to politicians, and furnished opposition with a fertile subject for censure, reproach and sarcasm.

This treaty, concluded the 14th of April, obliged the King of Prussia to join the coalition, in the month of May, with an army of sixty-two thousand men. He was to receive fifty millions. This sum had been granted to him, according to the terms of the treaty, *in order to facilitate to his Majesty the means of acting with vigour, and conformably to the zeal and interest with which he is animated for the common cause.*

His

His preceding declaration might give fome idea of his zeal, and the year afterwards his treaty of peace gave the Englifh miniftry complete proof of it. Before the opening of the campaign, a great council of war was held in Flanders. Mack, who came from London, was called to it; and the misfortunes of the laft campaign were ftill attributed to him, though not one of his plans had been adopted.

The Duke of York, always deftined by the adminiftration to command the Englifh troops, and almoft always condemned by Fate to be defeated, would not ferve under the command of an Auftrian Genreal. To put an end to this conteft, the Emperor Francis II. put himfelf at the head of his troops. His arrival at Bruffels reftored to him the affection of the Brabanters; and he acknowledged that he had been deceived by all thofe who had given him an account of this country, except Prince Charles, and Count de Metternich. His prefence re-animated the ardour of his armies, and their firft operations realifed the hopes to which fo many united efforts had given birth: the French were beaten at Cateau-Cambrefis; the allies laid fiege to Landrecy, and arrived in the commencement of the campaign, within

forty

forty leagues of Paris: but this was the termination of their profperity.

Europe was this year enfanguined by the moft numerous and moft formidable armies fhe had ever beheld collected together.

The following are the forces difplayed by the republicans and by the kings, reciprocally determined to deftroy each other.

REPUBLICAN ARMIES.

Army of the North . . . . . . 220 thoufand men
The united Armies of the Rhine and the Mofelle, } 280
Army of the Alps. 60
Army of the Eaftern Pyrénées. 80
Army of the fouth. 60
Army of the weft. 80

      Total 780 thoufand men.

ARMIES OF THE COALITION.

Army of the Prince de Coburg. 140 thoufand men
Army of the Duke of York . . . 40
Army of the Dutch. 20
Auftrian Army on the Rhine. . 60
Army of Pruffians. 64
Troops of the Empire. 20
Army of Condé. 12

      Total 356 thoufand men

It

It is not within the scope of the plan of this work to give an exact account of the skilful manœuvres, the numerous battles, the murderous sieges, which have occurred in the course of this celebrated epoch; the ability of the generals, the obstinacy of the parties, the importance of combinations, the brilliant actions of a host of warriors, require for these military details a separate work; it is to be wished, that the history of the commencement of this memorable war might be described by the same pen, which has just so brilliantly written that of the last two campaigns. Mathieu Dumas in this relation, leaves the reader nothing to wish for in the developement of plans, the series of operations, the accuracy of facts, the elegant perspicuity of style, and the richness of details. But we, in presenting to the reader the vast picture of the revolutions of European policy, during the space of ten years, can only take the results of military events, and we are forced to confine our observations only to their influence on the system of kings and on the fate of nations.

After several battles, and several alternate successes, Clairfait was repulsed near Tournai. The French, after having forced the passage of the Sambre, attempted in vain to drive General Kaunitz out of his position between Rocroy and

and Bitche. The Emperor then arriving at Tournai, a plan was formed for a general attack. It was to be made in three columns: the first under the command of the Emperor and the Prince of Coburg; the other, under that of Prince Charles and Clairfait; the Duke of York, Ott, and Colonel Mack were entrusted with the third. These three columns were defeated by the French: the Hanoverian cavalry, being put to the rout, threw into disorder the army of the Duke of York, who owed his safety only to the swiftness of his horse. After this disaster, the allies regained their position near Tournai; they were there again attacked by the French who lost in the action twelve thousand men. Kaunitz and Beaulieu obtained some advantages; one of them on the Sambre, and the other near Bouillon. All these engagements were but the prelude to more important actions and more decisive events.

The French, pressed by circumstances, stimulated by a terrible government, and animated by that enthusiasm which overcomes all obstacles, totally changed their system of tactics; taking advantage of their superiority of numbers, and not regarding the strong places they left behind them, they disconcerted by their bold marches the prudent and methodical system of their adversaries;

adverfaries; and their ardent and tumultuous valour triumphed over the order and difcipline of the Auftrians, who beheld French bayonets brave their artillery, and carry their moft formidable entrenchments.

Whilft Jourdan employed the attention of the enemy's centre, Pichegru, at the head of a French army, defeated the Englifh in Weft Flanders, took poffeffion of Ypres, and threatened the Low-Countries. Another French army marched towards the duchy of Luxemburg, and forced Kaunitz and Beaulieu to retire. The Prince de Cobourg, at this perilous crifis, wifhing to try a laft effort, and attempting to fuccour Charleroi, of the furrender of which he was ignorant, Jourdan totally defeated him at Fleurus. This victory, as celebrated as that of Jemappe, was ftill more decifive. The Prince de Cobourg, beaten by eighty thoufand men, and fearing to be turned by another army of feventy thoufand, which had juft defeated the Duke of York and Clairfait, and taken Ypres; threatened on the other hand by the third French army which had compelled Beaulieu to evacuate Namur, vainly attempted to hold out for fome time in the foreft of Soignes; he there loft feven thoufand men, was driven out of it, and retired towards Maeftricht. The Duke

Duke of York flowly fuccoured by Lord Moira, retreated towards Breda. The Emperor, lofing all hope, returned to Vienna, and fent orders to his army to return to Germany.

The French, during the reft of the campaign, took poffeffion without oppofition of all the Low-Countries; recaptured Valenciennes, Condé, le Quefnoy, Landrecies, which they had left behind them, and prepared to carry the war into Holland.

The Auftrians were equally unfuccefsful on the Rhine. The French threatened Manheim and Mentz; the army of Italy poffeffed itfelf of Oneglia. The republican troops, every where victorious, defeated the Spaniards at Saint-Jean-de-Luz, at Figuirés, at Irun, and made the Duke d'Alcudia, the then minifter and favourite of the King of Spain, repent of having oppofed the pacific fyftem of the Count d'Aranda, the credit of whofe antiquated policy he had ridiculed and overthrown.

In the courfe of this campaign, the clofe of which changed the deftinies of Europe, there were twenty-three regular fieges; the French gained fix pitched battles, and poffeffed themfelves of one hundred and twenty-four towns and cities.

The republic was as unfortunate by fea as

she had been triumphant by land. Nearly all the officers of the French navy had emigrated; and in a naval war, it is impossible for courage to supply the place of instruction: the English took possession of Corsica; Admiral Howe totally defeated the republican fleet and took seven ships of the line. The crew of the *Vengeur* gave on this day an immortal proof of the enthusiasm of the French; when this ship, pierced through and through by the enemy's balls, was sinking, the English, with a mixture of horror and admiration, heard these intrepid warriors make the air resound at the moment of death with the cries of *vive la liberté! vive la republic!* What wonders would a virtuous government produce at the head of such a nation!

The British squadrons possessed themselves of the islands of Saint Lucie, Guadaloupe, Marie-Galante, Martinico, and Deseada. The parliament passed a vote of thanks to Sir Charles Grey and Sir John Jervis. The French, by way of indemnification for these so serious losses, had only to congratulate themselves on the entrance into their ports of a convoy consisting of a hundred and sixty vessels, which brought them grain from the United States of America, and the capture of a great number of merchant ships

ships which their privateers took from the English. The Kings of Europe ought then to have perceived that they were no more than gladiators paid by Great Britain, in order to prolong, to the injury of their subjects and the peril of their crowns, a war of which the cabinet of London alone would reap the fruits.

The English and Austrian ministers have always maintained, in order to justify in the eye of humanity the prolongation of this disastrous war, that the general interests of Europe was to overturn a democratic tyranny so contagious by its principles, so powerful by its extent, and so evidently destructive of all social order; they have constantly repeated that it was impossible to make and to preserve peace with a government so ambitious and so unstable, which would not be subject to any of the rules consecrated by the law of nations.

These two assertions have been dictated by an excessive ambition and a false policy. Recent experience has but too strongly confirmed this truth in all ages, that democracies are consolidated by war, and dissolved by peace. The coalition united against the common danger all the divided parties; they gave to the tyrants of France all the causes they could wish to enable them to concentrate power in their hands, and all the pretexts that were neceffary to authorife their fpoliations and cruelties. Thus, the war, far from attaining it's objects, exafperated the minds which it ought to have calmed ; trained to war the democrats whofe ftrength it dreaded ; extended the territorial power of the country that it wifhed to diminifh ; and irretrievably loft, by the tranfition of property, the ariftocracy which they intended to protect.

The victories of the republic convinced all nations, that without nobility it could fight and conquer; the German foldiers might behold with envy an order of things where every brave man became a General; and the contagion of this example was a danger much more fubftantial to the Princes than all that had been alledged to juftify the war. The hope of fubjugating a million of men in arms was chimerical.

On the other hand, it was afferted without reafon, that it was impoffible to treat and live in amity with France. Sweden and Denmark, by their happy and tranquil neutrality, refuted this allegation: and a fhort time afterwards Pruffia and Spain proved beyond contradiction that they could negotiate with fuccefs and fafety. However barbarous the jacobin fyftem might be, France had need of peace ; and it is universally

universally known, that treaties unfortunately find a guarantee more certain in the interest of governments than in their fidelity.

It would appear certain, that had not the coalition armed, the King would never have perished; and that had not the emigrants been encouraged and deceived, they might have returned to France, and would neither have been proscribed nor stript of their property.

It is beyond a doubt, that at the moment of Dumouriez' defection, and till the commencement of 1794, if the coalition had been willing to make peace with the republic, the royal family would have been liberated, and the Low-Countries would have remained with the Emperor. But the abolition of royalty, and the death of Louis XVI. having inflamed the passions, prudent policy was no longer attended to; and England, taking advantage of the general hatred which existed against France, seemed resolved to perpetuate the war, in order to annihilate the commerce and the navy of France, to seize on the riches of the East and West Indies, and to establish unrivalled her domination over all the seas.

This ambitious plan was soon developed, and opened the eyes of the Spanish monarch. At the taking of Toulon, he was desirous that the

French ships of war found in that port might be confided to him, as belonging to Louis XVII. of whose rights the allies assumed the defence. The English retained the ships they had taken, and burnt those they could not carry away.

Corsica, conquered, ought to belong to the King of France; George III. took possession of it. At last, a Spanish register ship, carrying nine millions of piastres, having been taken by some republican privateers, and a few days afterwards recaptured by the English, was in vain reclaimed by the court of Madrid; that of London seized without scruple the property of her ally, of which it constantly refused to make restitution.

This conduct demonstrated to the Duke d'Alcudia that he was made the sport of the English ministry, and determined him speedily to dissolve an alliance so very uncertain, and to terminate a war so fatal to the house of Bourbon.

But, if the hatred of the English government desired to increase the internal evils of France, she ought to have been perfectly satisfied. Never had a country been the prey of a more bloody anarchy, or a more ferocious tyranny. It might have been supposed that the inhumanity

of

of the persons who oppressed her could not be increased; but the division that was established between them carried it even to delirium.

The club of Cordeliers, still more violent than that of the jacobins, endeavoured to destroy the latter, as suspected of aristocracy and moderation. Hébert, Chaumette, Vincent, Momoro, Ronsin, and the members of the *Commune* of Paris, guided this party, whose aim was, it is said, after having overcome their rivals, to place a new dynasty on the throne.

Since the 31st of May, the only means to arrive at power, and to avoid being hated as royalists, were to enrich the populace by pillage, to terrify energy by executions, and to propose laws the most sanguinary, absurd, and impious.

All housekeepers were compelled to inscribe their names over their doors; all persons of property were obliged to declare the extent of their fortunes, and to give in their specie; all the non-abjuring priests were transported; part of the ex-nobles were incarcerated; the others were put under the inspection of the police in appointed places, to wait their sentence. All the parliaments were destroyed, the merchants were all obliged to sell their commodities at a low price, by the law which fixed a *maximum*, and which produced a general scarcity. Atheism was preached every where; all kinds of dress and language were proscribed which announced some degree of decency, fortune, and education. A foreigner arriving at Paris, met in the streets only men of a hideous and ferocious aspect; women disgusting and lost to shame; nothing was heard but brutal speeches and atrocious blasphemy. In every *Commune,* in every section, were established clubs and revolutionary committees, consisting of banditti immersed in crimes: they had not the right to save any one, but their power to denounce, imprison, plunder, and send innocence to the scaffold was unlimited. The dregs of the people were paid to assist at assemblies, in order to encourage guilt, to terrify moderation, and to applaud executions.

The mind could find no relief from this horrible spectacle, but by penetrating into the prisons, with which the whole surface of France was covered; there were found united, virtue, beauty, talents, and that serenity which flies from tyrants but never abandons innocence.

In the same manner, as it is necessary to open the abysses of the earth, to discover the precious metals it contains, so was it then necessary to dive into dungeons in order to find constant love, faithful friendship, gentle piety, heroic generosity, and that philosophy whose name has

has been so much proſtituted, but which alone can give to minds a conſtant equanimity, to governments a true glory, and to nations a permanent happineſs.

If France has made Europe ſhudder by the crowd of wretches by whom ſhe has been polluted, ſhe ought alſo to excite its admiration by the number of brilliant actions, the efforts of virtue, the traits of generoſity, and the prodigies of courage, reſignation, and devotedneſs, of which ſhe has given an example.

Illuſtrious annals might be filled with the names of all the prieſthood who have died martyrs to their faith; of all the ſervants who have ſnatched their maſters from death; of fathers who have died for their children; of females who have ſhared the fetters of their lovers; of wives * who have braved chains, priſons, and executioners, to ſave their huſbands or to follow them to the ſcaffold. Never will be forgotten the hymns of the prieſts maſſacred in the month of September, invoking heaven for their murderers; the filial piety of *Mademoiſelle*

* *Madame de la Fayette,* an honour to her ſex and to her country, quitted the dungeons of Robeſpierre, in which her kindred had periſhed, only to go heroically with her daughters, to participate the bonds of her huſband in the priſons of the Emperor at Olmutz.

de

de Sombreuil, throwing herself between her father and his assassins; the courage of the young and beautiful Custine, vainly defying tyranny in order to defend her husband and her father-in-law; the stoicism of Malesherbes, who lived and died like Socrates; the modest firmness and the mild eloquence, pious and persuasive, of *Mesdames de Noailles**, who by their example and discourse restored courage and composure to a person condemned and overwhelmed by despair, and who went with them to execution. We shall ever call to mind the resignation of *Madame Elizabeth*, whose angelic purity, it is said, excited even the remorse of Robespierre.

In a word, history will tell, that during this fatal epoch, crime, virtue, wisdom, error, military valour, civic courage, every thing in the French nation, was marked by an impression of grandeur of which the most celebrated periods of antiquity furnish few examples; and which cannot be denied but by misfortune too much exasperated, and hatred too blind.

In the mean time, notwithstanding all the efforts of tyrants to conceal the truth, to enchain vengeance, to blind the nation, and to impose silence on pity, the eyes of the multitude

---

* D'Aguesseau, *ci-devant* Duchess d'Ayen, and Madame de Noailles her daughter.

began

began to be opened. The creditors of the emigrants saw their claims lost; the poor who thought they should divide the lands of the rich, found that they must purchase them; and that to them no benefit accrued. The law of the *maximum*, in favouring for an instant the shopkeepers at the expence of the merchants, had produced famine and the ruin of commerce.

The haughtiness of the nobility was forgotten, from the insolent cruelty of those who had come to preferment; and these nobles, imprisoned, stripped, sacrificed, were no longer the object of hatred from ceasing to be that of envy, and they began to excite pity. The priests, whose scandalous luxury had disgusted the nation, were venerated from the time they became poor and persecuted; and in several departments the blood of these martyrs regenerated devotion and carried it even to fanaticism. Even the emigrants, against whom the people had been so much more incensed, as to them were attributed all the evils of the war, appeared more excusable, since all their kindred who had remained faithful to their country had been assassinated. The decemvirs, instead of extending their rigours only over the aristocrats who had opposed the revolution, were compelled, in order to stop murmurs,

murs, to stifle the voice of humanity; and to prevent revolt, to send to the scaffold a crowd of plebeians, and of the poorest mechanics, when they dared to disapprove their tyrannical laws.

The long proscription and the great number of judicial assassinations, universally inspired as much wrath as terror. People were indignant to obey men who spoke of liberty accompanied by the noise of chains, of virtue only in the midst of plunder, and of humanity surrounded by executioners.

No one could awake in safety, nor sleep without dread; every man was apprehensive lest his fellow-citizen might be a spy, a denunciator, an enemy: the slightest noise at the door of a house spread alarm in families; they always thought they saw the arrival of robbers or gaolers. Men the most violent in favour of the revolution were not secured by the pledges, frequently criminal, which they had given; all were equally exposed to the suspicious fury of the new Syllas of France.

The same scaffold exhibited a scene in which were sacrificed the zealous royalist, the intrepid constitutionalist, the fanatical priest, the sanguinary jacobin, the opulent financier, the obscure artificer, the celebrated philosopher, the shameless prostitute, the innocent virgin, and the ferocious anarchist.

The

The government in its delirium resembled those cruel scourges, those fatal epidemical distempers, which rapidly depopulate a vast region by mowing down indiscriminately all ranks, all ages, and all sexes.

It appeared certain, that Robespierre himself at length felt the necessity of opposing a mound to this desolating torrent; but fearing to be struck by his inflexible accomplices in the attempt to arrest the scythe of death, he endeavoured to sound the opinions of the clubs and of the people, by engaging Camille Desmoulins to publish a pamphlet entitled, *Les Vieux Cordelier*; in which this deputy, formerly too factious, but then the victim of his humanity, quoted several passages extracted from Tacitus, which at once depicted in a lively manner the tyranny of the Roman emperors, and the frightful misfortunes of which Paris was the theatre.

This publication was rapidly circulated and eagerly received by all who preserved in France the smallest particle of sensibility; but it spread alarm in the clubs; the *brigands* bellowed against the audacious author, who thus dared to shew crime its image, and to afford a spark of hope in favour of virtue.

Robespierre feebly defended his friend, and dreading the fury of his rivals, basely sent to execution

execution this unfortunate man, whose pen he had first encouraged, and whose fear he had removed. From this moment Robespierre, exasperated and governed by dread, no longer set bounds to his fury.

Thinking himself threatened by Danton, Fabre d'Eglantine, Chabot, and a few bold deputies, he anticipated them, had them arrested and transferred to the revolutionary tribunal; these members of the Convention refused to answer their judges, till they had been confronted with their accuser. The multitude applauded their courage: they had a numerous party in the senate. Robespierre came thither, there spoke imperiously, and extorted through fear a decree which authorised the tribunal to condemn without formality every one accused who should fail in respect to it's members. Danton and his friends persisted in their resistance, and were hurried to the scaffold without any one daring to defend them.

A short time afterwards the Cordeliers attempted to erect the standard of revolt; they had covered the declaration of rights with a black veil; but the speedy execution of their leaders, Ronsin, Hébert, Chaumette, Momoro, was the punishment of their audacity. General Dillon, depending on the favour of the people, formed

formed in the prison of the Luxemburg, the chimerical project of breaking his chains; his indiscreet hope was denounced to the tyrants by the infamous La Flotte, who partook his imprisonment; and under the illusory pretext of this ideal conspiration, they sacrificed all the prisoners who were shut up in that palace, and a part of those confined in the convent of the Carmelites.

In a short time Robespierre, intoxicated with blood, and devoured by ambition, remorse, fear, and rage, finding the forms of the tribunal too troublesome, and his daggers too slow, procured the passing of a terrific law, which deprived the accused of any defender, and required only moral proofs for their condemnation.

A desperate citizen endeavoured to assassinate Collot 'd'Herbois; a young girl was suspected of having attempted the life of Robespierre; these two attempts occasioned the sacrifice of a crowd of unfortunates, who did not even know the name of the accused, and from that time each day witnessed the immolation of sixty or eighty victims at a time; the prisons were filled and emptied with the most horrible rapidity. The unfortunate father of a family, in the evening free and tranquil, was the next day suspected, arrested, tried, condemned, and executed,

cuted, before his children were able to learn the cause of his absence. The deputy, who the instant before made his fellow-citizen tremble, saw himself placed under the axe of the executioner. The judges trembled on their seat. The pro-consuls in the departments every where repeated the same horrors. Lebon depopulated the north, Carriere the west, others the south, and France throughout was no more than a heap of ruins and an ocean of tears and of blood.

Whilst Robespierre thus gave the signal of a universal destruction, he reflected how he might shift the horror of it on his colleagues and his instruments. For six weeks he conspired their destruction, and no longer appeared in the committee of public safety. Studying the dispositions of the multitude, he knew that they were weary of these cruelties, and above all, terrified at the outrages committed against religion and against God himself. Hypocritically declaring himself the defender of heaven, he obtained from the Convention a decree, that France acknowledged the existence of a Deity, and he ordained the celebration of a festival in honour of the Supreme Being.

This absurd and sacrilegious declaration, however, restored to Robespierre a part of his former popularity. Intoxicated with his success, he appeared

appeared at this feftival in the garden of the Thuilleries, in the midft of an immenfe crowd, with a haughtinefs contrary to his ufual diffimulation. It is even affirmed, that he had conceived the defign of then having himfelf proclaimed Dictator. But, whether his agents had not prepared the people as he wifhed, or whether he was ftopped by fear at the moment of attempting this coloffal enterprife, he did not put it in execution; but imprudently unmafked his ambition, without daring to fecure the fruit of it by a fkilful temerity.

His colleagues were neither ignorant of his hatred, nor their own danger; nine deputies, among whom were Barras, Freron, Rovère, Legendre, Bourdon, Tallien, Merlin (de Thionville), and Lecointre, had fworn to prevent their deftruction, and to put an end to the life of this monfter.

The hollow agitation which precedes ftorms, announced a great explofion. On the 8th Thermidor it burft forth, and on the 9th it ceafed.

Robefpierre, informed that they confpired againft him, being certain of the majority of the jacobins, of the affiftance of the *Commune* of Paris, of the favour of a part of the populace, of the fuccours of Henriot, commander of the national

national guard and of the attachment of Saint-Juſt and Couthon, his colleagues in the committee, thought that he could with impunity attack the other members of the government, obtain a decree of accuſation againſt them, involve in their deſtruction all the deputies whoſe energy he dreaded, and quietly ſeize by means of terror an abſolute power.

Aſcending the tribune, he pronounced a violent harangue on the ſituation of the republic, and bitterly complained of the calumnies ſpread abroad againſt him, wiſhing to perſuade the people that he aſpired to the dictatorſhip. *Oppoſing his public and private life to the reproaches of his enemies, he aſſerted that this impoſture was the work of the Engliſh, who had numerous partiſans in France; that if he had wiſhed to betray liberty and attain deſpotiſm, he would have been ſeconded by the ſame men who declared themſelves his accuſers.*

His love for the republic and the decree that he had obtained to annihilate atheiſm, drew on him, he ſaid, *as many enemies as there were traitors and infidels. Forced to be abſent during four decades from the committee of government, he did not leſs aſſiduouſly watch over the public welfare.*

But he ſaw with grief that the rigorous decrees againſt the Engliſh were not executed on the frontiers;

tiers; that the laws were without vigour, the finances without order, the poor without protection, innocence without support; that a crowd of victims were sacrificed without justice; that the efforts of the friends of liberty were palsied; that the Convention was amused by planting the sterile tree of liberty in Belgium, and by making pompous harangues on the victories of the armies, whose march they retarded; that Paris was unprovided with artillery; that there existed in this city dangerous conspiracies; that he was not incited by any other motive than the desire of saving the country, and that he was forced (however disagreeable these truths might be to certain persons who heard them) to unveil them to the Convention, in order that it might adopt the necessary measures to guard against the dangers with which it was threatened.

When Robespierre had concluded his speech, the proposition of ordering it to be printed was warmly opposed by Bourdon, Vadier, and Cambon, who accused him of falsehoods and perfidy, and constrained him, for the first time, to descend to justify himself.

Freron moved, that a report might be made of the decree which permitted the government to arrest the deputies; this courageous opposition called forth the most lively applauses, and awakened the sentiment of liberty. The terror however that Robespierre inspired, still dominated over the minds of the deputies, and the majority of the Convention decreed that his speech should be printed.

By this sitting, the tyrant foresaw that his influence in the senate was on the point of being overthrown. He repaired in the evening to the jacobins, whose passions he inflamed by the picture of their common danger.

The next day Saint-Just, depending on his eloquence, endeavoured to possess himself of the tribune, in order to attack the enemies of Robespierre; but he was driven from it by the general clamour. Billaud-Varennes accused Robespierre, Saint-Just, Cuthon, Henriot, and La Valette, of aspiring to tyranny, and of wishing to massacre the Convention. Robespierre in vain attempted to answer; his voice was drowned by the cries which were raised on all sides of *a bas le tyran*. Notwithstanding this general tumult, still no one dared to propose a formal decree against him. Tallien then rose, and in a vehement speech, painted in the most vivid colours all the atrocities under which France had groaned, and of which he regarded Robespierre as the principal author. After having recapitulated all the details of his bloody tyranny,

ranny, all the crimes he had authorised, all the atrocious laws of which he had been the author, all the victims which he had sacrificed, earnestly endeavouring to make the Convention blush at so disgraceful a slavery, and turning towards the bust of Brutus, invoked his genius, and drawing forth a dagger from his girdle, he swore that he would plunge it into the heart of Robespierre, if the representatives of the people had not the courage to order his arrestation, and to break their chains.

In vain did the monster, reddening with fury, attempt to repel this violent attack; the universal imprecations with which he was loaded, did not permit him to be heard; he vented his rage in ineffectual efforts, and the Convention decreed his arrest, and that of his accomplices. He was led to prison; the administrators, who were devoted to him, would not receive him, and the jacobins at the head of a furious populace, dispersing the guard which surrounded him, carried him in triumph to the *Hotel-de Ville*, where he saw himself at the head of the *Commune* of Paris, disposed to draw up the laws which he would dictate to it, and surrounded by a deluded crowd, which appeared ready to defend him.

At the same instant Henriot, who had been arrested

arrested at the committee of general safety, had just been liberated by eight hundred factious armed men; and if he had taken advantage of this moment to enter into the hall of the Convention which was not guarded, the deputies who had just signalised themselves by their energy would have been sacrificed without obstruction; and the terrified Convention, passing all the decrees which he might wish to extort from them, would perhaps have yielded irrevocably the victory and the empire to the ferocious tyrants, from whom it wished to deliver France.

Fortunately Robespierre, as cowardly as cruel, employed himself only in proscribing when he ought to have fought; and, instead of marching against the Convention, he contented himself with putting it out of the protection of the law by the resolutions of the *Commune*. Henriot on his part, at the head of the soldiers who had liberated him, thought only of running through the different parts of the city to call the people to his succour.

The Convention, then reflecting on the uneasiness which the late escape of Robespierre had caused, it unanimously adopted the most vigorous measures. Barras and some of his colleagues were entrusted with the command of Paris.

Paris. All the citizens were called to the defence of liberty; every one, seizing the opportunity of delivering himself from so odious a tyranny, flew to arms, and several deputies having assembled some of the sections, marched to the *Commune,* read to the multitude which surrounded it the decree that condemned the conspirators, and penetrated without opposition into the *Hotel-de-Ville,* where they seized all the conspirators.

Robespierre seeing all was lost[*], shot himself with a pistol; but the justice of Heaven did not permit the ball, which entered the lower part of his face, to terminate a life polluted with so many crimes. His wound rendered his punishment more cruel, and his sufferings longer. He beheld during twenty-four hours the universal joy inspired by his downfall, and the horror which his person excited; he heard the reproaches of his colleagues, whom he had abased, and over whom he had tyrannised; the cries of joy of the victims whom he still wished to strike, and the

[*] Others affirm that it was a citizen who wounded Robespierre. This however is certain, that at the very moment when the tyrant was extended on the earth, bathed in his blood, and surrounded by an irritated crowd that loaded him with injuries, a *Gendarme* passing near him, stopt, and without any imprecations nobly addressed to him these words: *Robespierre there does exist a Supreme Being.*

imprecations

imprecations of the whole people, whom he had for fuch a length of time deceived and oppreffed. An object of public execration, no kind remembrance could ftrengthen his courage, no friend by his tears foften his torments. He was compelled to appear before that revolutionary tribunal, by which his fury had commanded fo many affaffinations; condemned by his own accomplices, he was led to the fcaffold with his brother, Couthon, Saint-Juft and Lebas, his colleagues, Henriot his general, and the members of the rebellious *Commune*. An immenfe crowd followed him, reproached him with his crimes and his bafenefs, loaded him with outrages, and announced to him by their acclamations the judgement of pofterity, which would place him in the lift of the moft odious and contemptible tyrants. The executioner, tearing of with violence the bandage which covered his wound, drew from him a hideous fhriek, expofed him for fome time to the eager looks of vengeance and hatred, and at laft difpatched him by a death as infamous as his life.

The tyrant was dead, but tyranny was not deftroyed. Collot d'Herbois and Billaud ftill reigned; Barrère, in their name, had the audacity to propofe to fubftitute for the decemvirs who had juft been condemned, the deputies who
planned

planned the government. Had this proscription been acceded to, the same system of cruelty, despotism and oppression would have continued; the Convention would have remained enslaved, and France would have been lost. Fortunately, the deputies, whose energy had overthrown Robespierre, were not so weak as to lose the fruit of this revolution. They restored inviolability and liberty to the members of the Convention; they decreed that the committees of public safety and of general safety should monthly be renewed by scrutiny. Legendre, once a violent Cordelier, but at that moment an intrepid enemy of the tyranny to which he had nearly fallen a victim for having endeavoured to defend Danton, went, followed by some courageous men, to the club of the jacobins, drove them away from their den, and brought the keys of their hall to the Convention.

From this moment, terror by degrees ceased to spread her bloody veil over France. Innocence by degrees was seen to respire, justice to revive, and virtue to take courage. The judges and the juries, the executioners of the revolutionary tribunal, the proconsul, Lebon, the Nero of Aras, the infamous Carriere, the destroyer of la Vendée, expiated their crimes on the scaffold; the prisons were opened, the revolutionary

volutionary committees were diſſolved and purſued by public vengeance.

But this progreſs of the return from anarchy to ſocial order was ſlow, and often interrupted by formidable conſpiracies. The Mountain long predominated, and oppoſed with all its might changes which tended to ſtrengthen the Girondine party, whoſe vengeance it dreaded.

The Girondiſts, the moderate republicans, were themſelves afraid, leſt in accelerating too much the retrograde movement, the conſtitutionaliſts might take advantage of it to puniſh the revolution of the 10th of Auguſt.

Laſtly, there were ſeen moments when the conſtitutionaliſts alſo, experiencing theſe fears, dreaded leſt the public opinion, hurried away by their ardent zeal for juſtice which alarmed them, might carry the reaction ſo far, as imprudently to favour the royaliſts, a counter-revolution, and the vengeance by which it was likely to be followed.

Such is the unhappy lot of men, when with the view of attaining any object, they have employed violent means, and committed any injuſtice: they are always impeded in their progreſs towards the public good, by fear of the individual evil that may reſult to themſelves. This fear blinds them, and makes them forget, that

that justice is the only means to acquire general esteem; that by it every new government is strengthened, and without it all power is destroyed.

All the reasonings of fear against the dangers of equity are sophisms; private passions subside; the general interest is justice, which is immortal as truth. No force can for a long period control public opinion; success may give a momentary lustre, a brilliant celebrity; but esteem alone renders authority tranquil, and glory substantial.

Whilst the French, by a happy revolution, had escaped the monster anarchy, which threatened them with total destruction, a less fortunate nation made ineffectual efforts, in the other extremity of Europe, to break the chains of despotism, and preserve its existence.

We shall, in the ensuing chapter, proceed to give a sketch of this unsuccessful insurrection; which, in spite of the prodigies of valour displayed by Kosciosko and his unfortunate compatriots, terminated in the total partition of their country.

CHAP.

CHAP. XII.

Revolution of Poland.—Perfidiousness of the courts of Petersburg and Berlin.—Contradictory declarations of Frederic William.—His troops enter Poland.—Diet of Grodno.—Violence exerted over the Diet.—Treaty extorted.—Insurrection of the Poles.—Character and conduct of Kosciosko.—He takes Cracow, and defeats the Prussians.—Revolution at Warsaw.—The Russians are driven from that city.—Advantages of the Poles at Vilna, and in several other actions. Frederic William besieges Warsaw.—Insurrection in Great Poland.—Frederic William raises the siege of Warsaw and retreats.—Suvaroff enters Poland. Kosciosko betrayed, loses a battle fought against Fersen.—He is wounded and taken prisoner.—Suvaroff besieges Warsaw; takes by assault the suburb of Prague.—Horrible massacre.—Warsaw surrenders.—Dispersion of the Polish troops.—Stanislaus Augustus quits his capital, and goes first to Grodno, and afterwards to Petersburg.—Total partition and enslavement of the Poles.

AFTER having traced all the crimes of jacobinical tyranny, without regard for a party, the dangerous roots of which still exist, it becomes us to fulfil with the same impartiality the duty of the historian, by describing the scandalous perfidy, oppressive injustice, and sanguinary ambition of monarchs; who, without the smallest motive, and in defiance of their oaths, carried fire and sword into the bosom of a brave, just,

just, and generous nation, which, desirous of living in peace under their protection, merited their esteem by its energy, and their friendship by its moderation.

I am well aware of the severe censure to which an author exposes himself, who writes modern history with truth. Tacitus, whose boldness I venture to imitate, without being able to imitate his talents, says justly:

Antiquis scriptoribus rarus obtrectator; neque refert cujusquam Punicas Romanasve acies lætius extuleris: at multorum, qui Tiberio regente pœnam vel infamiam subiere posteri manent. Utque familiæ ipsæ jam extinctæ sint, reperies qui ob similitudinem morum, aliena malefacta sibi objectari putent. Etiam gloria ac virtus infensos habet, ut nimis ex propinquo diversa arguens.*

But to return to my subject.

It is necessary to mention briefly the motives which determined the Poles to make a great

---

* Writers of ancient history have few detractors; no one cares how much you extol the Carthaginian or Roman legions; but, of those who under Tiberius suffered punishment or disgrace, many have posterity existing; and should their families be even already extinct, you will find persons, who from a similarity of manners, would consider an account of the crimes of others aimed at them. Glory and virtue even have enemies, as being too strong a contrast with contemporaries.

change in their laws; which according to all probability would have confolidated their exiftence, but which, by an inconceivable fatality, occafioned their ruin. The misfortunes and partition of Poland* had convinced all the enlightened

* From the time of Boleflas the bold, Poland extended from the Oder as far as the Dnieper. It was at firft divided into feveral principalities, in the fame manner as France. Cafimir firft united them: he merits the title of Great, not, like many princes, from his conquefts, but from his juftice.

This people from its origin to its termination was diftinguifhed by a conftant love of liberty.

Twelve Woiwodes governed it fucceffively: although the fupreme power was vefted in the king, he was obliged, in important affairs, to confult the principal nobles of the country. On the prince's death, a fucceffor was elected from among his children.

The family of the Piaftes became extinct in the perfon of Cafimir the Great. According to his defire, he was fucceeded by his nephew Louis of Hungary. He affembled all the ftates of the nation, and charged them to draw up the laws which he thought adapted to fecure the profperity of Poland. The conftitution, which was the refult of the labours of this affembly, was refpected till the death of Sigifmond Auguftus; and as it protected all claffes of citizens, whilft it exifted the country was populous, the towns rich, the manufactures flourifhing, and the nation formidable and happy. The legiflation was vefted in the nobles and in deputies fent by the towns to the diet: the King was intrufted with the adminiftration, and the execution of the laws: he commanded the army, and enjoyed the prerogative of declaring war, and concluding peace. In important circumftances, he required the advice of the fenators.

Poland was for a long time confidered one of the powers of

enlightened perfons of that country, of the defects of their anarchical government, the danger of the firft rank; and from the fourteenth till the fixteenth century, the fciences flourifhed there perhaps more than in any other country.

This was the birth-place of the celebrated Copernicus. He was confidered a German, becaufe he was a canon of Warmié; but that country, one of the palatinates of Poland, did not fall into the power of the Houfe of Brandenburgh till the firft partition in 1773, and he was born at Thorn, of which Pruffia did not get poffeffion till 1793.

Orzechowfki, anterior to Maretus, was celebrated for his eloquence.

Kromer, the hiftorian, is little inferior to Livy.

Sorbieurfky introduced fo much beauty in his poetry, that it has been tranflated into feveral languages.

The poems of Kochanowfki, the moral treatifes of Fredzo, the political writings of Gorniki, the paftorals of Zimorowicz, have conferred a merited celebrity on their authors.

After the death of Sigifmund, the conftitution of Poland experienced a change. That prince was the laft male of the Jagellons. Till then, the kings had been elected from among the children of the deceafed monarch. At this time it became neceffary to feek another family, or a perfon who had married a female of the Houfe of Jagellon. It was debated whether the fenators only, or all the nobles were entitled to elect the new king. Zamoyfki decided the queftion by faying, that fince every Noble was obliged to fight for the country, they ought all to have the right of electing their chief.

This innovation, which afterwards occafioned fo many evils, at firft redoubled the national energy. The Poles were feen extending their conquefts as far as Mofcow, and giving laws to the Emperors of Ruffia. But in the fequel, the danger of an elective monarchy, and the necessity of reforming abuses, which, notwithstanding the nobles at each election acquired additional prerogatives. Every king sought to please them, in order to secure the crown to his son. In a short time the towns were oppressed, and the peasants reduced to slavery.

Under the reign of John Casimir, Poland was invaded by foreigners; and the king, having sought an asylum in the neighbouring country, there was introduced into the diet the right of the famous *liberum veto*, which completed the anarchy. This absurd institution, which paralysed all the assemblies, by giving a single voice the right of annulling every act, subsisted till the reign of Stanislaus Augustus, and was one of the principal causes of the tyrannical influence exercised over this country by foreign powers.

At the first partition, several changes were made in the constitution; but these changes, dictated by Russia, who declared herself their guarantee, had no other object than to increase the weakness, the misfortunes, and the dependance of the nation.

In this new constitution were carefully preserved all the abuses of the old one, without exempting even the *liberum veto*; and there was only added a permanent council, which diminished the authority of the King, and divided the executive power, whilst the tyranny of the Nobles, and the anarchy of the Diets, was allowed to subsist.

The government, limited, and not being able to do more good for the present, prepared it at least for the future. Never in any country was so much attention paid to the national education; but at the moment when the Poles were on the point of reaping the fruit of these institutions, which they owed to the writings of the most enlightened moralists in Europe, the ambition of Prussia and Russia dispelled all the hopes they had conceived from them, and extinguished all the knowledge which could now serve only to exhibit this hapless country to the extent of it's slavery and it's misfortunes.

ing the valour of the Polish nation, rendered it a slave to all it's neighbours.

But these neighbours being interested to prolong the weakness of Poland, it was difficult to emerge from it without danger. In 1788, a favourable opportunity occurred: the two imperial courts were at war with the Turks; the Kings of Prussia and England, wishing to encrease the embarrassments of Austria and Russia, excited the Poles to take advantage of this circumstance, and that nation, worthy of a better fate, abandoned itself with enthusiasm to the hope that was presented to it.

Never was there seen more concord in the wishes, more unanimity in the deliberations; more devotedness in the sacrifices: the nobles renounced their pretensions to the throne; they opened to the middling classes the avenue to all employments; all the citizens contributed to create an artillery and pay an army: at length the constitution of the 3d of May 1791 was the happy result of the labours of a Diet, as wise in it's operations, as it was enlightened in it's patriotism.

All the governments of Europe congratulated King Stanislaus and the Polish nation on this revolution, which, rendering the throne hereditary, and sufficiently limiting the royal power,

power, seemed to secure Poland both from the dangers of despotism and of anarchy, and the stormy influence which strangers had always exercised at the elections.

The Empress of Russia alone opposing her personal resentment to the general approbation, resolved to overturn this constitution, which released Poland from her yoke, and wrested it's prey from her ambition. She wanted a pretext; that which she employed was the opposition of some nobles enraged at seeing themselves deprived of their pretensions to the throne, and resolved to sacrifice their country to their vanity. These nobles were Felix Potocki, Severin Rzewouski, Braniski great General, the two brothers Kossawouski, Ozarowski Ankwitz, and a few others who became disgracefully celebrated under the name of the confederates of Targovitz, a town where they leagued against the constitution of 1791.

An opposition so weak and absurd would not have been dangerous, but for the support of Russia: but the Poles were to be secured against the enterprises of that power, by the protection of Frederic William, with whom they had concluded a treaty of alliance in 1790.

To obviate every objection, and to exibit in the strongest light the perfidy of Frederic William,

liam, when he abandoned the Poles to the resentment of Catherine, we shall here insert the whole of the 6th article of the treaty of 1790.

" If any foreign power shall attempt, in virtue of any antecedent acts or stipulations whatsoever, to assume a right to interfere in the internal affairs of the Republic of Poland or it's dependancies at any time, or in any manner whatever, his Majesty the King of Prussia will immediately employ his most effectual good offices to prevent hostilities in consequence of such pretention; but if these good offices are ineffectual, and hostilities shall on this occasion ensue against Poland, his Majesty the King of Prussia, being satisfied that the case comes within the alliance, will assist the Republic, according to the tenor of the 4th article of the present treaty".

1792.] It is true, that in 1792, at the moment the Empress attacked Poland, when King Stanislaus claimed the execution of this article, the Court of Berlin answered, that the constitution of the 3rd of May 1791 being subsequent to the treaty of 1790, the King of Prussia was not obliged to fulfil the conditions of it, *in as much as he had never approved this change of constitution, of which on the contrary he had foreseen the unfortunate effects.*

To appreciate the sincerity of this answer, it is necessary to contrast it with the official letter written to the Count de Goltz by Frederic William*, when he was informed of the complexion of this constitution, and of the choice made by the diet of the Princess of Saxony to commence the new dynasty, which was to reign in Poland.

He there says expressly, *that his plan is to cooperate for the prosperity of the Republic, and to consolidate her new constitution, which he admires; that he applauds this important measure which the nation has adopted; he considers it essential to its prosperity, and charges his minister to declare solemnly to King Stanislaus and the marshals of the Diet, that this choice of the Republic will for ever confirm the close connexion which subsists between the Polish nation and himself.*

We have often seen in politics justice sacrificed to ambition; but never have been witness to a person presuming to deny engagements so public and so recent, and to sport so openly with the faith of treaties.

Whilst licentiousness under the cover of philosophy led ambitious innovators to overthrow all

---

* See in the Appendix this letter, and also the letter of the King of Prussia to the King of Poland.

established

established governments, the infatuated Kings seemed to have conspired with their enemies to destroy in the minds of the people the respect for their authority which justice alone can render sacred.

The true motive of this change of system in the King of Prussia was, as has been seen, the alarm produced on him by the French revolution, and the fear of having to contend with Russia at the same time that he was obliged to wage war with France. The Empress having no longer any opposition to dread from the Prussian arms, in the month of May 1792, marched a strong army into Poland. Notwithstanding the number and bravery of her troops, she might perhaps have failed in her enterprise, had Stanislaus Augustus participated in the heroic ardour of his countrymen; but swayed by his usual weakness, and deceived by Catherine, who had always preserved a fatal ascendancy over him, he answered those who urged him to fight.

" That it was not against Poland that
" the Empress was irritated, but against the
" King of Prussia, whose destruction she had
" sworn; that she would renounce the war
" against the Poles, as soon as she saw the na-
" tion disposed to come to an amicable under-
" standing with her; that besides, it was better

"to continue the war with the pen than the
"sword."

He thus loft time in fruitless negociations; and notwithstanding the military operations were already commenced, he still hoped to appease his enemy; and in this confidence he arrested the impetuosity of the nation, who would have universally taken up arms; he retarded the march of his troops, notwithstanding the urgent intreaties of his nephew Joseph Poniatowski, their general, and paralized the efforts of the brave Kosciosko, who was forced to retreat before an enemy he had already repulsed in several rencounters.

The Russians favoured by this inactivity, advanced rapidly towards Warsaw. Catherine wrote to Stanislaus, *that she would not forgive him for having deceived her hopes, unless he joined the confederates of Targovitz, who came at the head of the Russians, to overturn the constitution of 3d of May, and restore that of which she had been the guarantee.*

Stanislaus Augustus, therefore, merited the misfortunes with which he was soon overwhelmed; he sacrificed his country by ordering his troops, under pretence of an armistice, to lay down their arms; and thinking himself in greater security among foreign satellites, than in the midst

midst of his countrymen, he allowed the enemies of Poland to enter Warsaw as allies, acceded to the act of the confederates, and left no other choice to the energetic men who wished to render his throne permanent, and their country free, than to crouch under Russian despotism, or to emigrate in order to avoid perpetual exile in the deserts of Siberia.

The confederates soon experienced the shame and misfortune which those incur, who deliver up their country to it's natural enemies: they thought to re-establish the former system in Poland; and imprudently made promises to Catherine; but the ambitious policy of that princess was in a short time unmasked, and their unavailing remorse could not extricate Poland from the abyss into which she had by them been plunged.

The Empress having felt the danger of the strength which Poland retained, resolved still to diminish it's territory. The Emperor was too much engaged by his war against France, to oppose her designs; and although he had agreed at Pilnitz, with the king of Prussia, to guarantee the integrality of this country: Catherine, who had not acceded to this treaty, readily found means to render it's effect nugatory, by proposing to Frederic William a partition as easy as it was beneficial. She had hitherto constantly opposed

opposed the views of this prince on Dantzick and Thorn, she then favoured them; and Frederic William eagerly seized the means of indemnifying himself for his expensive and unsuccessful expedition into Champaign.

The court of Vienna could not see without dissatisfaction, this new aggrandisement of Prussia; but it was informed that Frederic William would quit the coalition, if it did not consent to enable him to continue the war by the acquisition of these new possessions. To extenuate the infamy of this invasion, it was necessary to search for crimes in the nation that was to be dismembered; and its imaginary faults were the murmurs and complaints which oppression wrests from misfortune.

The Poles who had sought an asylum in foreign countries received the protection, some of *monarchical*, and others of *free governments*. They were every where pursued by the secret agents of Catherine. She accused those who were in France of a connivance with the coalition; and those who travelled through Germany, as zealous propagators of the jacobin system: it was this accusation of jacobinism which principally served the courts of Petersburg and Berlin as a veil to justify their invasion.

On the 25th of March 1793, the king of
Prussia

Prussia published a declaration*, to announce the entry of his troops into Great Poland. It is inconceivable that there are men so blind, as to be dupes to such documents. The King in his manifesto, *reproached the Poles with their resistance to his counsel, and the beneficent views of the Empress: he regretted the miseries of a country abandoned to the disorders of anarchy; and pretended to feel the greatest alarm for the safety of his own dominions, by the dissemination of French principles in Poland. These motives obliged him to adopt salutary precautions, and provisionally to take possession of Thorn, Dantzick, and a part of Great Poland, in order to ensure its tranquillity, and protect the well disposed Poles.*

The Prussians, in fact, notwithstanding the representations of the inhabitants of Thorn, forced the gates, and made themselves masters of that city. Dantzick was soon after obliged to submit, and the inhabitants of Great Poland, who were not prepared for this aggression, could oppose no resistance to these new enemies.

The confederates of Targovitz, extremely surprised at this invasion, demanded of the Russian ambassador, how they were to understand this aggression, and what must be done in

* See the Appendix.

so unexpected a conjuncture. The Russian minister answered them hypocritically, *that they ought to repose implicit confidence in the generous protection of the Empress; that he was unacquainted with the designs of Frederic William; but that they should beware of irritating that prince by imprudent hostilities, without previously consulting the court of Russia.*

The Empress, who did not yet wish to unmask and annihilate the confederacy of Targovitz, advised them to adopt certain defensive measures, which prolonged their blind security. If the Empress was then sincere, and was really ignorant of the plans of the court of Berlin, it is at least certain that her ignorance and her opposition were of short duration; for some time after, her ministers and those of Frederic William acted in concert, and proved the intimate connection that subsisted between the two co-partitioning powers.

In the mean time the confederates of Targowitz, who had betrayed their country by calling in the Russians, but who had never foreseen the fatal project of dismemberment, thought the occasion favourable for exculpating themselves in the minds of their countrymen: encouraged by the answer of the court of Russia, which they thought adverse to the designs of

the

the Pruffian monarch, they publifhed a proteft againft the entrance of the Pruffian troops into Poland. In this apology for their conduct, they lavifhed panegyricks on Catherine, abufe on the authors of the conftitution of the 3d of May, and moft frivolous promifes faithfully to defend the republic. To this proteft they joined circular letters, inviting the Polifh nation to rife, to take up arms, and to attack the enemy that invaded their territory.

This proteft convinced nobody; the confederates had loft the efteem and confidence of the public, but all the Poles were difpofed to profit by the invitation contained in the circular letters, and arm to repulfe all their oppreffors. Catherine II. informed of this general fermentation, prevented its explofion; and although fhe had herfelf advifed defenfive meafures, her troops had orders to reprefs, in concert with the Pruffians, all the movements of this unfortunate people, and to arreft all thofe who fhould attempt to oppofe any refiftance to their operations.

Thefe orders did not prevent the manifeftation of the national energy; feveral diftricts yielded to their ardour, and the Ruffian ambaffador fearing that this flame directed againft Pruffia, might burft out in all quarters, ordered

dered the confederates to recall the circular letters which convoked the ban and arrier-ban of the nobility. The confederacy, always servile, obeyed, and invited the Poles not to accelerate the annihilation of their country by imprudent measures: it recommended to them to act only according to the orders of Catherine, who alone could save them. This publication, which completed the opprobrium of the confederates, and unmasked the perfidious policy of the cabinet of Petersburg, overwhelmed the Poles with despair; seeing their destruction determined, they did not suppress their indignation, and they claimed the succour of all foreign powers against the unjust avidity of their oppressors.

The Empress, now convinced that the confederates of Targovitz were no longer useful instruments to her, ceased to temporize, and seeing that the time was come for acting openly, she ordered her ambassador Sievers to concert with the Prussian minister Bucholtz, to regulate the partition of the Polish possessions, which each of the two courts wished to obtain.

On the 9th of April 1793, these two ministers presented to the confederacy, a declaration which developed the fate of Poland.

In this declaration*, *after having enumerated*

* See the Appendix.

all

all the services rendered to the confederacy by the Empress, and all the efforts employed to restore peace and order to Poland; after having recapitulated the seditious resistance of the Poles, the two courts complained bitterly of the ingratitude of this nation once so flourishing, and now rent by anarchy, and led to ruin by the factious. The two ministers reproached these perturbators with having misled the people, and induced them to insult the Russian and Prussian troops, who came to protect them. Lastly, they accused them expressly of holding an understanding with the French revolutionists, who had already formed in Poland clubs affiliated to that of Paris, and by their intrigues rendered the fermentation general*.

In this state of disturbance, so alarming for the neighbouring powers, Catherine II. and Frederic William perceived no other means of extinguishing so dangerous a volcano than to confine Poland within more narrow limits, and reduce her to the proportions suitable to a power of the second rank. Such were the motives which determined them to

* This accusation was void of truth or probability: far from there existing Jacobin clubs in Poland, the most distinguished orators had spoken with energy against the principles of the French levellers; and the Polish Nobles, who had recently strengthened the aristocracy of their constitution, by rendering the monarchy hereditary, might rather have expected the indignation of democrats than of crowned heads.

take possession of the provinces contiguous to their dominions; they declared their immutable determination in this respect, and invited the confederacy immediately to convoke a Diet in order to co-operate towards this arrangement, as the sole means of procuring Poland a stable government and a permanent peace.

This document at length opened the eyes of the confederates. Felix Potocky in vain hastened to Petersburg, to implore Catherine to stop the current of the calamities he had drawn on his country. Rzewusky retired to Galicia, in order to escape both the perfidy of his protectors and the indignation of his countrymen. Branecky, nephew of Prince Potemkin, resolved to live under the Russian laws. The other confederates remained in Poland, to execute the orders of the usurpers.

They convoked at Grodno a Diet, consisting of men whom they thought most disposed to listen to all that was demanded. King Stanislaus Augustus then published a declaration, which bore the stamp of his character. Deploring the calamities of Poland, he declared that, compelled by circumstances, " having in vain solicited the
" support of foreign powers, and not enjoying
" the free exercise of his will, he submitted to
" the dismemberment of his country, without
" wishing

" wishing to co-operate in it." Absurd reasoning of weakness, which displeases all parties and multiplies the dangers it thinks to avoid.

Notwithstanding the care that had been taken to prevent the election of men of energy, still those elected were Poles, and the Russians were obliged to employ a display of arms to force them to sign the treaty of cession with Russia; they could not even thus induce them, but by promising that as the price of the present sacrifice, Catherine would assist them in their opposition against Prussia.

This trick was at the same time extremely palpable, and the declarations of the two ministers left no doubt of an intimate connection between the two powers. But in the extreme of calamity, we allow ourselves to be deceived by the most feeble ray of hope. Misfortune has, as well as happiness, its delirium: both are equally infatuating.

The treaty of cession in favour of Russia was signed the 22nd of July 1793. This affair being concluded, Frederic William required that a deputation should be chosen, to regulate the cession which he in his turn exacted.

The Diet warmly opposed this demand. After the most violent debates, the votes being equal, Stanislaus Augustus inclined the balance

to

to Pruſſia. He knew that it would be impoſſible to reſiſt two ſuch formidable powers, and he wiſhed to retain ſome remnant of his crown. But in ſuch circumſtances, prudence loſes glory without obtaining ſecurity; and in the midſt of extreme peril, temerity alone is wiſdom.

The Members of the Diet continued to reſiſt with obſtinacy; and in order to conquer their perſeverance, Sievers was obliged to inveſt the caſtle with troops and artillery. This menacing preparation could command only ſilence, not one member ſpoke to ſanction the diſgrace of his country; ſeveral were arreſted by the Coſſacks, for having proteſted againſt this violence.

Bialinſky, marſhal of the Diet, interpreting this general ſilence into a unanimous conſent, ſigned, at a deputation appointed for that purpoſe, the treaty that ceded to Frederic William the provinces of which he had proviſionally taken poſſeſſion.

Fear is always the conſequence of uſurpation. The King of Pruſſia and the Empreſs, knowing the indignation of the Poles, and dreading their vengeance, required that the Diet ſhould reduce the Poliſh army to the number of twelve thouſand men.

This reſolution increaſed diſcontent in place of

of repressing it; several regiments refused to deliver up their arms, retaining in their mind the plan and the hope of delivering themselves from this oppression.

Before it separated, the Diet of Grodno had re-established the military order instituted to reward the officers who had distinguished themselves in the war of 1792. General Ingelstrom, the new Russian minister, obliged them to revoke this decree, and required the abolition of all the acts which might awaken the Polish energy by the recollection of the constitution of 1791.

Catherine II. astonished to see that her despotic measures disposed the people of Poland rather to revolt than to resignation, sent thither fifteen thousand Russians; and Ingelstrom desired that the King and the permanent council should send troops to reduce Madalinsky to obedience, and arrest all persons suspected of rebellion. These demands were rejected; the obedience of a Polish soldier could not be depended on for executing such an order, and the laws opposed the arbitrary arrestation that was required.

Whilst the Russians, thinking to consolidate their domination by terror, daily multiplied their acts of injustice, pillaged the middling claſs, inſulted the nobles, and robbed the peaſants. All theſe acts of violence exaſperated the minds of the inhabitants, who were every where agitated, who murmured and ſought in deſpair reſources againſt tyranny. The conſtitutional deputies of 1791, Malachowſky, Sapieha, Ignatius Potocky, celebrated for his knowledge and eloquence, Kollatay and Mowſtowſky, had fled to foreign countries, whilſt Staniſlaus Auguſtus, abandoning them, had acceded to the diſgraceful confederation of Targovitz.

But their numerous friends remaining in Poland, ſecretly exerted themſelves to excite an inſurrection which might break their chains, and reſuſcitate their country. A committee of four perſons being ſent to Warſaw at the head of this conſpiracy ſoon ſpread its ramifications over all the ſurface of Poland. They were certain of being ſeconded by the whole nation, animated by the ſame hate for their deſtroyers; but they wanted a leader for this great enterpriſe. King Staniſlaus had loſt the general confidence, and all the troops ſwore that they would not join the inſurgents, unleſs the valiant Koſcioſko was placed at their head.

This man, who merited the love of his compatriots, and the eſteem of his enemies, had in his youth diſtinguiſhed himſelf by his zeal in
acquiring

acquiring military knowledge. Enamoured of a young lady, her relations opposed their passion. When he saw her married to Prince Lubomyrsky, his grief carried him far from his country, and he endeavoured to console himself for the disappointments of love by the favours of glory. He served in America under the command of Gates and Washington, who bestowed just praises on his courage and talents. Having returned to his country, he distinguished himself in the campaign of 1792, and in several skirmishes he repulsed the Russians, in spite of inferiority of numbers, the divisions among the Polish Generals, the versatility of the King of Poland, and the perfidy of some of his countrymen sold to Russia, who informed the enemy of all the movements of the Polish army.

Kosciosko, noble, but of a family which he was the first to signalize, of a middling stature, but bearing in his countenance the energy of his character, united all the qualities which can confer and fix glory. Intrepid, indefatigable, incorruptible, firm in adversity, calm after victory, cool in the midst of danger, feeling for misfortune, generous towards his enemies, zealous in the love of his country, a strict observer of justice even in the midst of civil war and the fury of parties, bold in his designs, resolute

resolute in his projects and rapid in his operations, he communicated his ardour to his companions, directed their exertions, modestly attributed to them all his success, and knew to inspire at the same time respect by his regulalarity, and attachment by his amenity. Thus he was alike esteemed by the soldiers, the peasants, the middle class, and nobles; he conciliated opposite interests, destroyed rivalship, and rallying all parties, be directed their energy towards his sole object—the emancipation of his country.

Corresponding secretly with the Court of Warsaw, and all those who were in Poland exciting a movement which he wished to effect, he gave them the instructions requisite for the success of this great enterprise. It was necessary every where to organise the corps which were to rise, to secure warlike stores and arms; and Kosciosko, who approached the frontiers of Poland, finding that all he had required was not yet ready, resisting the ardour of his friends, postponed the execution of his design, to make it's success more certain, and for some time longer withdrew from his country.

At length, having learnt that all was disposed as he wished, he returned to Leipsic, where he received the deputation from the patriots, who
came

came to requeſt him formally to put himſelf at their head, in order to regain their liberty.

1794.] In the month of May 1794, Madalinſki, as had been agreed on, erected the ſtandard of revolt. With eight hundred cavalry he traverſed all the country uſurped by Frederic William, and attacking all the Pruſſian troops who oppoſed his paſſage, he penetrated into the palatinate of Cracovia, at the moment when Koſcioſko arrived thither from Saxony.

On the 24th of March, all the citizens of Cracow muſtered and ſigned the act of inſurrection. Koſcioſko, being elected their chief, took the oath to the nation, and promiſed to obſerve the principles declared in the act. The garriſon of Cracow, and the troops which were near that city, ſwore fidelity to the nation and obedience to Koſcioſko.

By this act, the Poles declared war againſt the uſurpers of their rights and of their country, ſacrificed ancient prejudices, and beſtowed on all the inhabitants equal enjoyment of civil liberty. Koſcioſko was declared commander in chief of the national forces, without any other reſtraint to his power, but his virtue; he commanded the armies, appointed the officers, nominated the ſupreme council, directed civil and political affairs; but as ſoon as the enemy was driven from the frontiers, Kofciofko engaged to refign his power, and to affemble the nation, which fhould then adopt that conftitution moft conducive to it's happinefs and fecurity. Kofciofko was alfo to point out a fucceffor in the event of his ficknefs or death; but this fucceffor was to be fubordinate to the national council.

In any other hands this dictatorial power would have been dangerous to liberty; but the moderation of Kofciofko was known; he did not difappoint the confidence of his compatriots, and he was never reproached with having abufed his power.

Ten days after the proclamation of the infurrectional act, the general, learning that twelve thoufand Ruffians were advancing rapidly againft him, marched from Cracow at the head of four thoufand men, the greater part of whom were only armed with fcythes and pikes, and without artillery.

The battle continued four hours; Polifh ardour overcame the numbers and tactics of their enemies. The Ruffians, defeated and difperfed, loft three thoufand men, and twelve pieces of cannon. Such was their enthufiafm, that a corps of peafants armed with fcythes took poffeffion of a battery.

This

This victory of Wraclawice inflamed all minds, and soon rendered the insurrection general; the Poles every where assembled, took up arms, and swore to obey Kosciosko.

Grochowski undertook the defence of the frontiers of Gallicia; Giedroc raised Samogitia; Jasinski, with six hundred men, seized on Wilna, and drove out the Russians, of whom he took fifteen hundred prisoners.

The Russian ambassador, informed of these movements, in vain extorted from the weakness of King Stanislaus orders for suppressing the malcontents; this measure completely ruined the King in the opinion of the people, but did not abate the violence of the insurrection. The Russians, dreading the fermentation manifested in the capital, wished to get possession of the arsenal; the citizens then openly revolting, despair took place of terror. In vain did the Russian battalions, supported by a formidable train of artillery, pour down on the inhabitants; they were assailed on all sides, and after a battle of forty-eight hours, in which the Poles killed six thousand Russians, and took three thousand prisoners and one hundred and fifty pieces of cannon, the Russian Generals Ingelstrom and Opraxin were forced to abandon the capital.

All the citizens then hastened to repair the intrenchments

intrenchments and fortifications, in order to shelter themselves from the vengeance of their oppressors. Never was there displayed so much joy and ardour; old women, men, children, rich, poor, nobles and plebeians, all appeared animated by the same spirit, all partook of the same labours, and every one emulously offered whatever he possessed towards arming the soldiers, dressing the wounded, and consoling the families who had shed their blood on those glorious days.

Stanislaus Augustus, liberated from masters whom he dreaded, now wished to join the insurgents; but they had experienced his weakness too often to trust him with such important interests; he was treated with respect; he retained his guard, and enjoyed the honours due to his rank; but he possessed no authority.

Kosciosko, arriving at Warsaw, convened the permanent council, formed the supreme council, established tribunals, and published wise and resolute proclamations to prevent this great movement from serving as a pretext for disorders, and disturbing persons and property.

Frederic William, on the report of the Polish insurrection determined to fight in person, and having placed himself at the head of forty thousand men, he easily defeated the feeble detachments

ments of infurgents which he met. He was only interrupted in his progrefs by the intrepid Kofciofko who had the boldnefs to attack an army fo formidable, to which he could only oppofe twelve thoufand men, and thefe not yet completely armed. After an obftinate refiftance the Polifh General was defeated, and compelled to retreat into an entrenched camp which covered Warfaw, and was occupied by the divifions of Kofciofko, Dombrofky, Zayonczek and, Poniatowfky.

The Pruffians, after the battle of Szezekocin, availing themfelves of their advantage, marched to Cracow; Kofciofko not being able to march to the fuccour of that city, refolved to deliver it up to the Auftrians in order to excite fome rivalfhip betwixt the courts of Vienna and Berlin; but the Pruffians, by their celerity, prevented the execution of this plan, and took poffeffion of Cracow.

The news of this defeat tranfported the people of Warfaw with fury; fome agitators exciting the populace, who every where affembled, they erected on the 28th of June gibbets in the ftreets, forced open the prifons, and maffacred fome of the prifoners accufed of conniving with the enemies of the ftate. The conftituted authorities put an immediate ftop to thefe these excesses; but Kosciosko, not imitating the culpable weakness of the French government towards the Septemberizers, expressed in an energetic proclamation the indignation with which he was inspired by these atrocities, imprisoned the authors of the plot, and made them expiate their crime on the scaffold.

The King of Prussia, joined with the Russians, soon invested Warsaw; in order to reduce that city, and to subdue the army which defended it, employed all the means of force and all the wiles of policy; but the Poles proved themselves alike superior to fear and flattery.

Frederic William wrote to the inhabitants of Warsaw, assuring them of his protection if they submitted, and threatening them with total destruction if they resisted. They replied that they would share the fate of the army. That monarch promised that the Polish officers should retain their rank in his army, provided they would join him; they all swore to partake the lot of Kosciosko, and to conquer or to die with him.

After continual and bloody engagements, without any decisive success, the King of Prussia, who had taken Vola and beaten the division of Joseph Poniatowsky, commanded a general attack in order to force the Polish entrenchments.

ments. The action was long and obstinate. The King and the Prince Royal displayed on this occasion much bravery; but the resolution of the insurgents triumphed over the valour of the Russians and the Prussians, and compelled them to retire with loss.

At the same time a dreadful insurrection broke out in South Prussia, near Posen; the inhabitants of these newly-conquered provinces rising suddenly, attacked the dispersed troops, pulled down the Prussian eagles, seized the arms and stores which they found, and exerted themselves in organizing an army.

Frederic William informed of this event, and dreading, if he allowed the rebels time to increase their forces, to see his retreat cut off, took the resolution, after having ineffectually bombarded Warsaw, to raise the siege precipitately, and withdraw into his own dominions, abandoning his sick and wounded, and an immense quantity of warlike stores.

Thus the King of Prussia, always vehement in undertaking conquests, and ready to renounce them, expelled from Poland as he had been from France, would have experienced a similar destiny in both wars, if the forces of Russia and the fortune of Catherine had not repaired his errors, and revived his hopes. The retreat of the

the King of Prussia completed the glory of Kosciosko and his brave companions; but their position was as dangerous as their courage was ardent. The dangers which threatened them multiplied on all sides: although the General had given orders to respect the domains of the Emperor, he had not been able to preserve peace with the court of Vienna; and the papers found in the house of the Russian ambassador at Warsaw, proved the adherence of the cabinet of Vienna to the scheme of dividing Poland.

The national council published this treaty, according to which, Russia and Prussia were to possess the provinces which they had taken. Bavaria was to belong to Austria, and the elector of Bavaria was to receive as an indemnity Alsace and Lorraine.

Notwithstanding this official publication by the council, the existence of such a treaty may still be doubted, being too opposite to the real interest of Prussia to be supposed to have obtained her consent; it might have been merely a project, but facts demonstrate at least that Austria had a perfect understanding with the two co-partitioning powers with regard to vast schemes of dismemberment, and the ruin of Poland.

In

In this awful crisis, Kosciosko, was still obliged to manage with prudence the resources presented to him by the national energy. In determining the nobles to give liberty to the peasants, he had taken all the precautions which could prevent the danger of a too sudden emancipation. The peasants could not leave their abodes without paying their debts; they could not possess lands without making contracts with their old masters; and during the continuance of the war, in order that agriculture might not suffer, only half their accustomed labour was to be dispensed with.

Though the abolition of slavery had inspired a general ardour in the nation for the common cause, on the other hand, the necessity of leaving many hands employed in agriculture circumscribed the resources which could be employed in the defence of the country,

The following was nearly the force which the republic had at it's disposal. Zayontchik, with eight thousand men, defended the frontiers of Gallicia against ten thousand Austrians and against the Russians. Syrakowsky, at the head of ten thousand men, was charged to retard the progress of Suvarof, who was advancing into Poland with forty thousand men. Jasinski, commanding six thousand Poles, defended Lithuania,

thuania, which Ferfen marched through with feventeen thoufand Ruffians, and Dombrowfki, who had not yet organized four thoufand men in Great Poland, was to obferve with a crowd of peafants badly armed, the forty thoufand Pruffians who occupied this frontier. Kofciofko and Poniatowfki together had no more than eighteen thoufand men deftined to march wherever the danger might be moft preffing.

Notwithftanding this multitude of enemies and difproportion of forces, the enthufiafm for liberty might perhaps have triumphed over a coalition in which there reigned little harmony, and which the oppofition of interefts might in one inftant diffolve; but treachery rendered the efforts of Polifh valour ineffectual, and Kofciofko faw himfelf ruined at the moment when he believed he had fecured the independence of his country by a fplendid victory.

This General, being informed that Ferfen wifhed to effect a junction with Suvarof, marched rapidly againft him. Poninfki, who was ordered to difpute the paffage of the river, delivered it up to the Ruffians, and did not obey the orders which he had received to rejoin the army with his divifion. The Generaliffimo deprived of this fuccour, was attacked at Macieiowice by General Ferfen. Although the Ruffians

Ruffians were thrice the number of the Poles, the victory was difputed a whole day with the greateft fury. Kofciofko twice repulfed the enemy, and difplaying in this action the talents of a general and the bravery of a foldier, for a long time, by prodigies of valour, rendered fortune uncertain. But at length he fell pierced with wounds, and his troops in their retreat left him in the power of the enemy. When the Ruffian officers made him known to the Coffacks, who were about to terminate his life, on hearing his name, they teftified their admiration of his courage, and their pity for his misfortune. Kofciofko opening his eyes, and learning his defeat, in vain implored death which he preferred to captivity. The Ruffians treated him with the refpect due to his character, and as foon as he could bear the fatigue of travelling, they fent him to Peterfburg, where the Emprefs, too much irritated to be generous, confined this unfortunate warrior in a dungeon, whence he was not liberated till after the death of the Emprefs. Paul the Firft fignalifed the beginning of his reign by granting him his liberty, and by this magnanimous act obtained well-merited applaufe.

The Poles, on being informed of this tragical event, did not imitate the ferocious French jacobins,

jacobins, the misfortunes of whose generals were imputed to them as crimes :—they testified by loud lamentations their esteem for the talents and virtues of Kosciosko, and they listened with confidence to the advice which he gave them from his dungeon; they knew him too well to apprehend, that any menace could induce him to propose any measure unworthy of his glory and of his country. At length, while the Russians besieged the capital, on the birthday of their unfortunate General, all the streets of Warsaw were illuminated, and the Poles thus celebrated the remembrance of his triumphs on the very eve of their own destruction.

Fersen's victory did not abate the courage of the Poles. The national council adopted the most vigorous measures for the defence of liberty, and Wawrzecky was appointed commander in chief. But though their courage was the same, the same genius did not preside over their operations.

Zayontchik was defeated by the Russians at Chelm. Suvarof having completely defeated Syrakowsky and the Polish army at Brzesk, advanced rapidly towards Warsaw. The republicans, instead of imitating the example of Kosciosko, and always keeping the field, shut themselves

selves up in the fortifications of the suburbs of Prague. Suvarof reduced it after a murderous assault. Nine thousand gallant Poles perished in this action; but what must ever tarnish the glory of the Russian General is the carnage which succeeded the victory. The houses were pillaged, women violated, children murdered, thirty thousand victims fell a prey to the vengeance and ferocity of the Russian soldiers. The inhabitants of Warsaw without means of defence were forced to capitulate. Ignatius Potocki sent by them to negociate, proposed terms which were rejected; Stanislaus Augustus, who retained no more influence with his neighbours than authority over his subjects, in vain endeavoured to obtain mild and honourable conditions; the city was obliged to yield to the mercy of Catherine. The Polish troops refusing to submit, quitted the city, but being attacked on all sides by the Russians and Prussians, some were killed, some were dispersed, and some delivered up their arms to the conquerors. Madalinski, with a troop of resolute men, fled into Galicia. Suvarof had promised a complete amnesty; Catherine did not fulfil this engagement, she ordered Potocki and Mostoweki to be arrested. All those distinguished by their patriotism were proscribed; their property confiscated;

fiscated; a terrible inquisition pursued their actions, watched their thoughts, and punished this unfortunate nation for all the virtues it had displayed.

King Stanislaus received an order to quit Warsaw; he repaired to Grodno, and thence was called into Russia, where he survived but a short time the fall of his throne, and the humiliation of his country.

The Courts of Vienna, Petersburg and Berlin, relieved from all obstacles, quietly divided their ensanguined prey, and wished to annihilate even the name of Poland; but history will eternize the glory of the vanquished, and the injustice of the victors.*

* By the treaty concluded between the three co-partitioning powers, Brezesk became the central point of the frontiers of these three states.
Warsaw fell under the dominion of the king of Prussia, who had not been able to take it by arms. The Vistula separated Prussia from Austria. The Bog divided Austria from Russia. The Neimen marked the limits betwixt the possessions of the Russians and the Prussians. One half of the city of Grodno belonged to the King of Prussia and the other to the Empress.

CHAP.

CHAP. XIII.

Influence of the revolution of Poland on the minds of the French.—Their ardour against the coalition.—Conquest of Holland.—Flight of the Stadtholder.—Revolution in Holland.—Abolition of the Stadtholderate.—Conspiracy of the Jacobins.—Accusation and transportation of the Colleagues of Robespierre.—Revolution of Prarial.—Fortitude of Boissy-d'Anglas.—Errors of the Convention.—Reaction in the south.—New Constitution.—Events of the 13th Vendemaire.—Negociations of Barthelemy.—Treaty of peace between the Republic, the King of Prussia, the Landgrave of Hesse, and the King of Spain.—Neutrality of the north of the Empire.—Dissolution of the coalition.—Campaign on the Rhine.—The French forced to repass it.—Inaction of the King of Prussia.—End of the reign of Frederic William II.—His death, hopes conceived of his successor.—A slight view of the events which passed in the last two years of his reign.—Campaigns of Bonaparte and Moreau.—Conclusion of this History.

1794.] THE revolution which had just erased Poland from the catalogue of nations, might gratify the vengeance of Catherine II. and the narrow ambition of Frederic William. But it was extremely injurious to the great interests of the coalition. The reader may have observed in the course of this history, how much the violent passions which agitated the different parties blinded them, and induced them to follow the track which led to a point directly opposite to that which they wished to attain. Never was such infatuation more remarkable on both sides than at this period.

In fact, when it was the interest of the French revolutionists to prove to all nations the advantages of liberty, by rendering personal safety more inviolable, property more sacred, industry more active, mind more energetic, morals more pure, and justice more mild, the furious Jacobins adopting that state maxim, the usual excuse of tyrants, covered France with bastiles, confiscated or sequestrated all property, violated the secrecy of letters, suppressed thought, enchained talents, immolated innocence, protected every vice, proscribed every virtue, annihilated industry, drained the channels of agriculture and commerce; and lastly, exposed the lives of all the citizens to the rage of the vilest accusers, and to the ferocious caprice of a sanguinary tribunal.

The effect of this barbarity was to change the public mind to such a degree, that the liberty which was wished to be extended must be for ever lost; and that the deceived people, confounding principles and abuses, the friends of liberty and anarchists, Republicans and the tyrants who oppressed the Republic, no longer attached

attached juſt ideas either to words or to things, hated all that it ought to have loved, deſpiſed what it ought to have eſteemed, became indifferent to every thing by which it ought to have been moſt warmly intereſted, and ceaſed to avow that public opinion, the only baſis of liberty, the only ſtrength of inſtitutions, and the only guide of governments.

The nation, which had wiſhed to arm in order to maintain a war of the principles of reaſon againſt the injuſtice of arbitrary power, was governed by the maxims of deſpotiſm; and at the ſame time, the coaleſced Kings, whoſe object ſhould have been to demonſtrate the mildneſs and the juſtice of monarchical government, and to expoſe to general hatred the miſeries of anarchy, the cupidity of factions, and the cruelties of popular tyranny, impolitically imitated the demagogues whom they wiſhed to deſtroy.

Every moderate man was proſcribed by them, as the citizen ſuſpected of Ariſtocracy was by the Jacobins. They wiſhed to propagate the ſyſtem of arbitrary power, as in France the others preached the doctrine of perfect equality. Facts prove that they violated the faith of treaties, as much as the Decemvirs. They partitioned Poland, and pretended to diſmember

member France, as the French committees proposed to dismember Germany. The Convention ridiculously purposed to form the whole world into one Republic, and the English Government audaciously claimed the universal empire of the ocean.

The French Government put the emigrants to death who fell into their hands; and the coalesced Monarchs, who had armed them, gave them up to death with a weakness tantamount to perfidy, not employing any reprisals in order to save them, and abandoning them to their enemies in every capitulation.

In Poland they confiscated fortunes like Democrats, and like them created national domains, which they divided among themselves like the rulers of France; the duration of the coalition was not longer than that of the power of the committees. The allies defended the cause of Royalty with as little fidelity, as the Jacobins sustained that of true liberty. In a word, the unjust destruction of a people who had wished to establish a wise and solid monarchical government, proves evidently that the Kings were guided, not by justice but by ambition, that they attacked not every kind of anarchy but every species of liberty, and that they had conspired the ruin of every state which was

was not subject to the absolute authority of Royalty.

This comparison may seem severe, but it is not the less true. Thus all these errors produced their inevitable results. The French for a long time lost the liberty for which they combated, and rendered it the terror of those nations who were most disposed to receive it; and the coalition, far from accomplishing the subjugation and dismemberment of France, as they had projected, saw it extend it's territories at their expense. If the Republicans did not understand how to establish justice and liberty among themselves, at least they knew how to maintain their independence; and the alarming example of Poland induced the French, of almost all opinions, to swear rather to shed their blood than submit to the dictation of their enemies.

The French were too much elated by their victories to suspend their operations. The approach of a rigorous winter did not retard their progress; they availed themselves of the terror which their success spread in the allied army to complete it's defeat; and pursuing in all directions the Austrians, the English, and the Stadtholderian troops, who retreated in confusion, they profited by the ice to pass all the rivers and

and canals, which at any other time would have rendered the conqueſt of Holland impracticable to their courage.

Towards the end of 1794 Maeſtricht and Nimeguen had fallen into their hands.

1795.] In the month of January 1795 Pichegru attacked the allies at all points, from the ocean to the Rhine, and defeated them every where. The regiments of Orange, of Friezland, and of Hohenloe were taken priſoners, as was a corps of Swiſs in the pay of the States General. Clairfait was repulſed, and forced to retreat into Germany.

Frederic William did not ſend the ſixty-two thouſand men with which he had engaged to aſſiſt the allies. The Engliſh army, which coſt the Government enormous ſums, was deſtitute of clothing. It reſiſted, however, with courage the efforts of the French; but compelled to yield to the impetuoſity and the numbers of the Republicans, it ſuffered greatly in it's long retreat, in want of every thing, continually haraſſed by the French, and marching through a country where the miſeries of war inſpired a hatred againſt England, to whom Holland attributed all the evils ſhe ſuffered.

The Duke of York, diſſatisfied with the allies, and perceiving that there was no longer any hope

hope of regaining any advantage, quitted the army, and left the command to General Walmoden, who discovered much perseverance and courage in a position so critical; but his exertions could not retard the progress of Pichegru, whose plans were judicious, and whose means were immense, and who benefited at the same time by the division of the allies, the disposition of the Batavians, and the rigour of the season. In this crisis the Stadtholder contrived to be invested with a dictatorial authority; but the instant in which his invariable ambition was at length fully gratified, was the termination of his power; and as he did not possess genius to preserve it, his elevation only rendered his fall more mortifying and more complete.

The revolution of 1787 had deprived the Prince of Orange of the esteem and affection of all those who had a regard for the importance, the independence, and the laws of their country; the war in which he engaged the States General, contrary to their true interest, which was neutrality, completed the alienation of men's minds; and the danger of a total ruin at length inspired the whole nation with a decided aversion to the Stadtholderian house.

Several provinces had earnestly expressed their wish for the cessation of the war; but the
Stadtholder

Stadtholder, who dreaded that a peace might revive the patriotic party, opposed it, and arrested a great number of citizens, whom he was soon obliged to liberate. The English government, who directed his conduct, confirmed him in his opposition to peace: the Court of London was unwilling that the termination of hostilities should restore to France her influence in Holland; it preferred, should resistance be impossible, that this country, conquered by the French, should furnish England with pretexts for taking possession of the Dutch colonies in the East and West Indies.

In fact, events soon unmasked this ambitious policy; and William V. in the following year, saw his protectors seize the Cape of Good Hope and Ceylon, in order to augment their dominions, in the same manner as they had taken for themselves the island of Corsica, while defending the cause of the Bourbons. It is doubtful whether a generous enemy be not less dangerous than such allies.

The Stadtholder, contrary to the national wish, being determined to continue the war, was desirous that the Batavian people should rise in a mass in order to repel the enemy; but his orders were not executed: he also wished by inundations to stop the invasion of the French; but

but at first this was resisted ; and soon after the rigour of the season rendered this measure impracticable. Pichegru, availing himself of this long and intense frost, which favoured his designs, rapidly crossed all the rivers which might have retarded his operations, and took possession of Utrecht, Rotterdam and Dort. The fortress of Grave, after a vigorous resistance, was reduced. On the other side, Clairfait defeated, had repassed the Rhine. Thenceforward no obstacle impeded the republicans ; the Prince of Orange fled to England with his family ; Bergen-op-Zoom opened it's gates to the conquerors ; thirty hussars took possession of Amsterdam. All the patriots, relieved from the yoke which oppressed them, united with the republicans ; the persons of property, more wise than the aristocratic party in France, far from opposing, directed the national movement. The English always repulsed, and perceiving that the nation which they wished to defend, declared against them, retreated to Bremen where they embarked. In a short time the revolution was complete, the Stadtholderate was abolished, and the French government, though it might have considered all the United Provinces as a legitimate conquest, generously restored them their independence, reserving only some strong

ſtrong places, neceſſary for it's defence againſt the attacks of the coalition.

This entire and rapid conqueſt, the ſkill of the generals, the miracles of valour performed by the republicans, who, braving all dangers and ſufferings, fought fearleſsly over gulphs which a ray of the ſun might every inſtant open beneath them, excited the admiration of the neutral powers, and ſpread the moſt dreadful conſternation in the hoſtile courts. This people, whoſe ſlavery was commiſerated, on the 9th Thermidor ſacrificed it's tyrants; this nation, which it was expected would have been cruſhed, was every where triumphant; this country, intended to have been diſmembered, extended on all ſides it's frontiers, and ſeemed even to diſdain to keep all it had conquered.

The Britiſh miniſtry, by laviſhing the wealth of England, flattered themſelves they ſhould deprive France of Flanders, Lorraine, Alſace, Provence, Rouſſillon, and perhaps Brittany. But at the end of this campaign they had no other advantage to hold out to the Engliſh nation for ſo much expenſe, but ſome incomplete and inconſiderable conqueſts in the Weſt-Indies, whilſt the French republic had taken ſeven provinces from the Stadtholder, ten from the Emperor, Trèves, Cologne, Mentz, Liege, Spire

Spire and Worms from their respective bishops, a part of the Palatinate, the dutchies of Cleves and Juliers, Aix-la-Chapelle, the dutchy of Deux-Ponts, the dutchy of Savoy, the Comté of Nice, and the greater part of the provinces of Biscay and Catalonia. The French had gained 29 pitched battles, they had triumphed in more than a hundred less decisive engagements, taken possession of 152 cities and towns, 3,800 pieces of cannon, 90 standards, 70,000 muskets, had killed 80,000 men, and taken 90,000 prisoners. The King of Spain, disgusted with the English alliance, and tired of the war against France, meditated on peace.

Frederic William II. abandoning his ally the Emperor, England by whom he was subsidized, and even his brother-in-law the prince of Orange, whom seven years before he had so vigorously supported, negociated with the committee of public safety, and agreed with it in the month of Germinal, on a suspension of arms; the princes of the empire, who had not been dispossessed of their territories, were weary of a ruinous war, which, instead of stopping, extended the democratic spirit. The finances of the Emperor were exhausted; and the French government, in a similar situation, demonstrating by it's conduct towards Holland and it's decrees

crees against the anarchists, it's desire of terminating at once the war and the Revolution, it is probable that Europe might soon have enjoyed the peace which it so much wanted, if the English minister had not thought his existence identified with the continuance of hostilities.

Availing himself dexterously of the influence of money, and the irrationality of enraged passions, he reanimated the constantly deceived hopes of the Vendéans, the emigrants, the courts of Vienna and Turin; and thus succeeded in prolonging the miseries of humanity.

In order to avoid the imputation of partiality, it is necessary here to state the motives of public and national interest, which the cabinet of London might alledge in justification of it's hostile intentions.

1st, It was, said they, dangerous to acknowledge and to allow a great republic to subsist in the midst of Europe, whose democratic and levelling principles were incompatible with the safety and the existence of the monarchical and aristocratical governments.

2d, France extending her limits to the Rhine, possessing Brabant, restoring to the commerce of Antwerp the free navigation of the Scheldt, and enjoying in Holland a too preponderating interest, acquired in the balance of Europe, a weight too

too confiderable and too injurious to the interefts of England.

3d, It was effential to replace the Bourbon family on the throne, and to re-inftate the princes and the nobles in the rank and property of which they had been ftripped, to counteract in other nations the contagious example of an unpunifhed revolt againft the conftituted authorities.

4th, The French government, far from being ftable, prefented no fecurity for negociation.

The firft objection could not be maintained, either from principle or from fact; juftice forbad all interference in the internal affairs of an independent nation. And experience proved that democracy, feeble in peace, was ftrengthened by war; that by oppofing the fpirit of equality, it was converted into fanaticifm, and that if it's expanfion was to be dreaded, the glory of arms was perhaps the moft brilliant and dangerous means of it's propagation.

England might fee with regret the conquefts of France: but it had allowed the imperial and Pruffian courts to deftroy the equilibrium of powers by the iniquitous partition of Poland; fhe herfelf had continually been extending her dominions in the Eaft-Indies; and, in order to reftore restore the balance, it was natural that France should proportionably extend her possessions.

The re-establishment of monarchy and nobility in France, was rather a pretext than a motive. The coalition had demonstrated this by their restraining the efforts of the French princes, by never entrusting them with the command of an army, by not insisting on a cartel for the exchange of the captured emigrants, and by appropriating to themselves provinces which ought to have been held only in trust for them.

Besides, if with the aid of Spain and Prussia, the coalition had not succeeded even in the midst of anarchy, and during the detested reign of Robespierre, in forcing the French to submit to a foreign yoke, was it not evident that this project became chimerical when they were weakened by their defections and by misfortunes, and the republic strengthened by her victories and her conquests?

Finally, was it not perfectly absurd to assert, that a government, however unsettled, was not sufficiently stable to make peace, whilst it proved itself so powerful in carrying on war, and whilst it treated effectually with one of the principal members of the Coalition?—Through all these veils the truth is easily perceptible. The English

lish ministry disappointed in it's hopes of annihilating France, persisted in it's error with more passion than policy, and every where paid gladiators to accomplish it's purposes; and seeing, that notwithstanding the intestine disturbances which it fomented, the republic extended and consolidated her conquests, and endeavoured to indemnify itself for the disasters on the continent by usurping the exclusive empire of the seas.

Hitherto this scheme has been successful, but it justly alarms all the maritime powers; and the French government may one day, by uniting wisdom to strength, find itself at the head of a powerful confederacy which will punish England for her excessive ambition, emancipate commerce, and avenge Europe for all the blood which has been shed by British pride.

The historian, like the traveller, after having wandered over sterile plains, climbed steep mountains, and traversed stormy seas, enjoys a repose as delightful as uncommon, when he arrives at a more pleasant situation, a more temperate climate, and a more peaceful abode. We have acquitted ourselves of a painful task, by tracing a picture of the crimes of the jacobins of the frenzy of ambition, the injustice of courts, the infatuation of nations, and the ravages of war.

We are now arrived at an epoch more confolatory to humanity, and more honourable to a nation, which has alike aftonifhed the world by it's external energy and it's internal flavery; and has been equally celebrated for it's victories, and it's calamities.

The more rigoroufly we have depicted the fervile and culpable fubmiffion of the national Convention, during the life of Robefpierre, the more readily we ought, from regard to truth, to render juftice to the fame Convention, and applaud the wifdom of it's conduct for a whole year after the 9th Thermidor.

It then found itfelf, notwithftanding the fall of fome of it's tyrants, in a very critical fituation, being placed betwixt two violent parties who tended equally again to throw France into diforder, and through their folly to fubject it to the vengeance of foreign powers, always attentive to profit by thefe divifions to crufh it.

'The party of fanatic democrats and anarchifts, thirfting for blood and plunder, had loft fome leaders, but it was ftill formidable and numerous; and rallied to it all thofe who having committed themfelves to a certain point during the reign of terror, from fear, or from cupidity, dreaded the regeneration of liberty, and pretended ed to regard all return to principles as a step towards a counter-revolution.

By too suddenly and too strongly attacking this party, which possessed among the populace a crowd of infatuated disciples, and intrepid accomplices, the Convention hazarded restoring to it the strength of despair, and of falling again into it's slavery.

The royalist party, zealous, more weak, more divided, more indiscreet, less bold, still opposed a powerful obstacle to the good which the Convention wished to produce. Inflexible in it's opinions, blind in it's policy, contemptuously confounding under the name of rebels, all those who did not wish the total overthrow of the new laws, the return of the ancient system, and the punishment of the friends of liberty; their impatience occasioned their miscarriage, when every thing was united to favour them. Incapable of waiting or of coming to terms, they listened only to the voice of prejudice which rendered them inaccessible to reason. The progress of knowledge, the change of manners, the strength of the army, the interest of the officers, that of the new proprietors of lands, the crowds of citizens whose vanity or fortune supported the revolution: in a word, the danger of a violent commotion, and of a dismemberment which would deliver France to her enemies, and subject her to the fate of Poland; none of these considerations could make an impression on those violent men.

Such is the spirit of party which views every thing in profile, and never can perceive but the side favourable to it's wishes. In their eyes the unlimited return of the royal authority; the entire re-establishment of the nobility, of the dominant religion and of Parliaments, were as easy as indispensable; the idea of a republic, or even of any kind of free or representative government, offered to their minds only the image of anarchy, of crime, and of disaster; whilst a royal counter-revolution, recalling to their recollection tranquil times and delightful enjoyments, seemed to them no more than the return to order, to virtue, and to happiness.

This party incessantly thwarted the progress of those legislators who wished to repair existing evils, and to restore tranquillity; for when they destroyed some revolutionary laws, and did any act of justice, the triumphant royalists animated the people against the revolutionists, and indiscreetly proclaiming the return of the ancient system, they awakened the fears of the patriots, the inquietude of the army, and afforded

forded at once pretexts and strength to the jacobin party.

On the other hand, by listening too much to prudence, by keeping terms with the anarchists, by permitting the laws of terror to remain, it's credit was lost, it's misfortunes multiplied, and the nation, anxious for repose and justice, was impressed with a vehement indignation.

In this critical situation the Convention availed themselves of a combination of wisdom and firmness which deserves the highest eulogy, and which ought, in some measure, to compensate the numerous errors with which it has been reproached.

It laboured at first to consolidate it's own liberty, to amuse its furious enemies, and every where to change insensibly the principal authorities and their agents; it opened the gates of the prisons, and without attending to the alarms of the jacobins, and the very natural impatience of those detained, it by degrees restored to liberty all those whom the decemviral tyranny had plunged into these dungeons.

Whilst it preserved in it's body, and even politically placed in it's committees a certain number of suspecting *Mountaineers,* it calmed the public opinion by destroying the revolutionary committees, by abolishing the law of *Maximum,* by by purifying the pantheon, ſtained by the aſhes of Marat; in a word, by conducting to the ſcaffold Lebon, Carrier, Fouquier-Tinville, and that ferocious revolutionary tribunal which had ſacrificed ſo many human victims to terror.

Soon after the Convention, more ſecure in it's progreſs, recalled within its precincts the ſeventy-three deputies whom the anarchiſts had driven out of it. This reinforcement giving the moderate party a more certain majority, it determined at length to ſtrike a deciſive blow at the Mountain, and it paſſed a decree of accuſation againſt ſeveral of the old members of the decemviral government.

This decree entirely undeceived the anarchiſts; they were ſenſible that their deſtruction was at hand, and collecting together the wrecks of their forces, they attempted a laſt effort to ſeize again on their odious power. It was extremely eaſy to expoſe to demonſtration the crimes which called aloud for the condemnation of theſe deputies; the blood with which France ſtill flowed accuſed them, the ſhades of forty thouſand victims raiſed againſt them their plaintive voices; and the whole nation, in mourning, might ſerve as witneſſes, and atteſt their tyranny.

However the National Convention, which had liſtened

listened more to resentment than policy, in entering on this celebrated trial, was soon obliged to suspend it. Barriere, Collot d'Herbois and Billaud-Varennes, defending themselves with audacity, easily convinced the assembly that it could not judge crimes to which fear had in some sort rendered them accomplices, since they had every month sanctioned the acts of the committees of government by renewing their powers.

This consideration, and the discovery of the movements which the jacobins were preparing, determined the Convention to punish arbitrarily these men who had so continually violated all the forms of justice; and under the real or supposed pretext of a conspiracy, it in the month of Germinal decreed the transportation of the accused. Vadier and Cambon foreseeing their arrest, made their escape. Some of the *Mountaineers* who supported them were imprisoned. At the time they intended to convey the condemned deputies to the place of their destination, their carriage was stopt by numerous mobs, one part of which wished to liberate, and the other to massacre them. The guard who escorted them brought them back to the committee of General Safety; Pichegru, who was charged with the command of the capital, quickly

quickly re-established order: Collot d'Herbois and Billaud were sent off to Cayenne; Barrere, more fortunate or more favoured, after having remained a long time in prison at one of the sea-ports, made his escape, and was since comprised in an amnesty: a new decree excepted him from it, and fresh circumstances restored him to liberty.

The transportation of the colleagues of Robespierre roused the fury of his party, and became the signal for war between the republicans and the anarchists. A certain number of deputies, who had contributed to the revolution of the 31st of May, fearing the vengeance of the Girondist party, then unfortunately rallied round the wrecks of the decemviral tyranny.

Alarms were soon spread amongst the people; who, at the same time, were in dread of famine and a counter-revolution: the disastrous law of *Maximum* destroying confidence, had produced an actual scarcity, and the real authors of this scourge persuaded the populace that the aristocracy in the Convention was the cause of it. They inspired regret in the workmen for the forty *sous* that Robespierre gave them for the purpose of spreading terror in the sections; the orators of the jacobins were every where seen collecting together numerous groups, and by violent

violent harangues exciting them to revolt. The tribunes of the Convention again began to be befieged by thofe atrocious men, and thofe fhamelefs women, who had fo long terrified innocence by their afpect, fupported tyranny by their yells, and celebrated profcriptions with their ferocious joy.

On the 1ft Prairial a numerous troop of furious jacobins and deluded mechanics, preceded by a crowd of women intoxicated with brandy, and demanding bread, advanced towards the palace of the Thuilleries, forced the guard that defended it, penetrated into the hall of the Convention, intermingled among the deputies; infulted, threatened, and endeavoured to extort from them decrees to recall the decemvirs and revive tyranny.

Indignation and difmay predominated in the affembly. The Prefident, too aged and too feeble, could not make himfelf be heard, nor reeftablifh order in the midft of fuch a tumult; the members of the Mountain impudently infifted that the confpirators fhould be heard; all the deputies who wifhed to refift this infolence faw glittering around them the homicidal arms of thefe affaffins. Already had fome citizens, victims of their courage, fallen under their blows. Boiffy-d'Anglas, impelled by a juft indignation

dignation, braving all danger fuddenly rufhed forward to the Prefident's chair, ftopt by his noble and firm countenance the murmurs of this irritated multitude, and by a courage worthy of ancient times, faved his country from the fhame and peril with which it was menaced.

In vain they preffed on, and attacked him, in vain they held before him the bloody head of his colleague Ferraud, whom thefe *brigands* had juft facrificed: faithful to his duty, deaf to threats, infenfible to fear, braving the murderous bullets which flew around him, he alone prefented an immoveable mound to the torrent, and vowed that he would not fuffer any deliberation to take place whilft the interior of the affembly fhould be polluted by the prefence of the factious.

For eight days he conftantly fuftained this difficult ftruggle; and what is almoft inconceivable, the confpirators who, in fpite of his orders, remained in the hall, and had fo recently affaffinated one of his colleagues, dared not however to complete their triumph by depriving him of life: an extorted admiration, an involuntary refpect, feemed to reftrain their fury, and to reftrain their hands all ready to ftrike him. In the mean time his ftrength became exhaufted, his voice was no longer audible; the Prefident sident reclaimed, and again refumed his feat; the malcontents increafed in number and audacity, the tumult was gaining ftrength, and the Convention yielding from fear, and ruled by the Mountain, had already paffed fome decrees which recalled the exiled deputies, and reftored to anarchy its fatal empire; when at length feveral fections, to whom the refiftance of Boiffy-d'Anglas had given time to arm, called by the committees, came to deliver the Convention from it's oppreffors. The combat was not long; the moft cruel men are always the moft cowardly. Legendre at the head of fome armed citizens, pierced through the crowd, penetrated into the hall, and difarmed and drove out the *brigands*

The Convention, once free, repealed the decrees which the factious had extorted from them, and decreed an accufation of thofe deputies who had fhewn themfelves accomplices of the confpirators. The day following the *brigands*, furious at their defeat, communicated their rage to the infatuated populace of the fuburbs of Paris.

An immenfe crowd marched againft the Convention, arrived at the *Carroufel* in fpite of the refiftance of fome fections, and demanded from the legiflature the organization of the anarchical conftitution constitution of 1793, and of some decrees which might afford the Parisians the bread of which they were deprived.

The Convention, dreading to see a renewal of the bloody scenes of the day preceding, thought to oppose the Rebels by promising them to accede to their demands. This was attended with complete success; and the leaders of the sedition having no longer a pretext for keeping the people assembled, in a few moments after beheld disperse this multitudinous and tumultuous mob on whom they had founded so many hopes.

On the third Prairial the assassins of the deputy Ferraud, being conducted to execution, were forced away from the scaffold by the inhabitants of the *Fauxbourg St. Antoine*, whom the jacobins had excited; this audacity announced a great storm, and an insurrection more formidable perhaps than those which had preceded. The Convention, informed of the designs of the anarchists, and enlightened by it's own faults, at length adopted wise and vigorous measures in order to repress all these disorders, and to punish all the factious.

Having nominated General Menou Commandant of Paris, instead of imprudently waiting as heretofore the attack of the Conspirators, anticipated

anticipated them; and whilst some chosen battalions defended the avenues to the palace of the Thuilleries, Menou, at the head of a column, consisting of troops of the line, and of detachments drawn from some of the sections who were best disposed, placed himself at the entrance of the *Fauxbourg St. Antoine*, followed by a strong train of artillery, and by a wise and spirited proclamation threatened the seditious to cannonade them without mercy, if they did not consent to lay down their arms, and to deliver to him the assassins of Ferraud and the chiefs of the revolt.

The Rebels, in consternation, submitted; and this happy revolution, dissipating all the fears of the well disposed, and restoring complete liberty to the moderate party, at length totally annihilated the criminal hopes of the partisans of anarchy.

Crime from that moment every where ceased to show it's insolent boldness, virtue respired, liberty regained it's energy, and the representatives of the people, freed from their disgraceful fetters, finally dared to avow publickly their contempt for that constitution of 1793, invented to legalize anarchy.

They nominated a committee of eleven deputies to draw up a better constitution; and whilst they were thus employed, the Convention,

after

after having exerted a necessary rigour in bringing to trial, by military commissions, the authors of the revolt of Prairial, and the deputies who had evinced an inclination to take advantage of replunging it into slavery, fulfilled a more pleasing duty in healing the wounds which tyranny had inflicted.

They recalled the cultivators whom the tyrants had inscribed in the lists of emigrants; they opened a register for the claims of those who could prove their residence; they softened the barbarous laws passed against the priests, and they restored to families, who had been victims of the revolutionary tribunal, the property of which an atrocious confiscation had deprived them. All the citizens who had been compelled, in order to escape mandates of arrest, to expatriate since the 31st May 1793, were recalled to their homes.

Boissy-d'Anglas, Lanjuinais, Doulcet, le Sage and several other Deputies restored to the tribune the voice of reason, of policy, and humanity; they consoled the families plundered by the tyrants; they inveighed against the ferocious partisans of the Agrarian law, which ruined the nation by exciting an absurd hatred of the poor against the rich; they gave notice to the powers of Europe, that France, ceasing to be barbarous,

barbarous, was as ready to negociate as to continue the war. And the Convention, enjoying the happy advantages of this change of system, then received, for the first time, merited applauses, and universal and sincere congratulations.

Charette and the chiefs of la Vendée entered into a treaty, and made their submission. The coalition divided, lost several of their most powerful confederates: Prussia and Spain concluded peace; several courts acknowledged the Republic; the north of Germany declared themselves neutral; and the French nation, accepting a constitution as perfect as circumstances permitted, would probably have soon compelled Austria, in spite of resentment for her losses, and the British Government, notwithstanding it's ambition, to terminate a fatal war, if the fear caused by so many errors and misfortunes had not still interposed to blind the Convention, and to remove it by new storms from the haven which was opened to it by the almost unanimous efforts of all honest people.

Scarcely had the Conventional Deputies who had overthrown Robespierre, defeated the remainder of that formidable party, than they dreaded having given too great strength to that of the royalists; and this dread causing them to take

take false steps, gave birth to the reaction which they feared.

It seems that the fault of nearly all those who have ruled France since the revolution was, that they had studied books more than men, and continually deceived themselves as to the means of directing public opinion; they seem to have always been ignorant, that man is continually subjected to two opposite influences which sway him by turns; of attraction of novelty, and the force of habit: all the revolutions that we have seen supported and sanctioned by public opinion, have been those, where one of these two propensities has been gratified by a skilful government of the other.

At Rome, for example, in abolishing royalty, the senate, the tribes, the centuries, the augurs the pontifs, and the laws of Numa were preserved; and the people abandoning themselves with transport to the novelty which was offered to them, enjoyed the advantages of the republican system, so much the more completely as they did not in other respects experience any change which was repugnant to their inclinations or to their customs.

In America, we have seen recently a couragcous nation establish it's independence with zeal, terminate it's revolution with wisdom, and peacefully

peacefully enjoy it's liberty, becaufe it's legiflators poffeffed the prudence of making only indifpenfable innovations, and of refpecting the greater part of its ancient inftitutions. A contrary conduct left to the Englifh republic the duration only of the life of Cromwell.

But the Convention ought to have perceived, that in France the revolution which had at firft excited fo lively a national enthufiafm by the attraction of novelty, having been conducted by the paffions rather than by policy, had indifcriminately demolifhed all the parts of the ancient edifice, without examination of thofe whofe deftruction was not indifpenfable to liberty; the refult neceffarily was, that after the firft moment of enjoyment of each of thefe innovations, all the French, compelled to a total change of their laws, language, drefs, worfhip, fortunes, jurifprudence, calculations, opinions and manners, experienced at every inftant, and in all the circumftances of their lives, a conftraint, an inconvenience which at firft extinguifhed their ardour, and which might even foon impel them by the force of habit to regret every thing they had deftroyed.

If the National Convention, after the revolution of Prairial, had well underftood this fituation of the public mind, it would have profited by by the power which was in it's hands, and by the confidence that it inspired to consolidate liberty, by speedily repealing all the laws which might disgust the majority of the nation.

The legislators, in reverting to the ancient institutions compatible with the republican government, and in this respect wisely anticipating the wish of the people, had inspired them with the greater attachment for the new institutions, because they were so little contradictory to what they had been accustomed to; and far from giving by this strength to the enemies of the revolution, they had destroyed all hopes, for no person can flatter himself with raising an insurrection in a nation content with it's laws.

Unfortunately the conventionalists, blinded by their fear, the sole cause of the paucity of good governments, made a calculation the reverse of that which prudence should have dictated. Instead of inciting the enthusiasm of youth for the destroyers of jacobinical tyranny, they exhibited a distrust which irritated them; they disarmed the sections, whose force they had employed so successfully against anarchy.

Far from gratifying the just resentment of the people, and preventing private revenge, by quickly delivering over to justice the monsters who had in every department committed the greatest

greatest murders and robberies, and obliterating the less enormous crimes by a wise amnesty, they allowed fear to impend over the heads of all the subordinate agents of terrorism, whilst they protected the more guilty.

They prohibited the *Reveil du Peuple*, a hymn which reminded them of the fall of their tyrants, and they compelled the people to listen to those songs which they had rejected after they had been employed by the proscribers.

All the propositions tending to destroy any revolutionary law were strongly opposed by some distrustful deputies; instead of effacing all hatred and all distinction of classes, they shewed indulgence only to the tradesman and the peasant; the ex-nobles, the wealthy and their connections remained proscribed, whilst the others, suspected of the same guilt, were absolved.

Lastly, the most accredited journals treating violence as patriotism, and moderation as royalism, disgusted all judicious men, all the friends of principle, who saw with indignation an intention to perpetuate the revolutionary movement.

The death of the son of Louis XVI. who this year perished in his prison, furnished still new food for hatred. History ought not to adopt accusations without evidence, but the rigour of the captivity of this unfortunate child, and the fatal shade which enveloped his existence and his end, could not but inspire lively regret in those deputies, whose justice and humanity were then fettered by the fear of being suspected of royalism.

The result of this conduct was a general irritation against the Convention, and in several departments the royalists, availing themselves both of the resentment of those who saw the assassination of their families unpunished, and of the discontent of all those who eagerly wished to see an end to the revolution, misled the young men, inflamed their ardour, and occasioned a somewhat violent reaction, which drenched the southern districts with blood.

The Convention terminated its stormy career by a still more serious fault, which nearly occasioned it's destruction, and the fatal consequences of which produced new revolutions.

It had framed a constitution much better digested than the preceding ones, and, notwithstanding it's defects, calculated to afford the French for several years the tranquillity they required. By this new code, the legislation was vested in two councils elected by the people. The council of five hundred were to propose the

the laws, the council of two hundred and fifty, or ancients, were to accept or reject them. The supreme executive power was placed in the hands of five directors, named by the councils. The tribunals enjoyed a complete independence. The ministers, subject to the directory, were responsible for the execution of the laws. The directors and the deputies, alike inviolable, could not be accused and tried but by a decree passed by the two councils.

Whatever well founded objections there may have been to this constitution, it was the best that could then be possibly admitted amidst republican jealousy, and the clashing of passions; and it's duration in the time of intestine broils, and the rage of war, under the conduct of a directory, most of whose members were chosen contrary to the general will of the nation, sufficiently proves what it's solidity would have been, had the first directors been elected from among the most distinguished warriors, and the most wise magistrates.

All parties, excepting a small number of counter-revolutionists, and outrageous jacobins, were equally disposed to accept this constitution which offered them some hope of tranquillity after so many storms. In this instrument it had been wisely settled, in order to prevent too

violent

violent fhocks, to renew annually a third of the legiflative body; this was the fole means of avoiding in the legiflature too fudden and entire changes of fentiment; and this danger never could be more real, than at the moment when this new form of government was begun to be put in action.

We ftill remember the fault committed by the conftituent deputies, in abandoning their conftitution to the hands of a new affembly, who profcribed their perfons, and overturned their work. Thus we fhould have expected to fee two thirds of the National Convention form the new legiflative body.

If this determination had been comprifed and announced in one of the articles of the conftitution, it is certain that it would have paffed without difficulty. But the convention made a feparate law of it, fo that the primary affemblies thought they might accept the conftitutional inftrument, and reject this law of the 5th and 13th Fructidor.

This imprudence kindled all the paffions, and afforded the jacobins, counter-revolutionifts, and foreign powers, all the pretexts they could defire for renewing difturbances and inciting civil war.

All men liften to the voice of the paffions; very

very few attend to that of policy and reason. It was natural to be tired of an assembly, which for three years had so much abused it's powers, squandered so much treasure, and occasioned so many tears, and so much blood to flow. Men forgot that it had for a year expiated some of it's faults, and repaired a part of it's injuries; that it had still full power, and should be conciliated; that it offered with arms in it's hands a treaty of peace, of which prudence dictated the acceptance; that the troops obeyed it; that the new land-holders supported it, and that the more resentment it should attract, the less could it expose itself and it's laws to the vengeance of it's enemies.

A great part of the primary assemblies, excited by the malcontents, the ambitious, and the royalists, and perfidiously inflamed by the jacobins, who wished to make themselves necessary, declared themselves permanent, rejected the laws of the 5th and 13th Fructidor, and by their fermentation announced the approach of a new revolution.

The sections of Paris, more exasperated and violent, still less disguised their opposition and their projects, mutually inflaming each other, and manifesting their indignation against the tyranny of the Convention; they seized all the military powers, convoked the electors before the time

time fixed for their affembling, contemned the decrees which prohibited thefe illegal procedures, and abufed their power fo far as to fuppofe that nothing could refift them.

The Convention, terrified, brought troops to Paris, and armed the anarchifts, who, profiting by the opportunity for regaining their influence, offered it their affiftance. This arming of men who were detefted exafperated the fections. Without a leader, without artillery, without warlike ftores, on the 13th Vendémaire they ran to arms, and proceeded in a body to the palace with equal diforder and impetuofity; the regular troops and the artillery eafily repulfed this multitude ill organifed, ill conducted, and ill armed.

A great number of citizens, and even fome women, loft their lives on this day: fury was foon fucceeded by terrour; all the primary affemblies who had imitated the ardour of thofe of Paris, difmayed by this example, feparated and fubmitted; and the Convention, having no longer any oppofition to dread, put in action the conftitution, as it had intended.

It ufed victory even with more moderation than was expected. The military committees nominated to try the authors of the fedition, condemned few perfons, and were foon diffolved; but

but the most untoward effect of this abortive insurrection was the change of system of the Conventionalists.

Despairing to regain by mild laws the affection of a great part of the nation, they wished to restrain it by fear; they discharged from their employments, and excluded from elections, a great number of citizens, under pretext of relationship with emigrants, or of seditious acts in the late tumults.

This law of the 3rd Brumaire, contrary to the constitution, stifled it in it's cradle, destroyed equality, and under pretence of defending liberty, encompassed it with the chains of arbitrary power.

Lastly, the most powerful obstacle to the good they intended, was the choice of the persons to whom they intrusted the executive power.

The Convention, alarmed at the dangers it had incurred, forgetting that if violence produced revolutions, moderation alone can terminate them, did not consult the public wish, listened only to their fears, and named as directors, violent men, the choice of whom perpetuated the national discontent, and the agitation by which it was necessarily attended.

The history of their administration, of the struggle that took place between them and the
legislative

legiflative body, the recital of their momentary triumphs, of their divifions, of their cruel profcriptions, and of their fall, will be the fubject of another work. In this I purpofe only to trace a political picture of Europe to the end of the third year of the Republic, which terminated with the clofe of the fittings of the National Convention.

To complete the prefent work, therefore, I have only to retrace my fteps, and remark the changes that took place, at this epoch, in the fyftem of the Kings coalefced againft the Republic, as well as the laft operations of Frederic William II; for this monarch may be faid to have terminated his reign this year, though he lived upwards of eighteen months after.

The internal fituation of the French Republic was always little known, and improperly eftimated in Europe. It was at firft thought eafy to be deftroyed: fome time afterwards it was confidered impregnable: and whilft it was internally torn to pieces by the moft fcandalous factions, nothing ftruck foreigners but the fall of it's tyrants, the fplendour of it's victories, and the eloquence of it's orators.

Thus, notwithftanding the proteftations of the princes of the empire, whofe poffeffions the French had conquered; the intrigues of Ruffia;

Ruſſia; the complaints of the emigrants; the reproaches of the court of Vienna, and the ſeductions of the Britiſh miniſtry, moſt of the powers which formed the coalition began gradually to cool, to ſeparate, and to renounce a ruinous war, which extended the channel of the revolutionary torrent, inſtead of ſtopping it, and the ſole reſult of which was to increaſe the continental power of France, and the maritime power of England.

To the great aſtoniſhment of politicians, the Grand Duke of Tuſcany firſt acknowledged the French Republic, concluded peace, ſent the Count de Carletti as miniſter to Paris, and by a formal treaty, breaking his engagements with the coalition, promiſed in future to obſerve the ſtricteſt neutrality.

One crowned head ſoon followed the example of this prince, the regent of Sweden, in the name of his nephew, ſent the Baron de Staal to Paris, and that ambaſſador appeared in the Convention, and aſſured the French nation of the friendſhip which the court of Stockholm entertained for the Republic*.

* To the political inquirer it would be a curious ſubject, to conſider what would probably have been the comparative ſituation of Sweden with it's preſent one, had Guſtavus eſcaped the piſtol of Ankerſtröem, and lived to command the coaleſced armies.

If the committees of government had then possessed more money and more credit, this reconciliation might have produced the most important consequences. A negociation which was then begun, had for it's object to engage the regent to equip a fleet, in order to oblige the English to respect his neutrality; but the subsidies demanded were refused, and even those which were formerly due were not punctually paid; and by this impolitic economy, the opportunity was lost of securing the alliance of a maritime power, which might have favoured the so necessary renovation of the French navy*.

In calculating the effect of the passions, it might have been thought that Spain would be the last power to treat with France; that kingdom being governed by a Bourbon, it appeared that personal resentments, mingling family interest with that of royalty, would have destroyed every possibility of negociation with the assembly which had deprived Louis XVI. of his crown and life.

But the most striking circumstance in the his-

---

* Thus we see, that it is not to the friendship of Sweden, but to the momentary want of resources in France, that Sweden, and with her probably Denmark, till now abstained from presenting an armed neutrality.

tory of this aftonifhing revolution, is, that during its continuance the events have conftantly deceived the predictions of experience, the reafonings of policy, and all the calculations of tactics.

The coalition and the emigrants bitterly reproached Charles IV. for not having rather buried himfelf under the ruins of the Spanifh monarchy than treat with republicans; but pofterity, more difpaffionate, and more juft, will probably applaud him for acting rather as a monarch than as a Bourbon, and preferring his country to his family.

For a year the cabinet of Madrid had feen fortune favour the republicans, and their armies every where triumphant: after a bloody battle, in which the Spanifh General Count de la Union, and the French General Dugommier were killed, the republican troops had taken Figuieres. General Perignon, and General Servant, profiting by thefe advantages, threatened Spain with total ruin. Three provinces of Bifcay had fallen into the hands of the French; no fortrefs could ftop their efforts; and Spain, from it's fituation, could hope for no external fuccour.

The northern powers remained neutral; the Emprefs of Ruffia, who afterwards blamed in

rather

rather disrespectful terms the defection of the Catholic King, assisted the coalition only by promises.

The King of Prussia, contented with his new acquisitions in Poland, and disgusted with the war, forgot in the arms of his mistresses his former objects, his recent defeats, the danger of the Empire, the dispute of kings, and the interests of his sister, the Princess of Orange. England had in vain attempted to re-animate his zeal by subsidies; he was determined no longer to expose himself (not to dangers, for these he did not fear) but to the fatigues and *tedium* of a third campaign. Despairing to be able to reinstate a Bourbon on the throne of France, he saw without inquietude his rival Austria weakened; and although he had not yet made peace, he had quitted arms, and sent to the committee of public safety a counsellor named d'Harnier, whose pacific instructions evinced his intention of no longer being a party in the war.

Abandoning the Stadtholder, renouncing his possessions on the west bank of the Rhine, he hoped to render his repose honourable, by assuring the tranquillity of the north of Germany, and reserving to himself the office of a mediator.

It

It muſt indeed be acknowledged, that this arrangement, which divided the Empire, and ſubjected the half of it to him, had no grand political idea; and if his ſyſtem had been, like the neutrality of his ſucceſſor, the effect of a conſtant and firm prudence, he would have merited only praiſe; but as he had been the chief of the coalition, and had ſhewn himſelf the moſt eager of all the princes for undertaking war, and moſt averſe to liſten to the pacific miniſters who wiſhed to prevent it, this verſatility and defection drew on him the juſt reproaches of all the allies whom he had ſeconded in times of proſperity, and whom he abandoned in the moment when forſaken by Fortune.

Swedes, Ruſſians, Poles, Turks, Brabanters, Auſtrians, Dutch, Engliſh and French; all had, in their turn, ſeen him ſupport, fight, animate and abandon them; and this conduct, which deſtroyed all reſpect for him, made him univerſally conſidered as the moſt weak monarch, the moſt uſeleſs ally, the moſt deceitful ſupporter, and the leaſt dangerous enemy.

The court of Vienna, attentive only to it's own intereſts, feebly ſuccoured the King of Sardinia, and merely thought of taking advantage of the ſubſidies of England to reconquer the Netherlands, or ſecure elſewhere compen-
ſations

sations which might indemnify him for their loss.

It is evidently to be seen, that the great object of the coalition little interested those who directed it. The French Princes had never been intrusted with a command, to enable them to penetrate into France, and there incite a party. Even the chief of that House was not suffered to put himself at the head of the troops which were fighting for him. The Prince de Condé was restrained in all his operations, and constantly subordinate to the plans and the orders of Austrian Generals. The emigrants, whose courage had been misemployed, and their proscription occasioned by the coalition, in vain proved by prodigies of valour, that they were born Frenchmen; they were wantonly sacrificed as advanced guards in the attacks, and as rear guards in the retreats; they were shamefully given up in all the capitulations; and those who did not take up arms, almost every where deprived of protection and an asylum, found themselves reduced to misery by the abandonment of courts who pretended to support their cause.

England, more ostentatious in her protection, was not more just in her policy; she received generously the exiled priests, paid rather liberally the French officers who entered into her service,

service; but, after the capture of Corsica, Martinico, and the Toulon fleet for herself, and not for her allies, the Bourbons, she had left the insurgents in La Vendée to their own efforts, and never would consent to land on the coast of France a French Prince, in order to endeavour to terminate the revolution, which, on the contrary, she seemed desirous of being prolonged.

Afterwards, at last yielding to the entreaties of the emigrants, she debarked three thousand of them at Quiberon; and, without the support of any corps of troops, she, by this imprudence, not to give it a harsher name, abandoned them to the attacks of their enemies, and the rigour of the republican laws, which were then executed with a cruelty unexampled in history.

The Spanish ministry, convinced of the imminence of it's danger, the superiority of the republican force, and the ungenerous ambition of it's allies, thought it their duty to advise the King of Spain to sacrifice his personal resentments to the salvation of his country. It first founded, through the minister of the United States, the dispositions of the committee of public safety, and found them much more moderate in their pretensions than had been expected.

The Ex-Ambaſſador Bourgoing, the only Frenchman who has compoſed a good work reſpecting Spain, wrote letters to M. M. Oſcaritz and D'Yriarte, informing the cabinet of Madrid of the pacific intentions of the French government; and immediately more direct negociations were begun, the proceeding in which was ſo rapid, that England had notice of the concluſion of peace, almoſt as ſoon as ſhe heard of the negociation.

The perſons who had then the direction of the French government were too well acquainted with the ſituation of the republic, not to be ſenſible how much it required peace. Citizen Barthelemy, Ambaſſador at Switzerland, was authoriſed by them to take indirect means of diſcovering the diſpoſitions of the coaleſced powers.

They could not have made a better choice: Citizen Barthelemy, an experienced negociator, was, by his conciliatory diſpoſition, and the mildneſs of his character, the man of all others the moſt fit for moderating the moſt violent paſſions, and reconciling the moſt oppoſite intereſts. Eſteemed at Vienna, juſtly appreciated at London, beloved in Switzerland, he enjoyed univerſal reſpect, and merited it as much from the extent of his knowledge as the rectitude of his intentions

intentions; accordingly he afterwards experienced the fate his character necessarily attracted; he was called to the directory by probity, banished his country by tyranny, and recalled from his exile by glory.

As soon as Barthelemy had received orders from the committee of public safety, he availed himself of the arrival of a Prussian agent, who had come to Switzerland to treat respecting an arrangement for the exchange of prisoners, and made positive overtures for a reconciliation.

The cabinet of Berlin, after the assurances it had received of the pacific intentions of France, sent the Count de Goltz to Switzerland vested with full powers to treat of peace.

The committee of public safety, uneasy and distrustful, had first intended that this negociation should be conducted under their own inspection; they had, in consequence, required that the Prussian minister should repair to Paris with citizen Barthelemy, who was to have the charge of this pacification; but Frederic William refused this too obvious mark of deference; however he sent the Counsellor Harnier to Paris, and directed him to give the committee the most positive assurances of his disposition to remove all difficulties which might thwart the negociation.

The French government were satisfied from this step, that the King of Prussia did not consider the abolition of the Stadtholderate, and the revolution in Holland, as obstacles to peace; and that he did not insist on retaining his possessions on the left bank of the Rhine, although he had not yet definitively ceded them to the French, who occupied them provisionally.

The reason which induced him to postpone this definitive cession till a general peace, was, that he did not wish Austria, should her arms prove victorious, to be able to seize on this territory as belonging to France.

Conformably to the wish of the cabinet of Berlin, the town of Basle was appointed the place for negociation.

The conferences were there accordingly opened on the 5th Pluviose, year III. A melancholy incident almost immediately occurred to interrupt them: M. de Goltz fell sick, and died on the 17th. His death, by retarding the negociation, gave England and Austria time to intrigue, in order to prevent peace. However, the King of Prussia, disregarding their prayers and their threats, named as a successor to Count de Goltz, Baron de Hardenberg, the minister who had the superintendence of the Margraviates of Anspach and Bareith.

The

The Counsellor Harnier was at the same time directed to continue the negociation of M. de Goltz, and according to the same instructions; but those instructions were vague and limited. M. de Hardenberg, being obliged to go to Berlin for new orders before his proceeding to Basle, still retarded the business. The hopes of peace had already begun to vanish, when at length he arrived on the 29th Ventose, with instructions much more extensive than those of his predecessor. The conferences were immediately resumed, and carried on with the greatest activity; all obstacles were quickly removed, and peace was signed the 16th Germinal*.

The demand of a preliminary armistice, the evacuation of Mentz by the Prussians, the occupation of the Prussian possessions on the left bank of the Rhine, the neutrality of the King of Prussia, as a state of the Empire, and lastly, the establishment of the line of demarcation for the north of Germany, were the principal difficulties that were to be conquered in this negociation. M. de Goltz, whose dispositions in favour of France were known, had appeared reserved, minute, and fastidious, in the conferences; M. de Hardenberg, on the contrary,

* See the treaty with Prussia in the Appendix.

whose attachment to the English system was dreaded, exhibited, in terms of his instructions, as much facility in the negociation, as he displayed frankness in explaining himself respecting his private sentiments.

The principal articles were an engagement on the part of the King of Prussia to live in strict friendship with the Republic, both as King of Prussia, and as a member of the Empire; not to furnish succours or contingents, under any denomination whatever, to the enemies of France; to leave to the French the occupation of the Prussian possessions on the left bank of the Rhine, postponing every definitive arrangement with respect to these provinces, till a general pacification between France and the Empire.

France, on her part, engaged to withdraw her troops from the Prussian possessions situated on the right bank of the Rhine, and cordially to admit the good offices of the King of Prussia in favour of the Princes of the Empire, and not to treat as hostile territories the states of the Empire situated on the right bank of the Rhine, in whose favour the King should interpose.

This treaty equally satisfied the views of France and Prussia, and relieved the French of all dread

dread from the North, by submitting the northern part of Germany to the Prussian influence.

Peace was scarcely concluded, when measures were actively adopted to secure that neutrality on which the Court of Berlin set so great value, and which eased the French from all alarm for Holland, by keeping at a distance the English and Stadtholderians, who had then an army in Westphalia and the electorate of Hanover.

The principal and the most important conditions of this neutrality, were already agreed on by several articles, but the changes, modifications, and additions which were to be made on either side, obliged the contracting parties to execute a new instrument.

Such were the motives and the origin of the Convention, which was signed at Basle on the 28th Florial by citizen Barthelemy and M. de Hardenberg*.

The favourable clauses of the article, and treaty of peace, naturally induced the greater part of the states of the German Empire to take the advantage of the Prussian banner, in order to treat with the French government; and accordingly it was at Basle that negociations were begun with several of them. But the events of

* See the Convention in the Appendix.

war,

war, which were not favourable to the Republic this year, kept these princes from concluding peace, for fear of being exposed to the resentment of the Emperor.

The Landgrave of Hesse-Cassel, who had some troops and money, and was intimately connected with the Court of Berlin, was the only one that durst follow it's example. It was of importance to France to have him for a friend; he sent a plenipotentiary to Basle: Barthelemy negociated with him, and on the 11th Fructidor signed a treaty of peace, by which that prince withdrew his troops from the pay of England, ceded to France the country he possessed on the left bank of the Rhine, and disengaged himself of the obligation he was under to furnish his contingent as a prince of the Empire *.

The peace with the King of Prussia had broken the chain of the Coalition. Spain, authorised by that example, could not long hesitate in terminating a war, ruinous for her, and which was beneficial only to the English, her natural enemies. The Court of Madrid had, in the month of Germinal, sent the Chevalier d'Yriarte

* See the Treaty with the Landgrave of Hesse in the Appendix.

orders

orders to repair to Basle to citizen Barthelemy. Poland had just ceased to exist as a nation. M. d'Yriarte, who was at Warsaw as minister of his Catholic Majesty, had been obliged to quit that residence when the Russians entered it, and was then at Venice.

He was connected with Barthelemy by the strictest friendship; and the cabinet of Madrid had thought that this connection would accelerate the wished for conciliation. He arrived at Basle on the 15th Floreal, and the negociation was immediately begun. A somewhat extraordinary circumstance, however, complicated its progress; the courier who had been sent from Madrid to M. d'Yriarte, had gone first to seek him at Vienna, then at Dresden, then at Berlin, and lastly at Venice. M. d'Yriarte had immediately set out from Basle, and delayed, till his arrival at that city, to send back the courier with the answer he ought to have dispatched to his court.

This phlegm and silence will astonish only those who are unacquainted with the Spanish character. As there were then no communications through France, it was necessary that the dispatches should travel all round by Switzerland and Italy and cross the sea. The journey and return of this courier and his route through Germany,

Germany, took a prodigious time. The cabinet of Madrid became uneasy; they thought that either M. d'Yriarte or the courier had died. In this uncertainty they adopted the measure of sending the Marquis d'Yranda to the Pyrénées, with instructions to treat, in case M. d'Yriarte had not commenced negociation at Basle.

These two missions embarrassed the committee of public safety. They thought themselves obliged to send as plenipotentiary to the Pyrénées, General Servan; but this negociator made an unnecessary journey.

In the mean time, M. d'Yriarte had been permitted to dispatch couriers through France; he soon received from his court complete instructions and necessary powers to conclude peace; which was signed at Basle the 4th Thermidor*.

All Europe was astonished to learn the conclusion of this negociation in Switzerland, whilst general attention had been directed towards that of the Pyrénées which had been announced with some ostentation.

By this treaty France abandoned all her conquests, and Spain ceded to her the part it possessed of St. Domingo.

This moderation of the republic, and the

* See the Treaty with Spain in the Appendix.

common intereſt of oppoſing the ambition of England, diſpoſed the court of Madrid to renew its ancient connections with France, and enter into a treaty of alliance with her.

Citizen Barthelemy and M. d'Yriarte, having received powers for this purpoſe, they had diſcuſſed it's baſes, when M. d'Yriarte, already indiſpoſed, became ſo weak, that he was obliged to abandon the negociation, and returned to his country. Before his departure, he received letters which proved to him, by the rewards laviſhed on him, the joy which the concluſion of peace had occaſioned to the King and the prime miniſter.

The dread of feeing a continuance of the war, and the wiſh for it's termination, were ſo ardent through all Spain, that prayers were every where offered up for the ceſſation of the calamities which overwhelmed the kingdom; and the King of Spain, to whom the provinces he had loſt were reſtored at the moment when he expected to ſee the enemy arrive at his capital, beſtowed on the Duke d'Alcudia the title of *Prince of the Peace,* as Rome anciently granted to her generals the name of the provinces they had conquered.

M. d'Yriarte, who was appointed to the embaſſy of France, which he had always wiſhed, died

died, on his arrival in Spain, regretted by every one, whose passions did not lead them to oppose the re-establishment of general tranquillity.

Such was the conclusion of these important negociations: if they did not entirely extinguish the flame of war, they moderated it's violence; and although the ambition of England, and the resentment of the court of Vienna still so infatuated them; as to make them hope alone to vanquish a nation which had resisted all Europe, it was nevertheless evident to every wise politician, that from this moment the dispute was decided, and that if the French had not hitherto had the prudence to form a tranquil and permanent government, they possessed at least sufficient energy and resources to preserve their independence, and to receive laws from none.

The very result of all the events that had passed, proved that, if democracy in a great nation draws on it internally all the calamities occasioned by the rivality of unbridled ambition, and the weakness of a government without foundation, without concentration, and without permanence, it may give it externally an impulsion, not to be balanced by the limited and methodical means of monarchies.

Never, in fact, can a single will have so much action as a combination of wills; the former
experiences

experiences insurmountable resistance in procuring men and money; the latter admits no obstacles, and imperiously commands all sacrifices.

In monarchies, it is wise to employ a power that will be permanent, and the responsibility resting always on the same persons, they are obliged to economize their means by interest and by prudence. In republics, where elections are frequent, every one is desirous of deriving a brilliant eclat and prompt utility from his transient authority, and lavishes at the same time all his efforts and all his resources, without caring to leave any thing to his successor. These temporary chiefs wish that their reign of a year may exhibit all the glory which a monarch diffuses in his reign of twenty years; this desire gave birth to the prodigies we read of in the history of the Roman consuls.

Thus the more passionate than prudent policy of the cabinets of London and Vienna, by persisting in the chimerical project of subjugating the French republic, exposed Europe to imminent danger. These two courts, blinded by an animosity, the causes of which were very natural, did not perceive that in fact the question of the independence of France was decided by victory; and that in continuing the war, they

only

only put in jeopardy the exiſtence of monarchies.

In this conteſt againſt a numerous nation, elated by it's triumphs, which counted it's having the more ſoldiers, the more citizens it had ruined and workmen unemployed, and which was beſides, the more eager to invade foreign countries the leſs money remained in it's own; the monarchs had every thing to loſe and nothing to gain.

If conquerors, they would only enter a ruined country, where every man was a warrior, every wood a redoubt, every plain a field of battle; if conquered, they would ſee their treaſure pillaged, their magazines conſumed, their ſubjects incited to inſurrection, and their thrones overturned: every where the poor multitude and the ambitious underlings would be diſpoſed to deſire a change, which might diſplace the rich and powerful, and afford prizes to the fortunate and bold. And, if the French democrats, inſtead of allowing themſelves to be ſo often governed by unfit perſons, had taken for directors their impetuous warriors, the obſtinacy of the coaleſced Kings would, in a ſhort time, have rendered revolution univerſal.

Fortune, and the errors of the revolutioniſts, ſaved Europe from this general overthrow, which
would

would have overwelmed it with the evils of which France had been so long the prey, and afforded the French nation, after several other shocks, time to revert to more social principles, and constitute a government more concentrated, more happy for itself, and less alarming for others; but it is nevertheless true, that the coalesced powers, who neither foresaw nor wished this termination, had imprudently exposed social order to the danger of total destruction.

The year which saw the coalition dissolved ended by some military events, the indecisive success of which left in a state of uncertainty the hopes and fears of each party.

In the West-Indies, the French having excited the inhabitants of St. Lucia and St. Domingo, drove the English from these islands; whilst the latter suppressed a similar insurrection in Granada.

The army of Italy acted only on the defensive. In la Vendée, the affair of Quiberon had destroyed the hopes of the royalists.

Luxemburg, after a long blockade, surrendered to the republicans, who there took prisoner Marshal Bender, famous for the easy and rapid conquest of Brabant.

Jourdan, after having passed the Rhine near Dufsledorp, and invested Mentz, was under the

the necessity of raising the siege, and had been vigorously repulsed by the Austrians, who had not respected the line of neutrality marked by the King of Prussia in his treaty.

Pichegru, who had made himself master of Manheim, was defeated near that city, and constrained to abandon it to the Austrians, who had taken possession of it, reduced the Palatinate, threatened Landau, but were suddenly arrested in their progress by the French. At length this campaign was terminated by a suspension of arms, which was soon followed by fresh hostilities.

Frederic William, who had just completed the partition of Poland, and concluded a peace with France, disappeared about this time from the political scene of Europe.

He afterwards projected some farther disinemberment and secularization in Germany, which were proposed to him by France, who then believed it to be his interest to weaken the Emperor, and to augment the power of the protestant party in the Empire, at the expense of the catholic party; but these schemes, too complicated, would have required an activity which this monarch never possessed; and the declining state of his health augmented his natural indolence.

Aspiring

Aspiring to the character of a mediator, he made some fruitless attempts to bring about peace; but to this the passions of the coalition and the French directory were almost equally adverse.

The expenses of the war, the malady of the King, his profusion, and his mistresses, had deranged his finances, and he negociated a loan at Frankfort to relieve the exhaustion of his treasury, which he had lavished without glory. His infirmities daily increased his indifference for the storms with which he was surrounded; the *illuminati* amused him with deceitful promises, in the hope of recovering that health which excess of pleasures had irrevocably destroyed; at length the dropsy having decidedly declared itself, he died on the 17th November 1797, regretted by his family, and by a few friends who rendered justice to his mildness and his beneficence, but leaving behind him no trace of glorious rememberance.

His intrigues had exposed Sweden and Turkey to a ruinous war; his protection had destroyed Poland; the first to form the coalition, he was the first to abandon it. The Stadtholder might reproach him with the loss of his power, and Brabant with that of her liberty. His defects had diminished the lustre shed by his predeceffor over the Pruffian arms. His abortive enterprifes, and the avidity of his miftreffes, had diffipated the treafures of the Great Frederic; and although the partition of Poland had added feveral rich provinces to his dominions, Frederic William III. his fon, was obliged to exert the moft unremitting prudence, and to obferve the ftricteft economy, in order to repair the faults of his father, and to reftore to Pruffia her real importance and profperity.

On his acceffion to the throne, he arrefted Madame de Lichtnau Rietz, and thofe perfons who had impofed on the weaknefs of the late King to enrich themfelves. The juftice which he exercifed towards them, his choice of minifters, and the example which he fet of a regular life, infpired a juft confidence in his fubjects, to whom thefe augured a happier reign; and endeavouring rather to reftore tranquillity to Europe by his influence than to trouble it by his ambition, he firmly perfifted, in fpite of the intrigues of England, and the councils of fome violent men, in a fyftem of neutrality, which he purfued from prudence, but which his predeceffor had adopted only from inconftancy.

If during the laft two years of the reign of Frederic William II. Pruffia was not diftinguifhed by any important event, it was far

otherwife

otherwise with the rest of Europe, which became the theatre of the most sanguinary battles, the most brilliant exploits, and the most memorable conquests, recorded in the annals of modern history.

The recital of these new revolutions extends beyond the canvas which I proposed to fill: it presents rich materials for another work; but the more fertile and important the subject is, the less it ought to be ornamented.

The historian who undertakes to treat of it, will say, " that there appeared one of those men " whom Fate destines to celebrity, and whom " she seems seldom to create in the space of " ages, for the purpose of executing her decrees, " and changing the face of Empires."

He will recount the battles of Millesimo-Cerasco, the capture of Ceva, the sudden invasion of Piedmont, which forced the King of Sardinia to accept peace; he will describe the temerity of the French conquerors at Rastadt, Altenkirchen, and Rhincen, advancing to the centre of the Empire under the command of Jourdan, and afterwards forced to repass the Rhine; the talents of Moreau, who acquired as much glory by his skilful retreat as others have by their brilliant victories.

The battle of Fombio, that of Lodi, and of Rivoli,

Rivoli, the conquest of Lombardy, the capture of Mantua, the Austrian army of Provera laying down their arms, Rome emploring the generosity of the conqueror of Italy, will enrich this splendid picture.

The contest betwixt two celebrated generals, the battles of the Archduke Charles against Bonaparte, the victories of Tagliament, of the Wis, of Brixen and Clagenfurth, the capture of Gradiska and Trieste, will attest the courage of the French, and perpetuate the glory of their young and fortunate General.

The alliance of Spain with France, the secret efforts of England to prolong the war, her public overtures for restoring peace, the insolent and unconstitutional conduct of the French Government, the weak and imprudent course of the legislative body, the ardour and indiscretion of the Royalists, the revolution of the 18th Fructidor, the proscriptions which followed it will open a vast field for the reflexions of the Philosopher and the Politician on the delirium of human passions.

To relieve the eye from these dismal objects, the reader will accompany the conqueror of Italy, marching to the gates of Vienna, subduing Venice, and forcing the Emperor to conclude a peace; he will then hope that the

world,

world, weary of such continued tempests, is at length on the eve of enjoying some repose.

But this hope will suddenly vanish; and whilst he follows Bonaparte in his almost incredible conquest of Egypt, the defeat of the Mamelucks, the capture of Alexandria, of Damiotta, Cairo and Suez, the battles of the Pyramids, the invasion of Syria, the murderous siege of St. Jean d'Acre, the battles in Palestine, and the victory of Aboukir, will induce him to doubt whether these prodigies belong to history or to romance; he will at the same time perceive with regret the directory inflated by pride, and blinded by fear, exhausting all the resources of France by it's ignorance, irritate all minds by it's injustice, lose the fruits of the peace of Campo Formio by it's ambition, break up the congress at Rastadt by it's insincerity, ruin ensanguined Switzerland by the cupidity of it's agents, give birth to a new coalition by it's impolitic conquest of Naples, Turin and Rome, disgust the neutral powers by it's extortion, enfeeble the French armies and lose Italy by it's improvidence, fall at length through it's weakness, and in it's fall revive the monster Anarchy which would again have devoured the republic, had not the same hero who had carried his triumphant arms into Africa and Asia, returned with the velocity of lightening,

lightening, braving the English and the waves, to overturn this new tyranny, and by a fortunate revolution, restore hope and victory to France.

But all these facts are too recent to be faithfully depicted; they require a more distant period, happier circumstances, and a bolder pencil.

During their proximity the slightest censure would be imprudence; the best merited praise would resemble flattery. Besides, the future still conceals the plans and the fate of the warrior-magistrate who governs us. Whatever be his destiny, *The life of Bonaparte demands the pen of a Plutarch.*

THE END.

APPENDIX.

APPENDIX.

EXTRACT FROM MR. PITT'S SPEECH IN THE HOUSE OF COMMONS, ON THE 9TH FEB. 1790.

THE present convulsion of France must sooner or later terminate in general harmony and regular order; and notwithstanding the fortunate arrangements of such a situation might make her more formidable, it might also render her less obnoxious as a neighbour. He hoped he might rather wish, as an Englishman, for that, respecting the accomplishment of which he felt himself interested as a man, for the restoration of tranquillity in France, though it appeared to him as distant. *Whensoever the situation of France should become restored* it would prove freedom rightly understood; freedom resulting from good order and good government; and thus circumstanced, France would stand forward as one of the most brilliant powers in Europe, she would enjoy that just kind of liberty which he venerated; and the invaluable existence of which it was his duty, as an Englishman, peculiarly to *cherish;* nor could he under this predicament regard with envious eyes, an approximation in neighbouring states of those sentiments which were the characteristic features of every British subject.

LETTER

FROM THE KING OF PRUSSIA TO THE COUNT DE GOLTZ.

I HAVE received your dispatch dated 3d May, with a postscript informing me of a very important piece of intelligence, that the diet of Poland has proclaimed the Elector of Saxony eventual successor to the throne of Poland, by securing the said succession to his male descendants, and in default of them, to the Princess his daughter, and her future husband, when the Elector, in concert with the states of Poland, shall have chosen him. In consequence of a very amicable predilection which has always inclined me to co-operate for the prosperity of the republic, as well as to *consolidate it's new Constitution*, a predilection of which I have never ceased to give such proofs as depended on me, I admire and applaud *this important measure* which the nation has adopted, and which I consider

consider as essential to consolidate it's prosperity. The news which I have just received is to me so much the more agreeable, as I am attached by the ties of amity to that virtuous Prince, destined to render Poland happy, and that his house enjoys with mine the connections of good neighbourhood, and the most intimate union.

I am persuaded, that the choice of the republic will perpetuate this *harmony* and intimate connection betwixt it and me, I desire you may declare in the most solemn manner, my sincere congratulations to the King, to the Marshals of the diet, and to all those who have assisted in a work so important.

DECLARATION

OF THE MINISTERS OF RUSSIA AND PRUSSIA, TO THE CONFEDERATION OF POLAND.

THE designs which her Majesty the Empress of all the Russias has manifested in the declaration presented by her minister at Warsaw the 7th of May last year, on the occasion of the entry of her troops into Poland, were doubtless of a nature to merit the submission, the respect, and even the gratitude of the whole polish nation.

tion. Nevertheless, Europe has seen in what manner they have been regarded and appreciated. In order to smooth the road to the confederation of Targovitz, by which the Empress might attain the enjoyment of her rights and her legitimate power, it was necessary to have recourse to arms; but the authors of the revolution of the 3d of May, as well as their adherents, did not quit the field of battle to which they had provoked the Russian troops, until they were vanquished.

But although open resistance ceased, it only gave place to secret machinations, whose springs are so much the more dangerous as they often escape the notice of the most attentive eye, and that they even know how to elude the observation of the laws.

The spirit of faction and commotion has gained so wide an extension, that those who endeavour to render it general, having failed in the object of their intrigues in foreign courts, where they laboured to render the designs of Russia suspected, have turned all their efforts to delude the people, always disposed to allow themselves to be seduced. They have so far succeeded, that the same people has become accomplice in that enmity and hatred which they have sworn against the Russian empire, after having

having been frustrated in their criminal hopes. Without mentioning here several facts generally known, and which prove the bad dispositions of the majority of the Poles, it is sufficient to say, that they have been guilty of outraging the principles of moderation and humanity, which directed the Generals and officers of her Majesty the Empress in their operations and conduct, according to the express orders given them on this subject; so that they have experienced every species of insult, either by being maltreated or turned into ridicule, and that the most daring insurgents had even ventured to talk of Sicilian vespers, threatening them with a similar fate.

Such is the conduct that the enemies of good order and tranquillity, which her Majesty the Empress wished to re-establish and consolidate in their country, have opposed to the beneficent views of that Sovereign. Hence a judgment may be formed of the sincerity of the accessions of the greater number of the Poles to the confederation of Targovitz, as well as of the permanency and the stability of peace in the republic, both internally and externally

But the most serene Empress, accustomed for thirty years to struggle against the continual disturbances of that country, and confiding in the means with which Providence hath intrusted her, to confine within their limits the existing dissensions, would have persisted in her disinterested cares, and would have buried in oblivion all the grievances of which she has cause to complain, as well as all the just pretensions which those grievances authorize, if abuses of a more important and dangerous nature did not evidently display themselves.

The unexampled fury of a nation once so flourishing, now so humiliated, divided and placed on the brink of an abyss ready to engulph it; this fury, instead of furnishing these perturbators with motives for receding, on the contrary, appears to them an example worthy to be followed. They labour unremittingly to introduce into the bosom of the republic that infernal doctrine, which an impious, sacrilegious, and iniquitous sect has engendered to the misfortune and annihilation of all ecclesiastical, civil and political societies. Clubs affiliated with that of the jacobins of Paris, are established in the capital and in several provinces of Poland. They vomit their secret poison, infect the principles of the inhabitants, and foment their fermentations. The establishment of a furnace which feeds a flame so dangerous to to all the powers contiguous to Poland, ought naturally to excite their notice and attention.

They have already exerted themfelves in the common refearch of the moft efficacious meafures for ftopping the evil in it's fource, and for averting the contagion from their own frontiers.

Their Majefties, the Emprefs of Ruffia and the King of Pruffia, with the confent of his Majefty the Emperor of the Romans, have not been able to devife more effectual means for their refpective fecurity, than thofe of confining the republic of Poland within narrower limits, and fixing it's relative proportions to a degree more adapted to a power of the leffer order, and which may obtain and fecure her, without prejudice to her ancient liberty, a wife and regular government, and at the fame time fufficiently vigorous and active to obviate and appeafe all the diforders and troubles which have fo often interrupted her own tranquillity as well as that of her neighbours.

Being therefore perfectly united by a common concurrence of views and principles, their Majefties, the Emprefs of all the Ruffias and the King of Pruffia, are fully perfuaded that they cannot better prevent the total annihilation of the republic with which it is threatened by the diffenfions that prevail in it, and above all by the

dangerous

dangerous maxims which have deluded it's inhabitants, than by uniting to their respective dominions such of it's provinces as are adjacent, and immediately taking possession of them, in order to guarantee them in time, from the horrible effects of those maxims which are incessantly there propagated. Their said Majesties declare to the Polish Nation in general, their constant and immutable determination in this respect: they invite it to assemble as soon as possible in a diet, for the purpose of arranging this object amicably; as also of co-operating in effecting the salutary designs which they have formed for securing to it in future, a state of permanent peace, and a firm and stable Government.

Grodno, 9th of April 1793.

ANSWER

OF THE KING OF PRUSSIA, TO THE KING OF POLAND, DATED BERLIN, 8th JUNE 1792.

Sir, my Brother,

THE Grand Marshal of Lithuania, Count Potocki, transmitted to me the letter which your Majesty wrote to me dated the 31st May. I observe with regret the embarrassments in which the

the Republic is involved; but I alfo frankly avow, that after what has occurred during the laft year, they were to be expected. Your Majefty will recollect, that on more than one occafion, the Marquis de Luichefini was directed to manifeft both to yourfelf and to the preponderant members of government, my juft apprehenfions on this fubject.

From the moment when the re-eftablifhment of general tranquillity in Europe permitted me to explain myfelf, and that the Emprefs of Ruffia had fignified her determined opposition to the order of things eftablifhed by the revolution of the 3rd of May 1791, my mode of thinking, and the language of my Minifters have never varied: and in viewing with a calm eye the new conftitution which the Republic had adopted, *without my knowledge, and without my concurrence, I never meant to fupport or protect it.* On the contrary, I predicted that the menacing meafures and warlike preparations which the diet has unremittingly and fucceffively difplayed, would inevitably provoke the refentment of the Emprefs of Ruffia, and produce thofe evils in Poland which were pretended to be avoided. The event has juftified thefe appearances, and it cannot be diffembled at this moment, that, but for the new form of Government of the Republic,

public, and the efforts which she announced to support it, the Court of Russia would not have determined on the vigorous measures which it has embraced. Whatever may be the friendship which I have promised to your Majesty, and the part which I take in every thing which concerns him, he will himself be sensible that the state of things, being entirely changed since the alliance which I contracted with the republic, and the present conjuncture superinduced by the constitution of the 3rd of May 1791, subsequent to my treaty, *not being applicable to the engagements therein stipulated*, I am not bound to comply with the expectations of your Majesty, if the intentions of the patriotic party are still the same, and it persists in wishing to maintain it's work; but if, reversing it's views, it will consider the difficulties which arise on all sides, I shall be ready to concert with her Majesty, the Empress of Russia, and at the same time to consult with the Court of Vienna, in order to reconcile the different interests, and to concur in measures capable of restoring tranquillity to Poland.

I flatter myself your Majesty will recognize in these dispositions and assurances the sentiments of sincere amity, and the consideration with which I am, &c.

(Signed) FREDERIC WILLIAM.

DECLARATION.

DECLARATION

OF THE KING OF PRUSSIA, ON THE AFFAIRS OF POLAND.

It is known throughout all Europe, that the revolution which took place in Poland the 3rd of May 1791, without the knowledge or participation of the neighbouring and friendly powers of the Republic, did not fail to excite discontent and opposition in a great part of the nation. The adherents to the antient form of government have claimed the assistance of the august sovereign who guaranteed it; and her Majesty, the Empress of Russia, complying with their request, has not refused to support it by a respectable body of troops quartered in the different provinces where their presence was deemed essentially necessary. It is under their auspices that the preponderating members of the nobility have formed a general confederation, whose present exertions are calculated to redress the abuses of innovation, and to revive in full vigour the fundamental constitution of their country. These great events could not fail to attract the attention of Prussia, always interested in the fate of Poland, by the laws of vicinage,

vicinage, and the relations which subsist betwixt the two Empires; but, hoping the troubles which have occurred might speedily arrive at a happy termination, the King did not think it incumbent on him to interfere, especially at a time when other important cares engaged his attention elsewhere.

Much, however, was necessary to fulfil his expectation. The party, calling itself patriotic, instead of yielding to the salutary intentions of the Court of Russia, has dared to oppose an obstinate resistance to the imperial troops; but, though it's impotence soon compelled it to desist from the chimerical scheme of an open war, it does not the less persevere in it's secret machinations, which tend evidently to the total subversion of good order and tranquillity. The states adjoining those of the King have been but too much disturbed by excesses and reiterated violations of territory; but what merits still more his serious attention, and that of all the neighbouring powers, is, that the spirit of French democracy, and the maxims of this atrocious sect, which endeavours to make proselytes every where, begin to take deep root in Poland, to such degree that the manœuvres of jacobin emissaries are there powerfully supported; and that already several revolutionary clubs are formed, who openly profess their sentiments.

Great

Great Poland in particular is infected with this dangerous poison, and harbours the greatest number of zealots in false patriotism. Their connections with the French clubs cannot but inspire the King with just subjects of inquietude for the safety of his own dominions, and prescribe to him the absolute necessity of providing against them by suitable measures. Obliged to prosecute the war conjointly with the coalesced powers, and on the eve of opening a second campaign, his Majesty has therefore thought it his duty to concert previously with the Courts of Vienna and Petersburg on the part which it behoves him to take; and their Imperial Majesties have not refused their assent, that sound policy did not allow him to leave the hands of the factious free in Poland, and to risk turning his back on an enemy, whose desperate enterprises might become a fresh source of embarrassment.

To prevent this, the King has resolved to order a sufficient body of troops, the command of which he has entrusted to his General of Infantry, M. de Mollendorf, to march into the territory of the Republic, and particularly into several districts of Great Poland. This measure of precaution has for it's aim the defence of the provinces adjoining to those of his Majesty, and to repress the malevolent who foment troubles and insurrection, to establish and maintain public order and tranquillity, and to assure the well-disposed inhabitants of a powerful protection, which it will depend on themselves to merit, by a prudent and peaceable conduct, by receiving and treating amicably the Prussian troops, and furnishing them with the necessary succours and subsistance. The General Commandant, on his part, will not fail to preserve good and strict discipline, and to alleviate and assist the inhabitants in every respect which may depend on him, to remedy all their complaints, and to pay faithfully for the articles which may be supplied in case of their requisition. The King flatters himself that, with such pacific dispositions, he may rely on the attachment of a nation, whose welfare can never be indifferent to him, and to which he desires to give unequivocal proofs of his affection and benevolence.

In consequence, we have resolved, in concert with her Majesty of all the Russias, to take possession of the above-mentioned districts, as well as the cities of Dantzick and Thorn, and to incorporate them with our dominions. In making known to the public, the firm and unalterable resolution which we have adopted

on

APPENDIX.

on this head, we expect with confidence, that the Polish Nation will hasten to assemble in general diet, and that it will make all the dispositions necessary and suitable for the termination of this business in an amicable manner; and in order that the salutary end may be attained which was proposed to be procured for the Republic of Poland, namely, a solid and durable peace, and the guarantee of it's inhabitants from the horrible consequences of anarchy; at the same time we most seriously and affectionately exhort the states and the inhabitants of the districts of which we are about to take possession, not to oppose any resistance to the commanders of the troops whom we have ordered to take possession, inviting them *to submit willingly to our domination*, and to consider us henceforward as their King and lawful Sovereign, to conduct themselves towards us as faithful and obedient subjects, and *henceforward to break all ties and connexion with the Crown of Poland*. In return, we are resolved, and by these presents promise in the most solemn manner, to protect and maintain the dominions and inhabitants undernamed, all and each in their respective possessions, privileges and rights, whether secular or ecclesiastical, especially those of the Roman Catholic religion, who shall undisturbed enjoy the full liberty of exercising their worship, and generally to govern the said countries in the manner, that the sensible and well judging part of the inhabitants may have no cause *to regret their having passed under a new domination.* And still more to secure towards us the fidelity and attachment of our new subjects, we deem it our duty to exact from them the accustomed oath of fidelity and homage: but as our distance at present prevents us from assisting in person, we have charged and furnished with full powers for that purpose, and to represent us on this occasion, our General of Infantry, Joachim-Henry de Mollendorff, Knight of our several orders, Vice-president of the superior council of war, and Governor of our residence and city of Berlin, and likewise our Privy Minister of state and of justice, Adolphus-Albert-Henry-Leopold Baron de Deucklemann, Chief President of the superior tribunals of justice in Silesia.

In consequence, we most graciously command the aforesaid states and inhabitants to appear two days before the term fixed by our commissioners plenipotentiary for taking the oaths, at such places as may be pointed out by the said commissioners, to enrol their names in the public registers, as well as the full powers
with

with which they are furnished, and afterwards to take the oath of fidelity and submission; by which they engage to acknowledge us, our heirs and successors, as their lawful King and Sovereign. Moreover, our special will in this respect is, that the bishops, abbots, prelates, palatines, lords of manor, starosties, chamberlains, and provincial judges do all appear, personally, or by deputies sufficiently authorised, for this purpose. With regard to the other classes of citizens, this shall be by deputies chosen from among them, and furnished with powers duly legalized, that they will appear at the place above indicated; and particularly four deputies at least from every district for the equestrian order, four for the clergy and rector, six mayors of villages, and two burgomasters and a syndic for each city. These deputies shall also be furnished with an exact and authentic list, containing the names of all the individuals present and absent of the equestrian order domiciliated in their respective districts; as also the names of the magistrates, vicars, and preachers of every place, who shall all have truly sworn the oath of fidelity, which their deputies must take for them, and in their name. The regularity with which they shall have proceeded in this respect must be verified by an instrument signed

signed and dispatched in due and regular form by the magistrate or judge of each place, in order to be afterwards left by the said deputies in the hands of our commissioners plenipotentiary.

We doubt not but those to whom the present letters patent are addressed, will conform themselves punctually and obediently to every thing herein contained. If, however, contrary to our expectation, one or more orders, or citizens of the said towns or districts, dare to refuse taking the oath of allegiance required, and of submitting to our domination, or if they even attempt to oppose any resistance to our commanders and to our troops, then he or they, who shall render themselves culpable by such opposition, will infallibly incur the pains and penalties usual in such cases, without respect of persons.

In testimony of which, &c.

Berlin, 25th of March, 1793.

ANSWER

OF THE KING OF POLAND TO THE NOTES OF THE COURTS OF BERLIN AND PETERSBURG.

I DECLARE in presence of the States assembled, that when I acceded to the confederation of Targovitz, formed under the protection of her Imperial Majesty of all the Russias, I made it under the assurance that the possessions of the Republic should remain *inviolate:* this was the sole object of my measures, and this it is my duty to notify to the States in diet assembled, who, I hope still retain the same sentiments with me on the integrity of the territory of the Republic. I perceive that we are in a situation which requires that our answers to the notes in question should be very distinct, and couched in the most guarded terms. But all our demands resolve themselves into this single proposition. That our territories are restored to us; and I trust the wisdom and equity of her Imperial Majesty of Russia, and of his Prussian Majesty, will be convinced that our nation has not in any manner given pretext for the partition which the two Crowns pretend to be necessary.

(Signed,)
STANISLAUS-AUGUSTUS, KING.

LETTER

FROM THE DUKE OF BRUNSWICK TO THE KING OF PRUSSIA.

SIRE,

THE motives which induce me to folicit my recal from the army, are founded on the unhappy experience *that the want of concert, the egotifm, the fpirit of cabal and of diftruft* have fruftrated all the meafures which had been adopted during the laft two campaigns, and continue to difconcert all thofe which have been adopted by the combined armies.—Overwhelmed by the misfortune of being expofed, through the mifconduct of others, to the unhappy fituation in which I am placed, I feel with bitter regret, that the world appreciates Generals only according to their fuccefs, without giving itfelf the trouble of entering into any examination. The raifing of the fiege of Landau marks a period in the hiftory of this *unfortunate war*, and I have the ill fortune to be implicated in it. I am loaded with reproaches, and the innocent is confounded with the guilty. Notwithftanding fo many difafters, I fhould not have prefented to your Majefty my defire to renounce a profeffion profession which has been the principal study of my life. But, when a man has lost all the fruits of his cares, his labours, and his efforts; when there no longer remains a hope of accomplishing the purpose of the campaign, nor that a third promises a happier issue; what remains for a person the most attached to your Majesty, the most zealous for your interests and your cause, but to desist from exposing himself to extreme calamities?—The same causes which have hitherto divided the powers, divide them still: the movements of the armies will again suffer as they have suffered; they will experience delay and embarrassment; time will be necessary to recruit the Prussian army; policy absolutely requires it. These delays will, perhaps, prove the source of a train of misfortunes in the ensuing campaign, whose consequences are incalculable. I do not object to the war; it is not war I would avoid; but I dread the dishonour attached to my situation, by the errors which the other Generals will reflect on me, and because I can neither act according to my designs nor my principles. Your Majesty will easily recollect what I had the honour of representing to you the day you left Escheveilers; I explained to you all my difficulties, my troubles, and my misfortunes: I have made every exertion

tion to prevent all inconveniences; unhappily the event has proved their inefficiency. It is therefore from the thorough persuasion of my inability to render any essential service, that I am induced to intreat your Majesty to appoint me a successor as speedily as possible. But this determination, however distressing it may be to me, does not result from the melancholy reflections suggested by my situation. Prudence requires that I should retire, and honour commands it. When a great nation, such as that of France, conducts itself by the terror of punishments and by enthusiasm, the combined powers ought to be guided by but one sentiment and one principle; but if, instead of co-operating with this unanimity, each army acts separately and without concerting with the others, without fixed plans, without concord, and without principle, the consequences to be expected are such as we have seen at Dunkirk, at raising the siege of Maubeuge, at the capture of Lyons, at the destruction of Toulon, and when we raised the siege of Landau. May Heaven preserve your Majesty from great misfortunes! but every thing is to be dreaded, unless constancy, harmony, and uniformity of sentiments, of principles and actions assume the place of opposite sentiments, which, during the last two years, have occasioned

so

so many calamities. I offer up my most sincere prayers for your Majesty; your glory will be my happiness.

Oppenheim, 6th *January* 1794.

TREATY

TREATY OF PEACE
between
THE FRENCH REPUBLIC
and
HIS MAJESTY THE KING OF PRUSSIA.

Equally animated with the defire of putting an end to the war which divides them, by a folid peace between the two nations, they have named as their Minifters Plenipotentiary, viz.

The French Republic, Citizen François Barthelemy it's Ambaffador at Switzerland;

And the King of Prussia, his Minifter of State, of War, and of the Cabinet, Charles-Augustus Baron de Hardenberg, Knight of the order of the Red Eagle, the White Eagle, and Saint Staniflaus, &c.

Who, having exchanged their full powers, have agreed to the articles following:

Art. I. There fhall be peace, friendfhip and good underftanding between the French Republic and the King of Pruffia, as well confidered as fuch, as in his capacity of Elector of Brandenburg,

denburg, and a co-estate of the German Empire.

II. In consequence, all hostilities between the two contracting powers shall cease, from the date of the ratification of the present treaty, and neither of them shall, from the same epoch, furnish against the other in any quality, or under any denomination whatsoever, any succours or contingent, either in men, horses, provisions, money, warlike stores, or otherwise.

III. Neither of the contracting powers shall grant a passage through their territory to the troops of the other's enemies.

IV. The troops of the French Republic shall, within fifteen days of the ratification of the present treaty, evacuate those parts of the Prussian dominions which they may occupy on the right bank of the Rhine. The contributions, furnishings, and preparations for war shall entirely cease within fifteen days after the signature of this treaty. All the arrears due at this period, as well as bills and notes made or granted in this respect, shall be null and void. Whatever shall be taken or received after the above mentioned period, shall be immediately returned gratuitously, or paid for in cash.

V. The troops of the French republic shall continue to occupy that part of the dominions

of

of Pruffia, fituated on the left bank of the Rhine. Every definitive arrangement with regard to thefe provinces fhall be delayed until the general pacification between France and the Germanic Empire.

VI. Until a treaty of commerce fhall be entered into between the two contracting powers, all the commercial communications and relations fhall be re-eftablifhed between France and the Pruffian dominions, on the footing on which they ftood before the prefent war.

VII. The ftipulations in article VI. not being capable of having full effect but as far as the liberty of commerce fhall be re-eftablifhed throughout the north of Germany, the two contracting powers fhall take meafures to remove thence the theatre of war.

VIII. It fhall be permitted refpectively to the individuals of the two nations to recover the effects, revenues, or goods of every kind whatfoever, detained, feized or confifcated on account of the war which has been carried on betwixt France and Pruffia, as well as immediate juftice with refpect to any debts which thefe individuals may have in the dominions of the two contracting powers.

IX. All prifoners taken on either fide fince the commencement of the war, without regard
to

to the difference of number or rank, comprehending Prussian sailors and marines taken either in Prussian or other vessels; and, in general, all persons detained on either side, on account of the war, shall be delivered up in the space of two months at farthest, after the exchange of the ratifications of the present treaty; without any payment, except of the private debts which they may have contracted during their imprisonment. The same shall take place in respect of the sick and wounded, instantly after their cure. There shall immediately be appointed on both sides commissaries for the execution of the present article.

X. The prisoners of the Saxon, Palatine, Mentz and Hessian corps, including both those of Hesse-Cassel and Darmstadt, who have served with the army of the King of Prussia, shall be also comprehended in the above mentioned exchange.

XI. The French Republic will admit the good offices of his Majesty, the King of Prussia, in favour of the princes and states of the German Empire, who shall desire to enter directly into negociation with it, and who have for this purpose already requested, or shall hereafter request, the intervention of the King.

The French Republic, to give his Majesty,

the King of Pruffia, an immediate proof of it's defire to concur to the re-eftablifhment of the ancient ties of friendfhip, which have fubfifted between the two nations, confents not to treat as an enemy's country, for the fpace of three months after the ratification of this prefent treaty, fuch of the princes and ftates of the faid Empire, as are fituated on the right bank of the Rhine, in whofe favour the King fhall intereft himfelf.

XII. The prefent treaty fhall not take effect until after it has been ratified by the contracting parties; and the ratifications fhall be exchanged in this city of Bafle, within the term of one month, or fooner if poffible, from the prefent day.

In teftimony whereof, we, the underfigned Minifters Plenipotentiary of the French Republic and his Majefty the King of Pruffia, in virtue of our full powers, have figned this prefent treaty of peace and amity, and caufed to be affixed thereto our refpective feals.

Done at Bafle the 16th of the month of Germinal, in the year III. of the French Republic, (5th April 1795.)

(L S.) Signed, FRANÇOIS BARTHELEMY.
(L. S.) Signed, CHARLES-AUGUSTUS Baron de HARDENBERG.

CONVENTION

CONVENTION
BETWEEN
THE FRENCH REPUBLIC
AND
HIS MAJESTY THE KING OF PRUSSIA.

HAVING ſtipulated, in the treaty of peace and amity concluded between them, of the 16th Germinal laſt (5th April 1795,) ſome ſecret articles which refer to Article VII of that treaty, and which eſtabliſh a line of demarcation and neutraliſation, the object of which is to remove the ſeat of war from the whole of the North of Germany, they have thought proper to explain and definitively agree to the conditions by a particular convention.

For this purpoſe, the reſpective Plenipotentiaries of the two high contracting parties, that is to ſay,

ON THE PART OF THE FRENCH REPUBLIC, Citizen FRANÇOIS BARTHELEMY, it's Ambaſſador at Switzerland;

AND ON THE PART OF THE KING OF PRUSSIA, his Miniſter of State, War and the Cabinet, CHARLES-AUGUSTUS Baron de HARDENBERG, Knight

Knight of the Order of the Red Eagle, the Black Eagle and Saint Staniflaus; and have agreed on the articles following:

Article I. In order to remove the feat of war from the frontiers of the dominions of his Majefty the King of Pruffia, to preferve the repofe of the North of Germany, and to re-eftablifh the entire freedom of commerce between this part of the Empire and France, as before the war, the French Republic confents not to carry it's military operations, nor advance troops either by land or fea, into the country and territories fituated beyond the line of demarcation following:

This line will comprehend Osterisen and defcend along the Ems and the Aa or Alfa, as far as Munster, taking thence it's direction towards Coesfeldt, Borken, Bockold to the frontier of the duchy of Cleves, near Isselburg, following this frontier to Magenporst on the new Issel, and afcending the Rhine to Duysburg, thence running along the frontier of the Comté of Mark towards Werden, Gemarke, and along the Wipper to Homburg, Altenkirchen, Linburg on the Larn; along that river and that which comes from Idstein towards the city Epslein and Hoechst on the Mein, thence towards Raunheim, along the

Landgraben

LANDGRABEN towards DORNHEIM; afterwards following the rivulet which passes through that district to the frontier of the PALATINATE, thence to the country of DARMSEDT and the circle of FRANCONIA, which the line will entirely surround, to EBERSBACH on the NECKER, continuing the course of that river as far as WIMPFEN, a free city of the Empire, and running thence to LŒVENSTEIN, MURHARD, HOHENSTADT, NŒRDLINGEN, a free city of the Empire, and HOLZKIRCH on the WERNITZ; inclosing the Comté of PAPPENHEIM and all the circle of FRANCONIA and UPPER SAXONY, along BAVARIA, the UPPER PALATINATE and BOHEMIA to the frontiers of SILESIA.

II. The French Republic will regard as neutral countries and states, all those which are situated beyond this line, on condition that on their side they observe a strict neutrality, the first point of which shall be to recal their contingents, and not to enter into any new engagement which may authorise them to furnish troops to the powers at war with France. Those which do not fulfil this condition shall be exempted from the benefit of the neutrality.

III. His Majesty the King of Prussia engages to cause this neutrality to be observed by all the states situated on the right bank of the MEIN,

MEIN, and comprised within the line of demarcation above mentioned.

The King engages to guarantee that no troops hostile to France shall pass that part of the line, or go beyond the territory comprised in it, to fight the French armies; and to this effect the two contracting parties shall maintain on the important places, which shall be settled on between them, corps of observation, sufficient to make this neutrality respected.

IV. The passage of troops, whether of the French Republic, or of the Empire of Austria, shall remain always free, by the routes leading along the right bank of the MEIN by FRANKFORT.

1. To KŒNIGSTEIN and LIMBURG towards COLOGN.
2. To FRIEDBERG, WETZLAR and SIEGEN from COLOGN.
3. To HADERSHEIM, WISBADEN and NASSAU and to COBLENTZ.
4. To HADERSHEIM from MENTZ, and *vice versâ*.

As well as in all the countries situated on the left bank of that river, and in all the Circle of FRANCONIA, but without prejudice in any sort to the neutrality of all the states and countries comprised within the line of demarcation.

V. The

APPENDIX.

V. The Comté of SAYN-ALTENKIRCHEN on the WESTERWALD, comprehending therein the small district of BENDORFF above COBLENTZ, being in the possession of his Majesty the King of Prussia, shall enjoy the same securities and advantages as his other dominions situated on the right bank of the Rhine.

VI. The present Convention is to be ratified by the contracting parties, and the ratifications shall be interchanged in this city of Basle, within the term of one month, or sooner if possible, reckoning from this day.

In testimony whereof, we, the undersigned Plenipotentiaries of the French Republic and of his Majesty the King of Prussia, in virtue of our full powers have subscribed the present secret convention, and affixed thereto our respective seals.

Done at Basle, the 28th Floreal of year III. of the French Republic (17th May, 1795.)

(L. S.) Signed, FRANÇOIS BARTHELEMY.
(L. S.) Signed, CHARLES-AUGUSTUS Baron DE HARDENBERG.

TREATY OF PEACE.

BETWEEN

THE FRENCH REPUBLIC

AND

HIS MAJESTY THE KING OF SPAIN.

EQUALLY animated by a desire to put an end to the calamities of war which divides them; entirely convinced that there exist between the two nations respective interests, which demand a reciprocal return of friendship and good understanding, and wishing to re-establish, by a permanent and durable peace, the harmony which for a long time has constantly been the basis of the relations of the two countries, they have entrusted with this important negociation; videlicet,

THE FRENCH REPUBLIC, Citizen FRANÇOIS BARTHELEMY, its Ambassador at Switzerland;

AND HIS CATHOLIC MAJESTY, his Minister Plenipotentiary and Envoy Extraordinary to the King and Republic of Poland, DON DOMINGO D'YRIARTE, Knight of the Royal Order of Charles III. &c.

Who,

Who, after having exchanged their full powers, have agreed to the articles following:

Article I. There shall be peace, amity, and good understanding between the French Republic and the King of Spain.

II. In consequence, all hostilities between the two contracting powers shall cease, counting from the exchange of the ratifications of the present treaty, and neither of them shall from the same epoch furnish against the other, in any quality, or under any denomination whatsoever, any succours or contingent in men, horses, provisions, money, warlike stores, ships, or otherwise.

III. Neither of the contracting powers shall grant a passage through their territory to troops hostile to the other.

IV. The French Republic restores to the King of Spain all the conquests it has made from him in the course of the present war.

The strong places and the countries conquered shall be evacuated by the French troops within fifteen days after the exchange of the ratifications of the present treaty.

V. The strong places mentioned in the preceding article shall be restored to Spain with the guns, warlike stores, and effects, according to the usages of these fortresses, which shall exist at the time of signing this treaty.

VI. The

VI. The contributions, furnishings, and preparations of war shall cease entirely, reckoning from fifteen days after the signature of the present act of pacification. All the arrears due at that epoch, as well as the bills and promissory notes given in this respect shall be null. Those which shall be taken or received, after the aforesaid period, shall then be returned gratuitously, or paid in cash.

VII. There shall be immediately nominated on either side commissaries to proceed to a treaty of boundaries between the two powers. They shall, as much as possible, take for the basis of this treaty the brows of the mountains which form the divergencies of the rivers of France and Spain.

VIII. Neither of the contracting powers shall, within a month after the exchange of the ratifications of the present treaty, maintain on their respective frontiers a greater number of troops than they have been accustomed to do previous to the present war.

IX. In exchange for the restitution stipulated in Article IV. the King of Spain, for himself and his successors, cedes and gives up absolutely to the French Republic, all the Spanish part of the island of St. Domingo, in the Antilles.

One

One month, after the ratification of the prefent treaty fhall be known in that ifland, the Spanifh troops fhall hold themfelves ready to evacuate the forts, ports, and eftablifhments which they there occupy, in order to deliver them up to the troops of the French Republic, the moment when the latter fhall prefent themfelves to take poffeffion thereof.

The forts, ports, and eftablifhments, mentioned above, fhall be delivered up to the French Republic, with the cannon, military ftores, and articles neceffary for their defence, which fhall be there at the time when the prefent treaty fhall be made known at St. Domingo.

The inhabitants of the Spanifh part of St. Domingo, who, from motives of intereft or otherwife, prefer to tranfport themfelves with their property to the poffeffions of his Catholic Majefty, may do fo within the fpace of a year, reckoning from the date of this treaty.

The refpective generals and commanders of the two nations fhall concert the meafures to be taken for the execution of the prefent article.

X. It fhall be permitted refpectively to the individuals of the two nations to recover their effects, revenues, and other property whatfoever, detained, feized, or confifcated on account of the war that has been carried on between the French Republic and his Catholic Majesty, as well as prompt justice with respect to the private debts which those individuals may have in the dominions of the two contracting powers.

XI. Until a new treaty of commerce shall be entered into betwixt the contracting parties, all commercial communications and relations shall be re-established between France and Spain, on the footing on which they stood before the present war.

It shall be permitted to all French merchants to carry away and return to Spain their commercial establishments, or to form new ones, according as they think proper; being always subject, like other individuals, to the laws and usages of the country.

The Spanish merchants shall enjoy the same liberty in France, and under the same conditions.

XII. All prisoners made respectively since the commencement of the war, without regard to difference in number or rank, comprehending sailors and marines taken on board French and Spanish vessels, or those of other nations, as well as in general all those detained on either side on account of the war, shall be delivered up within the space of two months at farthest after the exchange

exchange of the ratifications of the present treaty, without any payment whatsoever on either side, except of the debts of individuals which they may have contracted during their imprisonment. The same shall be observed in respect to the sick and wounded, immediately after their cure.

There shall be instantly named commissaries on both sides, to proceed to the execution of the present article.

XIII. The Portuguese prisoners, making part of the Portuguese troops who have served in the armies and fleets of his Catholic Majesty, shall be likewise comprehended in this exchange.

A reciprocity shall take place in regard to the French taken by the Portuguese troops in question.

XIV. The same peace, amity, and good understanding, stipulated by the present treaty between France and the King of Spain, shall take place between the King of Spain and the Republic of the United Provinces, the ally of the French Republic.

XV. The French Republic, desirous of giving his Catholic Majesty a proof of friendship, accepts his mediation in favour of the Queen of Portugal, the King of Naples, the infant Duke of of Parma, and other ſtates of Italy, for the reſtoration of peace between the French Republic and each of theſe princes and ſtates.

XVI. The French Republic, knowing the intereſt which his Catholic Majeſty takes in the general pacification of Europe, conſents likewiſe to accept his good offices in favour of the other belligerent powers, who may apply to him to enter into negociation with the French government.

XVII. The preſent treaty ſhall not be in force, until after it is ratified by the contracting parties; and the ratifications ſhall be exchanged within the term of one month, or ſooner if poſſible, reckoning from this date.

In teſtimony whereof, we, the underſigned Plenipotentiaries of the French Republic and his Majeſty the King of Spain, in virtue of our full powers have ſubſcribed this treaty of peace and amity, and affixed thereto our reſpective ſeals.

Done at Baſle, the 4th Thermidor, year III. of the French Republic (22nd July 1795.)

(L. S.) Signed François Barthelemy,
(L. S.) Signed Domingo de Yriarte.

TREATY

TREATY OF PEACE
BETWEEN
THE FRENCH REPUBLIC
AND
THE LANDGRAVE OF HESSE-CASSEL.

HAVING accepted the good offices of the King of Pruſſia, in favour of his moſt Serene Highneſs, the reigning Landgrave of Heſſe-Caſſel, and being animated by the ſame ſentiments with the Landgrave, that a ſolid and laſting peace ſhould ſucceed to the ſtate of war which divides them, the two contracting parties have for this purpoſe named as their Plenipotentiaries, videlicet,

THE FRENCH REPUBLIC, Citizen FRANÇOIS BARTHELEMY, its Ambaſſador at Switzerland;

AND THE LANDGRAVE OF HESSE-CASSEL, his Privy-counſellor, FREDERIC-SIGISMUND Baron DE WAITZ D'ESCHEN, who, after having exchanged their full powers, have agreed to the articles following:

ARTICLE I. There ſhall be peace, amity, and good underſtanding between the French Republic and the Landgrave of Heſſe-Caſſel.

II. In

APPENDIX.

II. In consequence, all hostilities between the two contracting parties shall cease, reckoning from the exchange of the ratifications of the present treaty, and neither of them shall, after the same epoch, furnish against the other, in any quality, or under any denomination whatsoever, any succour or contingent, in men, horses, money, warlike-stores, or otherwise.

III. The Landgrave of Hesse-Cassel shall not, while war continues between the French Republic and England, either prolong or renew the two subsidiary treaties subsisting between him and England. This stipulation shall have effect from the day of the date of the present treaty.

IV. The Landgrave shall strictly conform, with regard to the passage of any troops whatsoever through his dominions, to the articles stipulated in the Convention concluded at Basle the 28th Floreal last (17th May, 1795) between the French Republic and the King of Prussia.

V. The French Republic shall continue to occupy the fortress of Rangole, the town of St. Goar, and the part of Domingo de Yriarte, lenbogen, situated
Rhine. Every def
gard to the

TREATY

the pacification between the French Republic and those parts of Germany still at war with her.

VI. All commercial communications and relations shall be re-established between France and the dominions of the Landgrave of Hesse-Cassel on the footing on which they were before the present war.

VII. There shall be granted respectively to the governments and individuals of the two nations, privilege to recover effects, revenues, or goods of any sort whatsoever, which may have been detained, seized, or confiscated on account of the war that has been carried on between France and Hesse, as well as prompt justice with respect to any debts whatsoever which they may have in the dominions of the contracting parties.

VIII.—All prisoners made respectively, since the commencement of the war, without regard to the difference of number and rank, shall be delivered up, within the space of two months at farthest after the exchange of the ratifications of the present treaty, without any payment whatsoever, except the private debts which they may have contracted during their imprisonment.

articles following: in respect to the sick
ARTICLE I. There shally are cured.
good understanding between appointed on ei-
ic and the Landgrave of Hesse-Ca the execution

cution of the prefent article, the ftipulations of which fhall not apply to Heffe troops in the fervice of England, made prifoners of war.

IX. The prefent treaty fhall not have effect, till after having been ratified by the parties contracting; and the ratifications fhall be exchanged in this city of Bafle within the fpace of one month, or fooner if poffible, reckoning from this day.

In teftimony whereof, we, the underfigned Plenipotentiaries of the French Republic and his moft Serene Highnefs the Landgrave of Heffe-Caffel, in virtue of our full powers, have fubfcribed the prefent treaty of peace, and affixed our refpective feals thereunto.

Done at Bafle the 11th day of the month of Fructidor, in the year III. of the French Republic (28th Auguft 1795.)

(L. S.) Signed, FRANÇOIS BARTHELEMY.
(L. S.) Signed, FREDERIC-SIGISMUND Baron de WAITZ D'ESCHIN.

SUMMARY NARRATIVE

OF THE CIRCUMSTANCES WHICH ATTENDED THE DETENTION OF LATOUR MAUBOURG, BUREAU DE PUZY, LA FAYETTE, AND HIS FAMILY*.

LA FAYETTE, Maubourg and Bureau de Puzy, having in vain endeavoured to support the Conſtitution of 1791, which they had ſworn to maintain, and finding themſelves compelled to emigrate, with ſome officers, in order to avoid the execution of decrees paſſed againſt them, meant to proceed to Holland; but, ſome leagues from the frontier, they were, notwithſtanding their proteſtations, arreſted by an Auſtrian poſt, and conducted to Luxemburg. Having ſent to aſk paſſports from the Duke de Saxe-Teſchen, they were refuſed, and thoſe who ſignified this refuſal, *barbarouſly informed them, that they were reſerved for the ſcaffold.*

As ſoon as the orders had been received from the court of Vienna, which determined the fate of the priſoners, and delivered them over to the King of Pruſſia, they were all three carried and confined at Weſel, where they were guarded by

---

* Communicated by one of the priſoners.

non-commissioned officers, whose orders were to observe them constantly, and not to answer their questions.

La Fayette had fallen dangerously sick. His fellow-sufferers were refused permission at Maubourg to see their friend ready to expire. A salutary crisis having rescued him from the jaws of death, the King of Prussia thought he might profit by his dejected state, and had a proposal made him, that his situation should be alleviated, if he would furnish him with plans against France; but he proved, by an energetic reply, his contempt of such a proposition. The rigour towards him was then redoubled, and soon after they were thrown into a cart and carried to Magdeburg, and were constantly refused any information of the existence of their families, respecting whom the proscriptions in France gave them the most anxious inquietude.

In travelling thus, their keepers thought to aggravate their distress and excite the public indignation against them. These wishes, however, were not fulfilled; they every where received marks of the interest excited by the injustice of their detention, and the constancy of their courage.

They remained a year at Magdeburg, in a damp and dark vault surrounded by high pallisadoes,

fadoes, fhut by four fucceffive gates, and faften-
ed with bars of iron and padlocks. However
their fituation feemed milder, that they were
fometimes allowed to fee each other, and were
walked out an hour each day on a baftion.

The King of Pruffia fuddenly fent an order
to remove La Fayette to Silefia; Maubourg
folicited and obtained leave to be confined
there with him: they were conducted to Glatz,
whither Bureau de Puzy was foon after fent.

Alexander Lameth, being dangeroufly ill,
could not be tranfported with his companions.
His mother, who enjoyed a refpect merited by
her virtues, obtained of Frederic William, after
ardent folicitation, that he fhould remain in
prifon in his dominions; and fometime after,
peace being concluded between that Monarch
and the French, fhe fucceeded in procuring his
liberty. The King of Pruffia granted it, becaufe he did not think himfelf longer obliged to
obferve the fame refpect towards the court of
Vienna which was irritated againft him for having
quitted the coalition. The prifoners were tranf-
ferred to Neifs; and, although the dungeon
which they there inhabited, was ftill more dif-
mal and unwholefome than any of the others,
this change appeared happy to them, as all the
three prifoners together were allowed to enjoy

the

the presence of Madame de Maisonneuve, who came courageously to share the chains of her brother, Maubourg.

The King of Prussia, who did not wish, on making peace with France, to be obliged from justice to release his victims, determined to send them into Austria; and they were carried to Olmutz.

On their arrival at this place, they were robbed of whatever the Prussians had left them, which reduced them to their watches and buckles; some of their books even were seized in which was found the word *Liberty*, particularly *Helvetius de l'Esprit* and *Paine's Common Sense;* on which La Fayette asked if these were contraband articles.

Each of them was told, on being shut up separately in his cell, " That they should
" hereafter see only their four walls; that they
" would have neither news, necessaries, nor
" visitors; that it was forbidden to mention
" their names even among the jailers, or in the
" government dispatches, in which they were
" distinguished by numbers; that they would
" never be informed of the fate of their fami-
" lies, nor of each other's existence; and that,
" as this situation might naturally lead them to
" self-

"self-destruction, they were forbidden knife, fork, and every means whatever of suicide."

After three certificates of physicians of the indispensable necessity of air for La Fayette, after three replies that he was not yet sufficiently ill, he was at length permitted to walk out unconditionally; for it is false that La Fayette enjoyed this liberty, as has been alledged, on his engagement of honour that he should not attempt to make his escape.

The public know the enterprise of doctor *Boleman* and the young *Huger*, the son of the man at whose house La Fayette first landed in America.

Boleman, after several months' unsuccessful attempts, succeeded in procuring a note to be secretly delivered to him, and executed a very bold plan: he repaired to Vienna, sent for the young Huger thither, and posted himself with him at the place where La Fayette was to be conducted to take the air; and these two attempted to rescue him at the moment when, having misled some of his keepers, they endeavoured to disarm the one that remained with him.

In this struggle, La Fayette gave himself a violent strain in the loins, and the corporal-jailer, with whom he contended, and whom he had disarmed, tore with his teeth his hand to the bone.

His generous deliverers succeeded in getting him on horseback, with such negligence of their own safety, that they could scarcely find their horses to escape themselves. This loss of time, and the alarms of the keepers, having attracted people and troops, Huger was immediately secured. La Fayette, separated from Boleman, was seized eight leagues from Olmutz, and with the less difficulty, as he had no arms. Boleman reached the Prussian territories, but the King of Prussia had the barbarity to deliver him up to the Austrians.

From this time the captivity of La Fayette was more rigorous, and his illness became more serious; he was left without relief, with an unremitting fever, during a remarkably severe winter, deprived of light, and not even allowed the linen which his situation rendered necessary.

To increase his suffering, he was constantly made to believe that his companions had perished on the scaffold.

The care that had been taken to keep La Fayette from the knowledge of every thing that might serve to inform him of the fate of his family, is remarkable in the following anecdote.

Latour

Latour Maubourg, having at length obtained permission to dispatch letters to his relations, learnt that Madame de la Fayette was alive; he requested the commandant to allow his friend to be told that his wife yet lived: the commandant, after answering *that his orders in this respect were too express,* from that time suppressed all the letters in which Madame de la Fayette was mentioned, and did not deliver them to him till near a year afterwards, when he quitted Olmutz.

Whilst La Fayette, reserved for the scaffold, was tortured in the prisons of Olmutz, his wife, uncertain of his existence, and condemned to perpetual grief in the prisons of Paris, daily expected to be led to execution, as had happened to the greater part of her family. The fall of the tyrant saved her life; but she did not, till long after his death, regain her liberty and strength sufficient to execute her designs. Having landed at Altona the 9th of September, 1795, she set out for Vienna under the name of Mottier, with an American passport; and arrived at Vienna before the court could be informed of her purpose, or prepared against her application.

The Prince de Rosenberg, affected with her virtues, obtained for her and her daughters an audience

audience of the Emperor, some detail of which it may be proper to give.

Madame de la Fayette, claiming the liberty of her husband, in the name of justice and humanity, that prince answered her, "This "affair is complicated; my hands are tied re- "specting it; but I grant with pleasure all "that is in my power, by permitting you to "join M. de la Fayette: I should act as you "do, were I in your place. M. de la Fayette "is well treated, but the presence of his wife "and daughters will be an additional in- "dulgence."

Madame de la Fayette spoke of other prisoners, and particularly of La Fayette's servants, who she knew had suffered much, and whose affair could not be complicated. The Emperor very graciously permitted her to write respecting those from Olmutz, and to address her applications directly to his Imperial Majesty; and Madame de la Fayette, reassured by the reception she had met with, then wrote on the road from Vienna to Olmutz, that she was astonished to find herself yet susceptible of all the happiness she was beginning to enjoy. But it was not long before sad experience convinced her that the Emperor was deceived, and was ignorant of the cruel and tyrannical abuse his

his barbarous agents made of his name and authority.

Mesdames de Maubourg and de Puzy, inspired by the same sentiments, wished also to partake the chains of their husbands; but they were never permitted to enter the Austrian dominions.

It is easy to imagine the impression la Fayette must have experienced at the sudden appearance of his wife and his children, whose existence had long been to him an object of fear and uncertainty, and that which his affectionate daughters and their mother must have felt at the sight of his emaciated figure and pale countenance; but they did not expect that their embraces would be interrupted, by the jailers robbing the travellers of all they had brought with them.

They took their purse, very ill supplied, and eagerly seized three forks, considered as instruments of suicide; for they well knew the temptation to it they had inspired. On this unexpected treatment, Madame de la Fayette desired to speak to the commandant; they answered, that he was forbidden to see her, but that she might write to him. She desired to write to the Emperor, conformably to the permission he had granted her; this they refused,
telling

telling her that her applications to the commandant would be forwarded to Vienna. They confisted in attending mafs on Sunday, having a foldier's wife to wait on her daughters, and being, as well as la Fayette, waited on by one of his domeftics. She received no anfwer to all thefe demands, nor to an application fhe fome time afterwards addreffed to the minifter of war, to fee Latour Maubourg, and Puzy, except this, " Madame de la Fayette has fubmitted to " fhare the captivity of her hufband."

At length, the health of this unfortunate lady, impaired by fixteen months' imprifonment, and dreadful vexation in France, difplaying fymptoms which denoted a tendency of the fluids to putrefcence, fhe thought it her duty to attempt fome means for her prefervation, and wrote to the Emperor to folicit permiffion from him to pafs a week at Vienna, there to refpire falubrious air, and confult a phyfician. After two months of a filence, which fuppofes the neceffity of medical advice as of no confequence, the commandant, till then unknown to the prifoners, entered their apartment, ordered, without giving any reafon, the young ladies to retire to a feparate room, fignified to Madame de la Fayette the Emperor's refufal for her ever to enter Vienna, and gave her permiffion to go out, on condition

condition of never returning: he desired her to write, and sign her option; she wrote:

"I considered it a duty to my family and friends to desire the assistance necessary for my health; but they well know that it cannot, at the price attached to it, be accepted by me. I cannot forget, that whilst we were on the point of perishing, myself by the tyranny of Robespierre, and my husband by the physical and moral sufferings of captivity, I was not permitted to obtain any intelligence of him, nor to acquaint him that his children and myself were yet alive; and I shall not expose myself to the horrors of another separation. Whatever then may be the state of my health, and the inconveniences of this abode for my daughters, we will gratefully avail ourselves of his Imperial Majesty's generosity, in permitting us to partake this captivity in all it's circumstances."

(Signed,) NOAILLES LA FAYETTE.

From this moment no complaint was expressed, and this ill-fated pair respired in their chambers, or more properly speaking, dungeons, an air so fœtid from the exhalations of a sewer, and of the privies of the garrison placed near Fayette's window, that the soldiers who brought their

their food held their nose on opening the door.

The constant answer of the persons of power, or interest, who heard their barbarities exclaimed against was; "Madame de la Fayette has "chosen to share the lot of her husband; she "has no right to complain." They might as well have said: "Every thing is allowable "against la Fayette; the life of his wife and "children is not worth arresting our vengeance "for a moment."

The three prisoners, Maubourg, la Fayette and Puzy, had been confined for three years and five months in the same corridor, without seeing each other, or their keepers giving them the least intelligence of each other's existence. When General Bonaparte and the French government testified an intention, conformably to the national wish, of restoring them to liberty, they experienced the strongest opposition. At last, an aid-de-camp of the conqueror of Italy, succeeded, after several months' tergiversation, in obtaining from the court of Vienna this deliverance.

The Austrian ministers wished to exact from the prisoners conditions to which they refused to submit. The Marquis de Chasteler being entrusted by the Emperor with this negociation, the following declaration was sent him by la Fayette.

"The commission with which the Marquis de Chasteler is charged, appears to me to be reduced to three points.

"1. His Imperial Majesty wishes to ascertain our situation: I am not disposed to trouble him with any complaint. Several details are to be found in my wife's letters transmitted or returned by the Austrian government; and if his Imperial Majesty be not satisfied on re-perusing the instructions sent from Vienna in his name, I shall willingly give the Marquis de Chasteler all the information he may desire.

"2. His Majesty the Emperor and King wishes to be assured, that immediately after my liberation I shall set out for America: it is an intention which I have often declared; but, as in the present moment my compliance would appear to acknowledge a right to impose this condition on me, I do not think it proper to satisfy that demand.

"3. His Majesty the Emperor and King has done me the honour to signify, that the principles which I profess being incompatible with the security of the Austrian government, he desires I may not re-enter his dominions
"without

"without his special permission. There are
"duties of which I cannot divest myself; I
"have such to the United States of America;
"I have particularly such to France; and I can-
"not engage what is contrary to the rights of
"my country over my person. With these ex-
"ceptions, I can assure General the Marquis
"de Chasteler, that my unalterable determi-
"nation is never to set my foot on any spot
"subject to the dominion of his Majesty the
"King of Bohemia and Hungary."

Maubourg and Puzy made similar declarations; and the three prisoners signed, in consequence, the following engagement:

"I, the underwritten, engage to his Majesty
"the Emperor and King, not to enter at any
"time his hereditary provinces, without having
"obtained his special permission, saving the
"rights of my country over my person."

After this engagement they were set at liberty and proceeded to Hamburg; and through their whole journey they received testimonies of regard which they will never forget.

NOTE

NOTE

RESPECTING POLAND.

AMONG the Polish authors who have done honour to their country, we forgot to mention *Krasichy*, Bishop of Warmie, whose pastoral poetry abounds in genius, grace and sentiment.

Malachowski, the constant defender of the interests of his country, excited the enthusiasm of his compatriots, and merited the respect of his enemies. *Boufflers*, an admirer of his virtues, made on him the following four lines, which he addressed to the Poles, deploring their misfortunes, and wishing to console their patriotism:

> A ce vrai citoyen sachez vous conformer,
> Et retenez de lui, Nation genéreuse,
> Que moins une mere est heureuse,
> Plus ses enfans doivent l'aimer.*

THE END.

---

* From MALACHOWSKI, of true patriot worth,
  Learn, gen'rous Poles! your ardent zeal to prove;
  The more unhappy she who gave you birth,
  The more her children should display their love.

INDEX.

A

Abbema, nominated by the Regency of Amsterdam Commissary of that city. His mission, vol. i. p. 198, *et seq.*

Ainslie, (Sir Robert) English Ambassador in Turkey. He engages the Ottoman Port, which he deceives, in a war with Russia against the wishes of France, i. 57.

Albert, Elector of Brandenburg, called Ulysses and Achilles. Why thus named, i. 21.

Alcudia, Minister of Spain. It was he who instigated the King to join the coalition, iii. 97. Derided by the British Ministry. He detaches Spain from the coalition, 102. Named Prince of the Peace on account of that which took place between France and Spain, 219.

Alliance, proposals for a quadruple, between Russia, the Emperor, Spain and France, ii. 5. Dispositions of the Empress of Russia on this head, ii. 5. Causes of the miscarriage of this project, 6; what were the consequences of it, 7.

Alsace, a province which becomes the pretext of the coalition. Why, ii. 355.

Amersfort. The Stadtholderian regency of this city suspend the functions of General Van Ryssel, i. 373. Desertion of the troops promoted by the English. Dissensions in the interior of this city, 380.

Amstel-Ween, loss of the Prussians in the attack of that village, i. 419.

Amsterdam, siege and capitulation of that city, i. 95. Assembly of the Burghers in order to form a committee to deliberate on the degree of influence which the people ought to possess in public affairs, 197. Mode by which the regents evaded the wish of the burghers, &c. Triumph of the Burghers, and recal of three new deputies whom the regency had sent to the States-General, 108. Dreadful commotion. Battle between the Stadtholderians and the Patriots, 261. Danger escaped by this city, 263. Commission of five in which the power is concentrated to watch over the safety of Holland, 267. Desperate resolution of breaking down the great dyke of Minden, rather than write a letter of satisfaction to the Princess of Orange. Suspected of having contrived the massacre of the patriots. It's capitulation with the Duke of Brunswick, 421. Proscriptions consequent on it, *ibid.* &c. 422. Recapture of that city from the Stadtholder and the coalition by thirty French Hussars, iii. 171.

Anarchist, a faction composed of the dregs of every class, ii. 233.

Ankerstroem, assassinates the King of Sweden at a ball, ii. 225.

Anselme, (General) takes possession of Nice, iii. 17. Accused of treason. Why he escapes his enemies, 43.

Antwerp, a congress held in this city, in order to concert the plans of the war against France, after the defection of Dumouriez, iii. 41.

Archenholz, (M. d') Colonel in the Prussian service, known by his attachment to the principles of the French revolution. He demonstrates that the Minister Pitt is the real aggressor in the war, by adhering to the declaration made at Pavia and to the treaty concluded at Mantua, ii. 323.

Argoerm, defiles occupied by Dumouriez, in order to stop the progress of the enemy, who would otherwise have reached Chalons, ii. 278.

Aristocracy, it's impolitic conduct. Serious errors committed by it after the loss of it's privileges, ii. 108.

Aristocrats, a name given to the partisans of the court of Louis XVI. Their hopes in the known dispositions of the king, the court, and the malcontents, ii. 96.

Armies, respective state of the republican and coalesced armies in 1795, iii. 93.

Armies, French, their exploits in the campaign of the second year of the Republic. Twenty-three regular sieges, six pitched

pitched battles won, capture of one hundred and twenty-four towns, iii. 97.

Arnheim, a town pillaged and laid waste by the troops of the Prince of Orange, i. 395.

Artois, (the Count d') his opposition to the councils given to Louis XVI. after the taking of the Bastille. His emigration, ii. 88.

Assembly, (*Constituent*,) it's composition. Inconveniences resulting from it, ii. 91. It's first proceedings, and the sentiments it inspired, 92. It's abolition of Nobility and of all it's privileges, 93. It's conduct respecting the government, 95. It's precincts forced by the *brigands* on the 5th October, 102. It established it's sittings at Paris, 103. The members who withdrew from it after the crimes committed at Versailles: their motives, 105. It's situation at Paris, and it's errors, 107. Influence of the Jacobins over it, 116. Parties and factions by which it was rent, 118. Contest established betwixt it and the King, 120. Suspension of the powers of Louis XVI. till he should accept the constitution, 129. It breaks up; Iit's last decree, and one of it's most serious errors, 131.

Assembly, (*legislative*,) defects of it's composition. Turbulence of it's minority, ii. 195. It's alarms and dispositions respecting kings, 196. It's seditious *manœuvres*, 198. The disgrace it incurs by protecting the assassins of Avignon, 201. It proscribes the refractory priests, to whom the law had given the choice of taking or refusing the oath, 202. Disposition of the people's minds respecting the King immediately previous to the *tenth of August*. Embarrassment of the conspirators it contained. Their small number; their artifices; their audacity, and success, 247, *et seq*. It condemns the royal family to be imprisoned in the temple, 254. It declares infamous and traitors to the country all agents of the executive power, all Frenchmen who should attempt, directly or indirectly, to modify the French Constitution, and to compound with the powers who had possessions in Alsace, 358.

Assemblies, (*primary*), *of Paris*, they accept the constitution of the year III. and reject the law of the 5th and 13th *Fructidor*, which led to the troubles of the 13th Vendemiaire, iii. 199.

Assignats, their mortgages on the spoliations of the rich, and on the place of the revolution, under the revolutionary government, 58.

August, (sittings of the 4th) abolition of nobility and of all it's privileges, ii. 97.

August, (the 10th) events which announced this day, ii. 245. Preparations of defence and of attack, 247. Prevailing dispositions in the legislative assembly, 248. Frightful observation of one of the conspirators, *ib.*

Austria (House of) saved by the wisdom of Leopold, ii. 140.

Austrians, they compel Pichegru to raise the siege of Mentz, take possession of Manheim after having defeated him near that city, and make themselves masters of the Palatinate, iii. 223.

Averhoult, Dutch patriot who defeated the troops of the Stadtholder at Juphatz, i. 85. He advances to meet another corps sent against the city of Utrecht, and disperses it, 217.

Avignon, this city and *le Comtat de Venaissen* were taken from the Pope, for having declared schismaticks all those who acknowledged the decrees of the National Assembly, ii. 181.

B.

BAILLY, victim of the revolution and of the Jacobins, first Mayor of Paris, quits that place when the Constituent Assembly finished it's sessions; an error which was common to him with la Fayette and several others, ii. 133.

Bâsle, a city of Switzerland, where the treaties of peace were signed between Prussia and France, and that of the same power with Spain, iii. 251, *et seq.*

Barnave, unites, as well as Dupont and Lameth, with La Fayette,

Fayette, in order to save Louis XVI. after his return from Varennes, ii. 129.

Barrere, Decemvir and colleague of Robespierre, condemned to transportation, is put in prison, escapes, and has since been pardoned, iii. 183.

Barthelemy, his character. He negociates peace in Switzerland with Prussia, iii. 211. Incidents which interrupt the negociations, 212. Interests to be regulated, *ib.* Treaty of peace, 215. His connections with M. d'Yriarte, 216. He signs with him a peace with Spain, 218.

Bastille, (taking of) a celebrated day in the annals of the revolution. This was the work of the people; the Governor was killed there, ii. 86.

Bavaria, the proposed exchange of it against the Low-Countries. War on this subject, ii. 138.

Beaurepaire, shoots himself through the head because he was not able to persuade the inhabitants of Verdun, of which he was commandant, to defend their city against the Prussians, ii. 260.

Bellonet, a French officer, of the corps of engineers, privately sent with a hundred cannoneers to Utrecht for the purpose of defending that city against the Stadtholder, i. 232.

Bender (Marshal de) re-establishes Flanders and Holland under the Empire of Leopold. The King of Prussia had abandoned them by the Convention of Reichenback, ii. 172. Taken at the blockade of Luxemberg by the French. Had rendered himself famous by his easy and rapid conquest of Brabant, iii. 223.

Bentinck, (the Count de) accompanies the Princess of Orange in her journey from Nimeguen to the Hague. They are refused a passage, i. 391. Commotion which he hastened to excite at the Hague, 309.

Bequelin, (M.) a distinguished academician, superintendant of the education of Frederic William II. King of Prussia, i. 22.

Berkel, (Van) Grand Pensionary of Holland. His speech to eth States, his address to Count Roonne, i. 211. Means
which

which he adopted in order to prevail on the patriots and popular focieties to agree to the mediation of France, 388.

Berlin, this city was taken by the enemy during the reign of Frederic the Great, i. 8. It becomes the focus of the politics of Europe under the Minifter Hertzberg, 36.

Berne, (Canton of) orders given to the Swifs regiments which were in the fervice of the United Previnces to preferve the ftricteft neutrality during the troubles of that country, i. 80.

Bernftorff, a prudent minifter of the King of Denmark. The Anglo-Pruffian league cannot induce him to renounce his fyftem of defenfive alliance with Ruffia, ii. 171.

Bertrand-de-Molleville, Minifter of Louis XVI. He conceals himfelf after 10th Auguft, and caufes a report to be fpread of his death, ii. 254. He proves in his annals of the revolution that there had been at Mantua a declaration of Leopold and the agents of feveral powers, in order to compel the French People to reftore Louis XVI. to liberty. The adherence of Pitt to that declaration, to the treaty at Pavia, and to the treaty at Pilnitz, would have been a proof that the cabinet of St. James's actually provoked the war againft France, 325.

Befenwald, (the Baron de) fervices rendered by him to the King after the taking the Baftille, ii. 88.

Beurnonville, Minifter of war. He denounces to the Gironde new maffacres projected by the Jacobins, and propofes to exterminate them, iii. 35. Delivered up to Cobourg by Dumouriez, 38. His junction with Dumouriez effected by an error of the Duke of Brunfwick, ii. 279.

Bialinfki, takes advantage of the terror impreffed on the Diet of Grodno, in order to fign the difmemberment of Poland in favour of Pruffia, iii. 144.

Bizot, hair-dreffer to the Stadtholder. The crime he commits to pleafe him; its confequence, i. 158.

Billaud-Varennes, Decemvir, condemned to tranfportation with feveral of his colleagues and accomplices, iii. 184.

Biren, how he eludes the demands of Ruffia and Pruffia, i. 45.

Biron,

Biron, he attacks the city of Mons. His misfortunes and the panic terror spread in the army, ii. 238. His situation in Alsace; and the utility of the diversion made by his army, 282.

Bischoffswerder, Minister and favourite of the King of Prussia, whose passions he flatters, and whom he irritates, by engaging him to declare war against France, ii. 212.

Bleswick, Grand Pensionary of Holland; his character and talents. The shameful act that he signed in favour of Duke Louis of Brunswick. Promise extorted from him by the Patriots, i. 123, *et seq.*

Bois-le-Duc, pillage and total devastation of that city, i. 425.

Boissy-d'Anglas, his courage and the extraordinary danger which he incurred at the tribune of the Convention in the commotion of the first Prairial, iii. 185.

Boleman, intrepidity of this physician, who attempted, with the assistance of young Huger, to deliver la Fayette from the prison at Olmutz. He succeeded in it, and had the good fortune to fly for shelter into Prussia, where the King had him arrested and delivered to the Austrians. La Fayette was retaken eight leagues from Olmutz, iii. 280.

Bonaparte, his victories in Italy, in Germany, and Egypt. Sieges and capture of towns and cities in this country, iii. 227, *et seq.* Interests himself in the deliverance of la Fayette and his companions who were languishing in prisons, 286.

Borck, (M. de) an experienced soldier, to whom was entrusted the education of Frederic William II. i. 22.

Borysthenes, festivals on the borders of this river, made in honour of Catherine II. on her journey into the Krimea, i. 55.

Boufflers, his courage at the court of Prussia. Predicts to the King the unfortunate issue of the war which he wished to undertake against France, and that it would endanger the life of Louis XVI. whom he wished to save, ii. 214.

Bouill,

Bouillé, a general officer who was to protect the journey of the King at the time of his escape, ii. 127.

Bourgoing, the only Frenchman who has written well on the subject of Spain; negociates and concludes a peace with that power, iii. 210.

Bouvine, the place where the Austrians attacked Gouvoin, who defended himself courageously, ii. 240.

Brabant, revolution of, occasioned by the exchange of Bavaria and the suppression of the privileges of the country, ii. 141. The confederated states of Brabant and Flanders declare their independence, 143. Character of that revolution, *ib*. The Belgic congress declare the sovereignty of the people, 144. Factions which divide men's minds. Food of these factions, *ib*. Innovation which the French democratic party wished to introduce there, 145. Aristocrats who became demagogues in order to crush the democrats, 148. Rapid success of this artifice, *ib*. Re-entry of the Austrians into the capital, 150. It's submission, 171. The conquest of that province. True cause of the war between France and England, iii. 29.

Brabanters, these people ask for a union with France as well as the Savoyards. Impolitic decree, which promised assistance to all nations that would rise in insurrection, iii. 18.

Brandenburg, Prussia, and *Pomerania*. State, manners and customs of the inhabitants of these countries after the fall of the Roman Empire, i. 17. Their worship before Christianity, and their superstition after adopting it. 18. The learned men who carried thither the first ray of knowledge. 19. Influence of the French refugees. Advantages resulting from their barter with the natives of the country, *ib*. Origin of the House of Brandenburg, it's purity and it's antiquity, 21.

Branicki, this Pole, nephew of Prince Potemkin, delivered up his country to the Russians, and took refuge in their country, iii. 142.

Brienne, (the Cardinal de) puerile system of this Minister, in order to save Holland from the invasion with which it was threatened

threatened by the Prussians, i. 94. He turns into another channel the funds prepared for the formation of the camp of Givet, 414. Pusillanimity of this Minister; his tardiness; the palsy which he introduces into the government, ii. 3, *et seq.* Terrors with which he inspired Louis XVI. Disarming proposed and carried into execution, 9.

Brissot, accuses Lessart, Minister for foreign affairs, of intelligence with the Emperor, and obtains a decree of accusation against him, ii. 218.

Broglio, (the Marshal de) assembles an army for the purpose of restraining Paris before the 14th of July. Use that he makes of it, ii. 86.

Brothers of Louis XVI. (letter of the) these princes acquaint him by means of printing that they have implored succours from some powers against the National Assembly; that the treaty for them had been signed at Pilnitz by the courts of Vienna and Berlin the 27th of August 1791, and that the other courts entertained the same dispositions, ii. 339.

Brunswick, (the Duke of) his portrait and conduct. Errors which he would have prevented in the King of Prussia had his advice been followed, i. 32. Sends to reconnoitre the camp of Givet. Remarkable speeches of this Prince respecting this camp. His rapid march into Holland, 94. He takes possession of Amsterdam and subjects the whole country to the Stadtholder, 95. Unlimited powers which he received from the King of Prussia, 241. Emissaries that he sent to Givet, *ib.* His entry into the territory of Holland, 251. Surprizes an impregnable post, 419. Compels Amsterdam to capitulate, *ib.* Is nominated General of the coalition. Imprudence of his manifesto, which disgusts and re-unites all the French, ii. 236. Takes possession of the towns of Longwy and Verdun. Error which he commits, 275. Contagious disease which carries off near twenty thousand men from his army, *ib.* Another error of this Prince, who ought to have pursued Dumouriez as far as Chalons, 279. Fresh error which facili-

tates

tates the junction of Beurnonville and Kellerman with him. *ib* After the affair of Valmies, he negociates a truce, which Dumouriez breaks. Lofs of more than twenty-five thoufand men, 281. He capitulates with Dumouriez. His retreat. Aftonifhment of Europe. Problem to refolve as to the caufes of this retreat, 283. He is abandoned by the Auftrians in Alface. Secret treaty to deliver up this province to the Emperor, iii. 83. Defeated by Hoche and Pichegru, *ib*. His complaints to the King of Pruffia of the want of union among the allies, 84. He quits the army. His departure and complaints occafion a coolnefs between the courts of Pruffia and Vienna, 84. His declaration to the inhabitants of France, impolitic and infolent from the promifes and the threats it contains. The pretexts of them are the fame as thofe of the declaration of the King of Pruffia, 386. In his additional declaration, the threats are ftill more extravagant, 376. His letter to the King of Pruffia to perfuade him to quit the coalition. Motives which induced him to refign the command of the armies. He complains of the coalition and predicts that it will not fucceed, iii. 250.

Brunfwick, (the Duke Louis of) has the charge of the education of William V. the laft Stadtholder. Shameful guardianfhip, which for ever binds the young Prince to his Mentor. His departure from Holland, i. 122.

Brunfwick, (Elizabeth de) firft wife of the King of Pruffia, repudiated on account of mifconduct, i. 36.

Bulgakof, he was one of the principal caufes of the war between Ruffia and Turkey, i. 56. He deftroys in the mind of the Emprefs of Ruffia, the infinuations of the King of Pruffia againft France, ii. 13.

Bureau de Puzy, his detention with la Fayette, Latour, Maubourg, and Lameth; circumftances that accompanied it. Horrible treatment they experienced in Pruffia and in the fortrefs of Olmutz. It is to Bonaparte that they owe their deliverance, iii. 286.

Burke, colours in which he paints the Conftituent Affembly, ii. 91.

ii. 91. What he said respecting France and Mirabeau's observation on it, iii. 18.

C

CAILLARD, *Chargé des Affairs* of France at the Hague, &c. Excellent memorial drawn up by him relating to the revolution of the United Provinces, i. 99—433.

Callemberg, (the Count de) a Dutchman attached to the Stadtholder. *Bon-mot* which the Rhingrave of Salm made to him, i. 252.

Calonne, (M. de) his prodigality towards the Rhingrave of Salm, i. 248. Convention of the Notables. Imprudence of his choice, ii. 41.

Camille Desmoulins, author of *Le Vieux Cordelier,* which he wrote at the solicitation of Robespierre. The astonishing reception of this pamphlet by the public draws on him an accusation from the Cordeliers and the Jacobins. Robespierre, who seemed to defend him, condemned him to execution, iii. 109.

Camus, Bancal, Quinette and Lamarque, Commissioners from the Convention, sent to seize on Dumouriez. He arrests and delivers them up to Coburg, iii. 37.

Capellen, (the Baron de) a Dutchman distinguished by his patriotism. Danger which he encounters at Gatphen. His flight. Devastation of his property, i. 394. Dies from the barbarous treatment he received at Utrecht, where he commanded, 255.

Carletti, signs a treaty of peace with France in the name of the Grand Duke of Tuscany, who was the first that acknowledged the republic, iii. 203.

Carnot, revolution made by him in tactics; author of several plans for a campaign ingeniously conceived, iii. 71.

Carrier, an atrocious proconsul, whose cruelties were recognised under the name of Republican marriages, iii. 80.

Cassimir the Great, gave a constitution to Poland, which rendered it happy and flourishing, iii. 126.

Cateau,

Cateau Cambresis, battle gained by the allies, who arrive within forty leagues of Paris, iii. 92.

Catherine II. her threats to the Duke of Courland, i. 44. Alarms spread over Europe by her project of a journey to the Krimea, 44—52. Imposture and deception of that journey, *ib*. Her stay at Kief. Her interview with the King of Poland. With the Emperor Joseph II. at Catherinowslaw, 54. Her scheme of reviving the Greek Republics, 58. Motives which induced her to postpone the execution of it. Plan of conciliation, 59, 60. Her motives for revenge against the Courts of London and Berlin, ii. 5. She consents to the project of a quadruple alliance, 6. Storm formed against her in the North, 17. Her situation in regard to Sweden, 20. Affront which she received from Gustavus through the medium of his minister, 21. Her infatuation and security respecting the King of Sweden, 23. Her alarms, and the dangerous crisis of her empire, 24. She excites an insurrection in the Swedish army, 27. Loses the fruits of this measure, 28. Refuses the mediation of Prussia and England, her enemies, 31. Proposes to Stanislaus-Augustus a treaty of alliance between Poland and Russia, 32. This proposition is rejected, 39. She ineffectually addresses herself to the Court of France, 41. Propositions for peace with the Turks through the medium of *Choiseul-Goffier*, 50. Her fleet is defeated by the King of Sweden, 155. Threatened by the King of Prussia and Poland, at war with Sweden and the Turks, without hope on the part of the Emperor, 156. Makes peace with the King of Sweden without the intervention of any other power, 169. Rapid progress of her armies in Turkey, 174, *et seq*. Fresh league against her, in order to compel her to make peace with the Ottoman Porte, and to oppose the French revolution, 176. Peace of Sistovia, which saves the Turkish Empire, 178. Her views in supporting the opinion of the French Princes, who are desirous of a war, 187. She protests against the constitution of Poland, 191. Her policy in the war of the coalition against France. She directs her views against

against Poland, under the pretext of grievances which never existed, 229. Under what unjust pretexts she takes possession of Poland, iii. 75. She declares war against Poland for having formed a constitution guaranteed by the King of Prussia, and afterwards abandoned by that Prince, 130. She betrays the confederates of Targovitz, who wish to re-establish the ancient government of Poland. In order to engage the King of Prussia not to oppose her conquest of this country, she promises him Great Prussia with the cities of Thorn and Dantzick, and persuades the Emperor that it is the only means of retaining the King of Prussia in the coalition, 134. Her ungenerous and unworthy conduct in respect to General Kosciosko, wounded and taken in battle. Law of nations and of war violated in his person. Revenge satiated in Poland after the taking of Warsaw, 161. Letter which she causes her ministers to address to the confederacy of Targovitz, 233.

Cottemburg, a quarter of the city of Amsterdam inhabited by the sailors. Riot and battles between them and the Patriots, i. 262.

Chabot, frightful proposal of that conspirator in order to render the King odious to the people, and to bring about the 10th August, ii. 250.

Champ-de-Mars, federation. Assembly of the seditious. Petetion for judgment on the king, ii. 129.

Charlemain, liberty of the French people under his reign, ii. 57.

Charles IV. King of Spain. Motives which engaged him to peace, and to acknowledge the Republic. Reproaches made against him by the emigrants and the coalition, iii. 205.

Charette, organises and conducts the war of *la Vendée*, iii. 80.

Chasteler, (the Marquis de) charged by the Emperor to negociate with la Fayette and the other French prisoners the conditions to which they were expected to submit, in order to depart from the prisons of Olmutz, iii. 286.

Château-Vieux, indignation and contempt which this regiment inspired in the national guard, because the pike men had hadurched in triumph into Paris. The Swifs condemned for the revolt of Nancy, ii. 198.

Chauvelin, the minifter fent to London, in order to folicit the mediation of England, between France and the coalefced powers, ii. 227. Machiavelifm of the cabinet of St. James, *ib*. Though accredited by the executive power, England refufes to acknowledge him as ambaffador, after the death of the King, iii. 23. He offers in vain a reparation of Grievances complained of; receives an order to quit the kingdom, 27.

Chivalry, What it was in the feudal ages. Proof of the barbarifm and the ignorance of thofe times, ii. 60.

Cicero, (John) Elector of Brandenburg, founder of the univerfity of Franckfort, i. 19.

Clairfait and Coburg, thefe Auftrian Generals furprize the French cantonments, take poffeffion of Liege, defeat General Valence, raife the fiege of Maeftrich, and compel Dumouriez to evacuate Holland and the Low Countries, iii. 31—34.

Clergy, (the) it's power under the feudal hierarchy, ii. 59. Union of the inferior clergy with the minority of the nobleffe, 83. In what fpirit the new conftitution of the clergy was decreed, 108.

Club of Cordeliers, it's leaders, and their divifions with the Club of the Jacobins. Picture of the dreadful fituation into which France was plunged during their reign, iii. 10?. Heroic traits which have done honour to France during thofe times of infernal atrocity, 170. Veil thrown over the Declaration of Rights. Ronfin, Hebert, Chaumette, Momoro, their chiefs, fent to execution, 110.

Coalition of Powers, their errors as to the refources of France, at the epoch when war was declared, ii. 231. General indignation excited by this event, 234. Caufes of the frightful jacobin anarchy which for a moment threatens to overthrow focial order throughout the world, 235. Effects of the firft fucceffes of the coalition, 275. How it has feconded the wifhes of the revolutionifts of the 10th Auguft, iii. 3. It forms ftricter connexions, after the decree

decree of the Convention which promised assistance to all nations who would rise in insurrection, 19. New allies which it acquires, 27. Strange system adopted by it after the defection of Dumouriez, 73. It's conduct in regard to the Vendéans and the French Princes, 74. System of spoliation, 75. Pretext which the emigration of a few Poles furnished it for the conquest and partition of Poland, 75. Coolness between the cabinets of Berlin and Vienna, 84. Defection of the King of Prussia, 87. His motives, *ib.* He returns to it in consideration of the subsidies given him by England, 91. Double pretext which he uses; the contagious tyranny of democracy, and the instability of an ambitious government, 76. Falsity of these two assertions and how very fatal they were to himself as well as to France, 76, 77. They are only of advantage to England, *ib.* It loses the King of Prussia, *ib.* Parallel of the conduct of kings with that of Jacobins, 166. Provinces which it wished to take from France, 172. Detail of the losses it experiences in the campaign of 1795. Allies which it loses, 203, *et seq.* It's conduct more than equivocal in respect to the French Princes and the Emigrants, 208. What it might have effected against France; what it has not effected. Reproach addressed to it by the Duke of Brunswick. A defect of plan and of concert causes it to miscarry at Dunkirk, Maubeuge, Lyons, Toulon, and Landau, 240.

Coblentz, collecting of the Emigrants, ii. 203. With what joy they there receive the King of Prussia, 236.

Cobourg, His victories over Dumouriez, iii. 32–34. Manifesto to the French, which he draws up in concert with him, in order to give a King to France, 38. He besieges and takes Valenciennes, 43. He disavows the manifesto of Dumouriez when he learns that General's want of influence, 72. His inaction after the capture of Valenciennes and Condé, and having summoned Cambray to surrender, 77. He loses the battle of Fleurus, and seven thousand men in the Forest of Soigners; he marches the wreck of his army beyond the Rhine, 96.

Cockade

Cockade (National,) presented to Louis XVI. after the taking of the Bastile, ii. 88.

Collot-d'Herbois, one of the Decemvirs, a comedian and execrable executioner; fires on the inhabitants of Lyons with cannon loaded with langridge shot, and wishes to destroy that city to it's foundation, iii. 78. A desperate citizen endeavoured to stab him; this attempt caused a crowd of unfortunates to be massacred, iii. 111. Robespierre uses the same pretext. See *Robespierre.* Transported to Cayenne with Billaud his colleague and accomplice, 183.

Comedians (French,) gallantry of the King of Prussia respecting them. In what circumstances he ordered them to be driven out of Berlin, i. 37, 38.

Commerce, (the treaty of) between France and Russia, one of the grievances of England against this latter power, and one of the pretexts employed by the Anglo-prussian league to kindle the war between the Russians and Turks, i. 48.

Committee of public safety, a branch of the revolutionary government, iii. 55. A barbarous order and worthy of these cannibals of not making prisoners of the English but of murdering them on the field of battle, 81. Treaties of peace concluded by another Committee with Spain, Prussia and the Landgrave of Hesse-Cassel, 209. &c.— See *the Treaty of Peace.*

Commune of Paris, formed on the night of the 9th and 10th of August by the commissaries of sections, ii. 251. It seizes on all the powers and effects, the triumph of crime, till the moment of it's fall with Robespierre, 255. Atrocious circular notices sent into the departments by the Committee of Public Safety of this commune, to announce to them the massacres of September, and to extend them throughout France, 270. These massacres are exhibited to them as the work of the people and an act of justice, *ib.*

Condé, (the Prince de) his emigration on the 14th of July, ii. 88. His letter in concert with the Princes de Bourbon and d'Enghien to Louis XVI. in which they assure him

him of their fidelity and of their determination to perish, rather than suffer the overthrow of the monarchy, 337.

Confederacy of Poland, letters written to it by the Ministers of Russia and Prussia. Under pretext of jacobinism and to establish order, they declare to this guilty confederation that the project of the three courts is to contract the limits of Poland, iii. 233.

Constitution of Poland, it's proclamation. Wisdom of the diet in it's compilation, ii. 189, *et seq*. Protest of the federates at Targovitz, 191.

Convention between the French Republick and the King of Prussia. His object for France to cover Holland and the Low-Countries, and for Prussia to place the war at a distance from his dominions, by securing the neutrality of the north of the Empire, iii. 250.

Convention, National, (the) divided from its origin into two parties, the Gironde and the Mountain, iii. 5. It decrees the trial of the King. Heads of accusation, 7. It's incompetence, 9. Motives of those who wished the death of the King, 10. It declares war against England and Holland, 27. Grievances of the belligerent parties, 28. War declared some time after against Spain, 29. Situation of France at that period, *ib*. Arrestation of twenty-two of its members. Subjugated on the 31st of May by the party of the Mountain, it makes useless efforts to prevent the arrestation of the Girondists, 46. Origin of the most odious and bloody tyranny, *ib*. After the 9th Thermidor, the Convention becomes placed between two violent parties which equally tend to overthrow France and to deliver her up to foreign enemies; these are the anarchists and the royalists, 178, *et seq*. Wise conduct of the Convention in this critical situation, 179. It's arbitrary and impolitic conduct in the trial that it institutes against the colleagues of Robespierre; not daring to condemn them to the scaffold, it sentences them to transportation, and gives their partisans an opportunity of exciting the populace to insurrection. Besieged in it's hall, it had liked to have been destroyed there on the 1st Prairial. Delivered by the courage of some sections, it attack and disarms the factious, 180, *et seq.* Principles which it misconceived; faults which brought on the 13th Vendémiaire, 192, *et seq.* Errors that were the consequence of it, and which had influence over the government during the whole continuation of the constitution of the year III. 198.

Corday, (Charlotte) assassinates Marat. Observation of Madame Roland thereon, iii. 60.

Corps (free) militia of Burghers established in Holland in order to restrain the abuses of the Stadtholderian authority i. 160.

Corsica, capture of this island by the English, iii. 98. They take it in the name of the King of England, 102.

Counter-revolution, the meaning given to this word in the revolutionary clubs and committees, iii. 71.

Court of France, the errors committed by it at the commencement of the States-General, ii. 81. Orders the States to quit the place of their sittings, 82. It's consternation at the news of the capture of the Bastile, 87. It's opinion on the augmentation of the power of the Constituent Assembly after the 4th of August, 94.

Cracow, act of insurrection, drawn up and signed by all the inhabitants of this city who swear fidelity to the nation, and obedience to Kosciosko, iii. 149. Dictatorial power that it entrusted to him, 150. His victories, *ib.*

Custine, his conquests in Germany, iii. 17. Suspected of treason, 43. Takes the command of the wrecks of the army commanded by Dumouriez, *ib.* His rapid and bold march to Spire, Capture of Mentz and it's recapture by the King of Prussia, ii. 289.

Custine, (Madame de) her courage in order to save her father in law and her husband, iii. 106.

D.

Dampierre, heroic death of this General at the battle of Famars, iii. 42.

Danton, one of the principal authors of the massacres of the 2nd

2nd of September, ii. 268. His ferocity during the trial of Louis XVI. iii. 13. His character. What he said of Louis XVI. Wishes to terminate the revolution by giving the crown to the Duke d'Orleans. Compelled by Robespierre to quit the Committee of Public Safety, though his death is adjourned, 61, 62. Loses his power, and then ceases to be terrible, 65.

Dantzick, pretensions of the King of Prussia to this city, i. 45. He takes possession of it as well as Thorn, under the pretext of discarding jacobinism from his dominions, iii. 187.

Decemvirs, (the) name given to the Members of the Committee of Public Safety after the death of Hérault and Simon their colleagues, iii. 69. Picture of their government, 103, *et seq*. Robespierre considers the means of stopping it in it's excesses or of profiting by it, *ib*. Act of accusation brought against those who had escaped the 9th Thermidor. They are condemned to transportation, but find, with the exception of Billaud and Collot-d'Herbois, the means of escaping from it, 182. Seditious movements excited by their partisans, on the 1st Prairial. Assassination of Ferraud, and danger of the Convention, 186.

Degrave, the only constitutional Minister of Louis XVI. who remained Minister at War from attachment to the person and misfortunes of that monarch, ii. 219. Information which he gives on the attack directed by Dillon, and on the incomplete state of the army, 239.

Demagogues, their tactics and their secrets in order to agitate the populace, iii. 44.

Democrats, a name given to the popular party. Their influence over the Constituent Assembly. Serious errors which they occasioned it to incur, ii. 96.

Denmark, declares in favour of Russia. The Prince Royal enters Norway, ii. 25. Defection of the Danes, 27.

Denunciations, Decemviral weapons, decree of proscription, or death, iii. 59.

Dessaux,

Dessaw, (the Prince de) of the sect of *Illuminati*, and favoured by the King of Prussia, i. 38.

Deseze, defender of Louis XVI. iii. 11. The simplicity of his plea. What it might have been if Louis XVI. had not opposed it. Observation of the King when Deféze presented to him the peroration: *I will not appeal to the passions*, 13.

Dewitt, Grand Pensionary of Holland. Resolution adopted in order to authorize every Member to give his vote with impunity, i. 170.

Diet, *(Polish)* wisdom of this assembly in the Constitution which it gives to the Poles, ii. 189.

Dillon, (Arthur) forces the Prussian army to make a long *detour*, which makes it lose more than eight days, ii. 275. Accused of a design of conspiracy at the Luxemburg: the tyrants use this as the pretext of sending a crowd of innocent victims to the scaffold, iii. 110.

Dillon, (Theobald) massacred by the corps which he commanded, and which fled at the first discharge of artillery, ii. 239.

Directory of the French Republick, picture of its operations contrasted with those of Bonaparte, iii. 227, *et seq.*

Dogger-Bank, naval engagement betwixt the Dutch and the English, where the latter, though superior in strength, were obliged to bear away, i. 138. Grief of the Stadtholder, and joy of the Patriots on learning this news, 139.

Dombrowsky, defends Great Poland with an army of peasants against forty thousand Prussians, iii. 158.

Domingo, (St.) this island, fallen into the hands of the English, rises in insurrection and drives them off, iii. 223.

Duisburg, capture of this city by the party of the Prince of Orange, i. 395.

Dumouriez, Minister of Louis XVI. His character, ii. 219. What advantages the court might have reaped from his popularity, *ib.* Is deceived as to the dispositions of the King of Prussia, and provokes the war against

against the Emperor, 220. This Minister alters the plan of the campaign concerted between Luckner, la Fayette, and Rochambeau, *ib.* Shameful quarrel between him and the three other Ministers. He gives himself a command as Lieutenant General under the orders of Luckner, 240. His disobedience to la Fayette facilitates the first progress of the enemy, 259. He attains the supreme command of the army, *ib.* Advantageous position taken by him to stop the combined army of Prussia and Austria, 275. His letter to General Biron as to the measures he had adopted to repel the enemy from the frontiers of Champaigne, 277. Believes himself certain of ruining the enemy whether they advance or retreat, 280. Battle of Jemappe, and a complete victory over the Austrians. Capture of Mons, iii. 17. He takes the Low-Countries, *ib.* Threatens Holland, and, by dividing, weakens his forces, 18. His conquests in Holland, 30. Title he assumes in his letters to Lord Aukland, 31. His fall as rapid as his elevation had been sudden. Loses his cantonments: compelled to quit Holland, he abandons it and loses the battle of Nerwinde, but retires to the camp at Mauld, 32. He betrays the republican cause and wishes to give a king to France, 33. Is accused of treason by Marat, 36. He attempts the fidelity of Beurnonville, and orders him to be arrested with the four commissioners whom the Convention had sent to him in his camp, 37. He delivers them up to Cobourg as a guarantee for the safety of the Royal Family, 38. His Austrian escort irritates the army, 39. He is obliged to fly the French territory, 40.

Duranthon, Minister of Louis XVI. distinguished by the moderation of his principles, ii. 219.

E.

Eckeren-de-Zurdras, a zealous Stadtholderian. Motive of his journey to the Hague, i. 398.

Edicts,

Edicts, on the liberty of the press and of consciences, i. 8. Contradictions in these edicts, *ib.* Edict of religion, 437. Edict of Censorship, 451.

Efferen, a battalion of the Prince of Orange defeated by a detachment of the burghers of Utrecht, i. 218.

Elbourg, Hattem, troops sent against these two towns. Signal of civil war, i. 78—187. All the inhabitants, men, women and children take refuge on the other side of the Yssel, 173. Pillage of Elbourg, 395.

Electors, their assembly at the *Hotel-de-Ville*, at the commencement of the revolution, ii. 895.

Elizabeth, (Madame) Her angelic purity inspires remorse even in Robespierre, iii. 106.

Emigrants, (the) their assembly at Worms and at Treves, ii. 192. Second revolution, which they might have prevented, 199. Their ardour for a war whose near issue and termination they ventured to predict, 201. Decree of proscription which assimilates them all without distinction of age, sex, or the motives of their absence, 202. Their retreat and armament at Coblentz, 203. Declaration in their favour by the Emperor and the King of Prussia, 206. Louis the XVI. solicits the other powers to prevail on them to disarm, 207. Consideration which they enjoyed at foreign courts, 214. Their recal into France. Sequestration of their property, in case of disobedience, 220. Pretexts and reasons for not conforming to this decree, 221. Their intoxication and false hopes on the news of the declaration of war, 222. They receive the King of Prussia at Coblentz as a Saviour, 235. England abandons them at Quiberon. Three thousand perish there. Those shot, whom the sword had spared, iii. 209.

Emigration, after the arrestation of the King it becomes very numerous. Hope of the arming of foreign powers, and of regaining their privileges, ii. 121.

England, it's conduct and want of faith in regard to the United Provinces during the American war, i. 126. The connivance of the Stadtholder with the cabinet of St. James's,

St. James's, 127. Motives of the war which it declared against Holland, *ib.* It's reasons for relying on the connivance and partiality of the Stadtholder, 128. Perfidious councils which the cabinet of St. James's gives him. Interested councils which France equally gives the Patriots, 132. Parties which divided it, iii. 19. The Whigs and Republicans applauded the first efforts of the French towards liberty, 20. The Convention, not being able to conciliate the British Ministry, declares war against it as well as Holland and Spain, 27—29. It takes possession of several of the French Islands in the West-Indies, and of Toulon. It scatters it's forces and undertakes too many enterprises at once, 79. Violates the rights of nations in the port of Genoa. It's tardiness in succouring the Royalists of la Vendée. Errors which it commits in this respect, which are the cause of the failure of it's project to ruin and dismember France, 91. It's interest in the Coalition. Solely reaps the fruit of it. It's favourite but hidden scheme of totally ruining France, 101. It's ambitious policy relative to the Dutch. It opposes the peace which they ask, only to seize on their possessions in Africa and India. System that was realised by the capture of the Cape and Ceylon, 172, *et seq.* Provinces of which it endeavoured to strip France, 172. It's motives for opposing peace, 174. After having taken Corsica, Martinico, and the ships of war at Toulon, it abandons the Vendéans to their own efforts, refuses to land a French Prince on the coasts, and concludes by deserting the Emigrants at Quiberon, 208.

English, driven from St. Lucia and St. Domingo by the inhabitants, 223.

Enhof, (Countess de) the third of the living wives of the King of Prussia, i. 37.

Ephraim, (the Jew) conduct of the King of Prussia respecting him, i. 26.

Esterno, (the Count d') Minister of France in Prussia. Plan of conciliation which he there proposes to the king in order to appease the troubles of Holland, i. 81—190-1-2.

Eton

Eton, (Mr.) errors of this historian as to the Empress of Russia, ii. 5. And also relative to the Prince de Nassau, 17.

Europe, Political picture of it when Frederic William II. ascended the throne of Prussia, i. 13. Policy and conduct of the several powers at the time of the rupture between the Porte and Russia, 62. Situation of the powers of that part of the world at the death of Frederic the Great, 13. Why the history of modern Europe has interested us so little during so many ages since the fall of the Roman Empire.

Ewart, (Mr.) his influence over the Court of Prussia. Alarms which he spreads there as to the project of the quadruple alliance, ii. 8.

F.

Famars, (camp of) battle in which General Dampierre gloriously fell, iii. 42. Error of the Coalition after the dispersion of the camp, and the terror which was the consequence of it, 76.

Federation at the Champ-de-Mars, situation of men's minds at that epoch. Enthusiasm of the people for the constituent assembly, ii. 111.

Ferraud, killed in the midst of the Convention, and his head carried on a pike, iii. 186.

Fersen, he gains the battle of Macjejewice, where Kosciosko was wounded and taken prisoner by the Russians, whom he had thrice repulsed, iii. 158.

Feudal, system, resemblance it gives the modern nations of Europe to the Tartars and inhabitants of Caucasus, i. xx.

Fink, (the Count de) Minister of Frederic the Great. His niece was mistress of the King of Prussia, i. 37.

Flanders, situation of this country prior to the insurrection of the Brabanters, ii. 144. Troubles and massacres which took place after the arrestation of General Vandermersch, 149. Re-entry of the Austrians into the insurgent country, 150. Submission of the Low-Countries, 172.

Flessingue,

INDEX.

Flessingue, commotions and massacres directed by the Orange party, i. 397.

Fleurus, victory gained over the Prince de Cobourg: this battle fought by Jourdan was decisive and forced the Austrians to repass the Rhine, iii. 96.

Florida-Blanka, (M. de) seconds the Anglo-Prussian league by his influence on the timid character of Brienne, ii. 11.

France, state of minds under the reigns of Louis XV. and Louis XVI. ii. 68, *et seq.* Interests of this power in the disputes between the United Provinces and the Stadtholder, i. 190. Proposition made by it to the states of the United Provinces to interfere in their favour, and put an end to their disturbances, 387. Circumstance which renders this intervention nugatory, 390. Attempts of the court of Petersburg with Louis XVI. to join it and the Emperor against the league formed in the North; picture of France at this epoch, ii. 40, *et seq.* It's gradual loss of consideration, 48. The Anglo-Prussian league endeavours to direct all the powers against it, and in this hope strives to pacificate those at war, 154, *et seq.* France offers to support Spain with all it's strength against England, which wishes to declare war against it, 171. It's resources against the coalition; error of the powers in this respect, 232. Number of factions who divide it, and their character, 233. After having struggled against the coalition, repulsed and beaten the foreign armies, invaded the Belgic provinces, delivered Holland and subjected all the left bank of the Rhine, it enters into negociations for peace with Prussia, Spain, and the Landgrave of Hesse-Cassel; the treaties with these powers prepare the ruin of the coalition, and consolidate the French Republic, iii. 208, *et seq.*

Francis II. succeeds Leopold; he answers with acrimony the menacing dispatches of Dumouriez; interested views of the House of Austria at the epoch of the war, ii. 223, *et seq.* Grievances complained of in his manifesto, 234.

He

He demands a levy in mass throughout all the Circles: the King of Prussia opposes it, iii. 85. Imprudence of this demand, 86. He takes the command of the troops in Flanders; defeats the French at Cateau-Cambresis, and advances within forty leagues of Paris; the termination of the Austrian success in France, 92. He forms a plan of a general attack near Tournay, where the allies are twice defeated, 95. Violation of the law of nations in the persons of la Fayette, Puzy, and Mauburg: he grants an audience to Madame de la Fayette, and permits her, as well as her daughters, to share the captivity of that illustrious prisoner; conditions annexed to their liberty, 275, *et seq.*

Fraser, (Mr.) an extraordinary courier sent by him to London concerning the quadruple alliance proposed by the Court of Versailles, ii. 7.

Frederic I. Elector of Brandenburg, abates the feudal and anarchical tyranny of the country, i. xxx.

Frederic IV. Elector of Brandenburg. He makes prisoner Frederic of Austria in 1332. The epoch from which may be dated the rivalry which has since so often shown itself between this House and that of Brandenburg, i. xxxiv.

Frederic iron-tooth, Elector of Brandenburg, example of moderation given by this Prince in the times of barbarism. He refused two kingdoms, i. xxxv.

Frederic William, elector of Brandenburg, repaired all that his predecessor had lost; presages of his greatness; war which he sustained; he merited and obtained the surname of Great Elector, i. xl.

Frederic I. King of Prussia. All his ambition was to be a King. He obtained this title from the Emperor Joseph I. who created for him the Duchy of Prussia into a kingdom, i. xli. Placed between the Great Elector and Frederic William, he appeared the more pitiful; his character, i. xlii.

Frederic William I. King of Prussia. It was to a pleasantry of two Englishmen that was owing the creation of a military power which changed all the political system of Europe.

Europe: wars which he undertook; numerous treaties which he signed: his severity towards his son; his character by Frederic the Great, i. xliv.

Frederic the Great, King of Prussia, difference existing between him and Frederic William II. i. xlviii. His character and qualities, *ib*. In what situation he left Prussia. Summary of his life; imprisoned at Curin; obliged to be present at the punishment of Katt, his friend, i. 1. He offers his succours to Maria Theresa, which she refuses; he declares war against her, and seizes on Selesia; his Machiavelism with regard to France, 3. His dangerous situation in the war of 1741, 4. Victory which stamps his reputation, *ib*. Letter which he writes to the English Ambassador; his dispositions with regard to the King of Poland; laconic letter to the Marshal de Bellisle on making peace without his ally, France, 5. He supports war against the half of Europe, sees his capital taken, and triumphs over his enemies, 6. He opposes the conquest of Bavaria, 10. His policy after the peace of Hubertzberg, 30. Conciliation between the courts of Versailles and Berlin; cause which prevents the effect of this political revolution, *ib*. His parting observation to his niece when become Princess of Orange, 116. *Bon-mot* or the subject of peace respecting the navigation of the Scheldt, 143.

Frederic William II. mounts the throne at the age of forty-two; hopes entertained by his subjects of his reign, i. 21. Flattering expression addressed to him by the Great Frederic his uncle, 23. Surname which he wishes to deserve, *ib*. He gives the first idea of the Germanic league, *ib*. His conduct towards the Ministers of his uncle; aim he proposes to himself at the beginning of his reign, 25. His motto, *suum cuique*, 26. Operations which excite much content in the interior, 27. How he represses the intriguing, *ib*. Just observation he addresses to them; edicts for liberty of conscience and of the press, *ib*. Contradiction in these edicts, 28. Change of conduct in his politics, 32. He neglects his uncle Prince Henry, and
keeps

keeps him from interference in state matters, as well as the Duke of Brunswick, *ib*. He repudiates his first wife, and humiliates her successor by giving himself up to his mistresses, 36. The number of his lawful wives living at the same time, 37. Power which the sect of the *Illuminati* have over him, and faults they induce him to commit, 38. Striking contradictions in his conduct; the causes, 141. Reparations which he requires of the States-General of the United Provinces: he is disposed to declare war against them, 90. His opinion respecting the war between the Turks and Russians; he intimidates France, and makes her renounce her plan of alliance with Russia, ii. 8. His impolitic conduct; ills it would have produced in favourable circumstances, 14. His influence in all the cabinets of Europe, 15. He foments the troubles in Liege, and supports the people against their bishop, 152. Artful policy of the King in the support he affords the demagogues, 154. He changes his political system, and dismisses Hertzberg from the ministry, 159. Reason which determines him to this change of system, 160, *et seq*. Note which he writes on this subject, 163. He congratulates Stanislaus Augustus on the constitution given to Poland; his scandalous contradiction, 192. He allows himself to be led by the counsels of the emigrants and his ministers, who hold up to him the conquest of France as a work of a couple of months, 212, *et seq*. Brilliant illusions of the King on the nature and issue of that war, 223. He abandons the Poles whose constitution he had approved, and whom he had himself incited against Russia, 230. His manifesto and march with an army of 50,000 men, 235. His unworthy and cruel treatment of la Fayette, Bureau de Puzy, Latour-Mauburg, and Lameth, 261. Having got possession of Longwy and Verdun, he advances imprudently to the frontiers of Chalons in Champagne, 266. Critical position of his army, 275. His position in Champagne, 276, *et seq*. His letter to his mistress, 287. Probable cause of his retreat, 288. Secret Convention, 289. He ratifies it after the recapture of Mentz, and separate separates from the coalition, 290. His complaints in an answer to the King of Poland of the loss of the cities of Thorn and Dantzick are to the commerce of Prussia, 301. He demands the cession of these two cities, 303. He complains of the Diet's refusal of them, 305. His letter to the Archbishop of Liege on the occasion of the disturbances excited between him and his subjects, 309. His motives for taking up arms against France; suppression of the rights and possessions of the German Princes in Alsace, 359. The propagation of anarchical principles, 360. War declared against the King of Hungary, *ib*. Invasion of the territory of Basle and Liege, and for maintaining the balance of Europe, 361.—and to re-establish the monarchy of France on it's former footing, 363. Serious fault he committed in exasperating a part of the French nation, iii. 2. Complete revolution in the national mind after his retreat, 16, *et seq*. He drives the French from Frankfort, makes himself master of Mentz, forces the lines of Weissemburg and kills 15000, French, 56. He possesses himself of the cities of Thorn and Dantzick, and a part of Great Poland under the pretext of jacobinism, 75. He counteracts Francis II. in his demand to the circles of Germany; just cause of his complaints, 84. He renounces the coalition; causes of his defection, 87, *et seq*. New subsidiary treaty with England who brings him back to the coalition, 91. Treaty of alliance in 1790 with Poland; he refuses the succours stipulated by the 6th article of that treaty; praises which this Prince had bestowed on the Polish constitution; falsity with which he denies his promises and betrays the Poles, 131. He pretends alarms respecting the opinions of a people whom he wanted to strip, and under the pretext of disarding the contagion of them from his dominions, he takes possession of Dantzick, Thorn, and Great Poland, 136. He seizes on Cracow after the battle of Szczehocin, where he repulses General Kosciosko, *ib*. He besieges Warsaw, takes Vola, and defeats Joseph Poniatowsky.

He

He abandons the siege, his sick and his ammunition, 138. He refuses the subsidies offered to him by England; abandons the interests of his sister, and the Stadtholder; renounces his possessions on the left bank of the Rhine, and secures the tranquillity of the North of Germany, 206. Nations whose interests he has supported and betrayed, 207. He grants the Count de Goltz full powers to treat for peace, and sends him to Switzerland to negociate with Barthelemy. Mark of deference which he refuses to the Committee of Public Safety, 211, *et seq*. His letter to Count de Goltz on the acts of the Polish Diet, 282. Declaration of his and the Russian Ministers to the confederation of Poland, *ib*. His answer to a letter of the King of Poland, 238. His declaration on the affairs of Poland, 241. Treaty with the French Republic, 254. Convention with the French Republic, 259.

Friesland, it's attachment to France; it's hereditary aristocracy, 272. Division and rupture between its regents and those of the towns in the provinces of Holland, 273.

G.

GARDES-DU-CORPS, banquet given to the regiment of Flanders—insurrection at Paris and tragical consequences of that banquet, ii. 101.

Gecomitarde-Raad, or council committee. Riot quelled by it's orders—Powers with which it is vested, i. 146.

Generality, (country of the) it's political relation with the States-General of the United Provinces, i. 101.

George William, Elector of Brandenburg. The State of the army before him, under him, and under the first Kings of Prussia, i. 21. His reign was a series of disasters and weakness. He was on the point of losing all his predecessors had acquired, 26.

Gironde, (deputies of the) cause of their mistakes—became the victims of the faction they seconded, ii. 199.

Girondists, the name given to the party that attacked the constitutional

constitutional throne, which occasioned the day of the 20th June. Republicans from principle, they formed the great majority of the Convention, iii. 5. Presages of their fall, 6. Their first defeat, 7. First fault of this party, and of those who would not vote for the death of the King, 9. Their conduct in the trial instituted against him. They voted in vain an appeal to the people; thus by the day of the 20th of June they undermined the foundations of the constitutional throne; in acknowledging the King guilty, they led him, against their own opinions, to the scaffold, 13.

Gislaer, tumult excited against him at the Hague, i. 76. He justifies to the Envoy of the King of Prussia the conduct of the Dutch Patriots, 97. Conspiracy against his life, 150. His generosity, 160. His speech to the States at the Hague, 170. Resolution taken to suspend the Stadtholder, if he persisted in his usurpations, 172. His conference with the Prussian Ambassador concerning the pretended insult offered to the Princess of Orange, 407, *et seq.*

Givet, (camp of) intended to support the Dutch Patriots against the invasions of the Prussians, i. 90. Expression of the Duke of Brunswick relative to that camp, 94. Motives of the court of France in wishing to form it, 412. Brienne prevents its formation, 413.

Goertz, (the Count de) sent from Prussia to the Hague; his conduct in that city, i. 80. His character; his talents, 179. Strange style of his letters of credence, 180. Partiality of the King of Prussia, 181. Instructions less defective and more pacific, 191.

Goltz, (the Count de) sent to Switzerland to treat for peace with the Minister of the French Republic, iii. 211. His death suspends the negociations, and revives the intrigues of Austria and England to prevent peace, 212. This Prussian Minister gives in the King's name the most complete approbation of the new constitution of Poland, ii. 230.

Gorcum, a town in Holland which surrenders to the Prussians on the first shot, i. 367.

Gouffier, (Choiseul) French Ambassador at the Porte; he advises the Turks to put themselves in a state of defence; unforeseen accident which accelerates this war, which France wished to avert, i. 55. Causes which render his mediation between the Turks and Russians unsuccessful, 59. New plan of conciliation which he induces the court of Russia to adopt, causes of this war, 61.

Gouvion, his courageous conduct at Bouvines, ii. 240. killed in the advance-guard of la Fayette's army, *ib*.

Gower-Welsche-Sluys, the place where the Princess of Orange, who was proceeding to the Hague in order to excite an insurrection there, was ordered to go back, i. 391.

Grand-Pré, a defile occupied by Dumouriez with a handful of men to stop the Duke of Brunswick, ii. 280.

Greece, project of Catherine and Joseph II. to renovate the Grecian Republics, i. 58.

Greig, (Admiral) first sea-fight between the Russians and Swedes; he there distinguishes himself, ii. 25.

Grey, (Sir Charles) and Admiral Sir John Jervis receive the thanks of the British Parliament for taking the French islands, iii. 98.

Grodno, a city where the confederates of Poland met, to finish the ruin of their country, by the orders of Catherine II. whom they had had the imprudence to call to their assistance, iii. 142. Arrestation of several Members who opposed the measures concerted between Russia and Prussia, 144.

Gueldres, revolution in that province, and its situation, i. 167. Suppression of the liberty of the press, 169. Composition of the States, 170. Singular demand of the States of this province to the States-General, 272.

Gustavus III. King of Sweden. Caution given him by Frederic the Great, ii. 18. His passion for war and offensive alliances, 19. Causes which determine him to declare war against Russia, *ib*. Pretext which he makes use of, of, 21. Cruel and puerile stratagem, 22. His arrogant note and ridiculous pretensions, *ib*. His delays and the inactivity of Prussia save the Empire of Russia, 24. Discontent of his army, 27. Activity, prudence, and firmness of the King in this danger, 28. Celebrated victory which he obtains over the Russian fleet, and imminent dangers to which he is exposed, 155. Peace with Russia, 157. He takes the part of the French Princes; he insists on war against France, 184. Assassinated at a ball, ready to put himself at the head of the emigrants to march against France, 225.

H.

HAGUE, (the) to whom the military command of this city ought to belong, i. 144—149. Political negociations on this subject, 150. Plan of commotions and burnings, 397. Causes of the failure of this atrocious plan, 399. Another attempt to massacre the Patriots all in one night, 401. The Patriots who composed the States fly to Amsterdam as well as the three Pensionaries, 253. Massacres and arsons renewed on the approach of the Prussian army, 256. Outrages at the Hotel of the French ambassador, *ib*.

Hailes, the English Minister at Poland; in concert with the Prussian Envoy, he occasions the rejection of the alliance between the Russians and Poles, ii. 39.

Hardenberg, (Baron de) this Minister is charged to continue the negociations for peace begun in Switzerland. It is signed the 16th Germinal at Basle, iii. 212. Principal difficulties in this negociation, 213. Treaty of peace between France and Prussia, 254.

Harlem, this city proposes to the States of Holland to agree to grant the people a certain degree of influence in state affairs; fright of the aristocracy, consequences of this proposition, i. 197, *et seq*.

Harnier, (d') Prussian negociator sent to the Committee of Public

Public Safety to announce the pacific dispositions of the King, whom England wished to attach to the coalition, iii. 206, *et seq.*

Harris, (Sir James) English Ambassador; his character; his intrigues to excite civil war in Holland, i. 82. Insurgents paid by him in favour of the Stadtholder; stratagem he employs to engage the King of Prussia to declare against the Patriots, 88. His detestation of France; he becomes the confidant and adviser of Count de Goertz, 181. A ball proposed to celebrate the anticipated triumph of the Stadtholderian party, 214. His absence at play, and the cause, 398.

Hassan-Pacha, the Sultan Selim, has his head cut off as a punishment for his defeat by the Prince de Nassau, ii. 175.

Hattem, Stadtholderian troops sent against this city and that of Elburg; signal of civil war, i. 78. Capture of Hattem and flight of it's inhabitants, 175. Devastation in this city by the Orange party, 395.

Helvet-Sluys, violent sedition excited there by the Orange party, i. 397.

Henry, (Prince) his portrait; his conduct with respect to the King, his nephew, i. 32. He wishes to determine the King against war with France, ii. 178.

Henriot, what he did to secure the success of his party on the 31st of May, against the Girondine deputies, iii. 45. Arrested and conducted to the Committee of General Safety; rescued by a factious mob; imminent danger of the Convention, 117.

Herbert, Austrian internuncio, concerts with Bulgakof and the French Minister Ségur to conciliate Russia and the Porte, i. 59.

Hertzberg, (the Count de) the most able Minister of Frederic the Great; manner in which Frederic William II. repays his services, i. 24. The enemy of Prince Henry and the Duke of Brunswick, he is alone at the head of affairs; his partiality for the cabinet of St. James's; principal cause of the great events which have disordered Europe

35. His character, qualities, and talents; services which he renders to different powers, 36. Principal cause of the revolution of Holland, *ib.* He persuades the Turks to declare war against the Russians, 60. He foments the disturbances in Brabant, 61; and those in Holland, 80. He supports, with Frederic the Great, the cause of the Stadtholder against the States General, 150. Instructions given to the Count de Goertz, 179. He allows himself to be governed by the English Minister; opposes the quadruple alliance projected by the cabinet of Versailles, ii. 8. He irritates the Poles against Russia, who had proposed a treaty of alliance with them, 37. He quits the ministry, 157. The causes, 160, *et seq*; 168.

Hesse, (the Princess of) second wife of the King of Prussia. Her prudence and her disgrace, i. 36.

Hesse, (the Landgrave of) decision against him by the tribunal of the Empire, i. 26.

Hesse-Cassel, this Prince makes peace with the French Republic; yields up the country he possesses on the left bank of the Rhine, and ceases to furnish his contingent to the Emperor, iii. 216, *et seq.*

History. Why the history of modern nations has so much dryness and so few attractions, i. 9, *et seq.* What it was formerly; the interesting pictures it has to paint, 12. To what they are reduced in the fall of the empire, and the general invasion which gave birth to new monarchies, 13. What it became on the revival of the arts, 15.

Hoche, this general greatly contributes to gaining the famous battle fought with the Duke of Brunswick near Hagueneau. iii. 83.

Hohen-Friedberg, victory of Frederic the Great in Silesia; letter which he wrote to Louis XV. after that victory, i. 4.

Hohenzollern, (House of) a branch of the Kings of Prussia; to what it ascends, i. 21.

Holland, causes of the troubles of that country, i. 67. Summons of the States to the Prince to withdraw his troops, and

and threat, in case of perseverance, to suspend him, 174. Provisional suspension of the Stadtholder in his functions of Captain General, 177. Pacific dispositions of the States 192. The States establish a supreme committee; gratification it gives to the soldiers who remain faithful, 382. Answer of the States to the imperious note of the King of Prussia, 242. Demand they make to Count d'Esthérazy, *ib.*

Holland (States of) their declaration to the States General that they consider the *Union* as broken by the hostility committed against the territory of Utrecht; order given to General Van-Ryssel to suspend every officer that should refuse to march to the succour of that city, i. 220, *et seq.*

Hood, (Lord) gets possession of Toulon; debarks there an army too weak to join the insurgents of Lyons, iii. 80.

Hooft, a respectable veteran of the Regency of Rotterdam. Honours paid him by the people, whose cause he had served, i. 204.

Horn, (Lilieu) one of the conspirators against the life of the King of Sweden; remorse and caution unavailing, ii. 225.

ouchard, relieves Dunkirk besieged by the English; complete victory rewarded with the guillotine, iii. 80.

House in the wood, villa of the Prince of Orange; plots planned at this place to destroy all the Republicans at one blow, i. 398.

Howe, (Admiral Earl) defeats the republican fleet, and takes seven ships of the line; immortal proof of the enthusiasm of the French, iii. 98.

Hugar, Son of the person at whose house la Fayette had first landed in America; bold project which he undertakes to liberate la Fayette from the castle of Olmutz, iii. 279.

I

ILLUMINATI, a sect of visionaries in Prussia; faults to which they lead Frederic William II, i. 38. Cause of his premature death, ii. 16; iii. 225.

Ingelstrom,

Ingelſtrom, the Ruſſian General, requires of the Diet of Grodno to annul all the acts which could renew the energy of the Poles, iii. 145.

Iſmael, taking of that city; horrid maſſacre there by the Auſtrians, ii. 175.

J

JACOBINISM, the pretext Catherine II. makes for ſeizing Poland; ſhe conſiders as propagandiſts all the Poles who take refuge in France or Germany, iii. 136. Colours under which it is repreſented by the Empreſs of Ruſſia in her declaration to the Confederates of Targovitz, 236. It ſerves as a pretext for the Courts of Berlin, Peterſburg, and Vienna to eraſe Poland from the liſt of nations, 237. Declaration of the King of Pruſſia, 241.

Jacobins, their origin; a dangerous power which raiſes itſelf beſide the Conſtituent Aſſembly; inquietude of the enlightened Patriots on account of the multiplicity of clubs, and the union of that of the Jacobins, ii. 112. Their influence on the National Aſſembly; their principles, 115. New language they introduce, 119. They demand the depoſition of the King, 129. The death of the Emperor Leopold is falſely imputed to them, 212. Dreadful anarchy with which the world was threatened, 235. They demand that Louis XVI. be dethroned, 237. They diſorganiſe the army, and paraliſe it's firſt operations, 288. Legendre ſhuts up their club the 9th Thermidor, iii. 121.

January, 1793, (21) the day when Louis XVI. periſhed on the ſcaffold, iii. 14. Terrible conſequences thence reſulting, 15.

Jaſinſki, weakneſs of his army in Lithuania againſt General Ferſen and ſeventeen thouſand Ruſſians, iii. 157.

Joachim II. prudence with which this Elector of Brandenburg conducts himſelf in the time of Luther; to him are owing the rights of the Houſe of Brandenburg over Pruſſia, i. 25.

Y 4

Joſeph

Joseph II. his interview with the King of Poland, i. 53. With the Empress of Russia in her journey to the Krimea, 55. Flatteries of this Prince, 57. Project concerted with Catherine II. to revive the Greek Republics, 58. Causes which occasion it to be postponed; plan of conciliation, *ib*. His pacific conduct at the commencement of the rupture, 60. Shameful bargain of this Emperor with Holland under the arbitration of France; *bon-mot* of Frederic the Great on this subject, 143. His mediation between the Russians and Turks changes into hostilities, ii. 12. He engages personally at the taking of Sabach, 16. Error and defeat which oblige him to retreat before the enemy, 49. His death; his character; his political errors; his conduct with regard to Bavaria and the Netherlands, 137. With regard to the Brabanters and the Flemings; suppression of their privileges; cause of the Brabantine and Flemish revolution, 141.

Jourdan, gains a complete victory over the Prince de Coburg at Fleurus, iii. 95. Passage of the Rhine; the siege of Mentz raised, he is warmly repulsed by the Austrians, 223.

July 1789, (14) taking of the Bastille; this day in some degree prepared by that of the 23rd June, when all Paris rose because the King in his declaration did not offer a sufficient guarantee for liberty, ii. 85.

June 1791, (24) Flight of Louis XVI. ii. 184.

June 1792, (20) the day when an unbridled and ferocious populace penetrated into the palace of the Tuilleries under the pretext of obtaining the sanction of some decrees, ii. 141. The work of the Girondists who wished France to be governed by their ministers, iii. 5.

Juphatz, a place where the troops of the Stadtholder were defeated by the patriots, i. 85.

K.

KARLSKREUTH, interview at Franckfort between this Prussian General and the French commissioners. Conciliation between

tween the court of Berlin and the French Government iii. 87.

Killerman, his junction with Dumouriez; he occupies the heights of Valmies, where the combined army was repulsed in the attack of 20th November, ii. 281. He penetrates into the Electorate of Treves, after contributing to repulse the King of Pruſſia from Champagne, iii. 17.

Kief. Diſmal proſpect this country preſents to Catherine II. on her journey to Krimea; artifice of Potemkin to render Romanzoff leſs agreeable to the Empreſs, i. 53.

Kilburn, victory gained there by General Suvarof over the Turks, ii. 13.

Kiſberg, a great naval character; his conduct to an old Admiral, i. 137. His intrepidity in the battle of the Dogerbank, 138.

Kinkel, excites diſturbances in Holland under the direction of Sir James Harris, i. 227.

Koſcioſko, a Poliſh General, celebrated for his victories over the Ruſſians; he receives the fatal order to withdraw his army, and Poland paſſes under a foreign yoke, ii. 231. His politic conduct, iii. 152. He defeats the King of Pruſſia with a handful of men, 153. Defeated at Szezekocin; he cannot ſuccour Cracow, *ib.* He puniſhes the authors of an inſurrection, 166. Diſcovery of a treaty of partition between the two Imperial Courts and the King of Pruſſia, 154. Alarming criſis in which he is between theſe three powers, 157. Made priſoner by the Ruſſians, after prodigies of courage, by the treachery of one of his generals, 159. The Empreſs has him confined in a dungeon; Paul I. reſtores him to liberty; he gives advice to the Poles from the heart of his priſon; honours paid him by the city of Warſaw on a feſtival day whilſt it was beſieged by the Ruſſians, *ib.*

Krimea, the Empreſs's journey to that country, 49.

Krimpener-waard, a diſtrict in Holland celebrated for the inſult offered to the Princeſs of Orange, who was prevented from proceeding on her journey to the Hague, in order to excite the people against the States, i. 391.

L

La Fayette, proposes the declaration of rights, ii. 83. He is chosen commandant of the national guard, and restores quiet in Paris, 86. The commune send him to Versailles, he saves the Royal Family but arrives too late to prevent the horrors of that day, 102. At the *Champ-de-Mars*, he orders the troops to fire on the seditious, 130. His complaints of the weakness of the means provided for him for the first campaign, 238. Arrived at Givet, he receives an order not to continue the operations that were begun, 240. He denounces to the National Assembly the disorganization of the army by the Jacobins, 241. He goes to Paris and presents to the assembly, in the name of the army, a petition against the authors of the day of the 20th June; council which he gives the King, and answer of the queen, 243. Means employed to ruin him, 258. He orders Dumouriez to quit the camp of Maulde, and wishes to arrest him for disobeying that order; he arrests at Sedan the commissioners from Paris who had disorganised his army; on a decree of accusation, he flies from France, 261. Taken prisoner by the Austrians and delivered over to the King of Prussia; treated and carried as a criminal,' 262. Confined at Wesel, iii. 275. Transferred to Magdeburg, and thence to Glatz in Silesia; delivered to the Emperor, who causes him to be confined at Olmutz, 276, *et seq*. Carried off by Boleman and Huger, and immediately retaken, 279. His wife and daughters come to share his captivity, 282. Unavailing solicitations to the Emperor, 285. Conditions put on his liberation, 286.

La Fayette, (Madame de) her journey to Vienna to obtain the liberty of her husband: not being able to soften the Emperor, she applies for, and obtains leave to share

his

INDEX. 313

his imprisonment, with her two daughters, iii. 281, *et seq.*

Lafitte, a French engineer in the service of Turkey. He sends notice to France that Otchakof could not hold out three weeks; the siege of that place for ten months, ii. 29.

Laflotte, to save his life, forms the chimerical plan of a conspiracy among the prisoners in the Luxemburg, iii. 111.

Lally-Tollendal, quits the National Assembly after the crimes of the 6th October, ii. 105.

Lamballe, (the Princess de) massacred in the *September days,* ii. 269.

Lameth, (Alexander) his captivity at Magdeburg, iii. 276. Having fallen dangerously ill, he does not follow la Fayette and Mauburg to the prisons of Olmutz; Frederic William II, permits him to remain in Prussia, and grants him his liberty after the conclusion of peace, 277.

Lascy, (the Marshal de) serious fault committed by the Emperor through him in the campaign against the Turks, ii. 49.

Latour-Manburg, his captivity with la Fayette and Lameth, iii. 275, *et seq.*

Launy, chief of the French administration established at Berlin for the direction of the finances, i. 39.

League, (Anglo-Prussian) plan of this league directed against the courts of Versailles, Vienna and Petersburg, ii. 10. Arms the King of Sweden against the Empress of Russia, 17. Foments the disturbances in Flanders and Brabant, 141. Wishes to establish there a petty Republic which it might govern, 145. Change of principles and system; abandons the Brabantines to turn it's views against France, 148. The immense ambition of this league directed against Russia, the Emperor, France, and Spain; it changes it's system and objects; it's efforts to unite all powers against France, 153. Baffled in the North by the peace between Sweden and Russia, 170. It

excites

excites the Poles to profit by the embarrassments of Russia and Austria, during the war with the Turks, to establish a stable government and free themselves from their yoke, iii. 129.

League, (Germanic) what was the first origin of it, i. 23.

Legendre, shuts the Jacobin club, iii. 121. Frees the Convention from the factious who besieged it and had assassinated one of it's members on the day of the 1st Prairial, 1st year, 187.

Leopold, critical and weak situation in which he found the House of Austria on his accession to the throne, ii. 140. His politic and pacific conduct secures to him the empire, and brings back the rebellious provinces to their duty, 158, *et seq.* After the convention of Reichenback he marches 40,000, men into the Netherlands, 167. He quells the disturbances in Hungary, and is elected Emperor without opposition, 172. At Mantua, he concerts with the ambassadors of England and Prussia the means of conciliation between Louis XVI. and the French Nation, 182. His interview at Pilnitz with the King of Prussia, Count d'Artois, and the Elector of Saxony, 183. Suspension of hostilities advised by Louis XVI. 185. His convention with the King of Prussia, 187. His joint declaration with the King of Prussia, that he should consider the entrance of the French into the Electorate of Treves in order to drive out the French Emigrants, as a declaration of war, 206. His complaints; his preparations for war; advice which he gives to the Elector of Treves, 210. Congress which he wishes to open in order to reconciliate the interests of the kings with the French Constitution; his death; suspicions against the Jacobins respecting it, 211.

Lessart, succeeds Montmorin in the ministry refused by Ségur and Barthelemy; he dies on the scaffold, ii. 203. His trial decreed on pretence of an understanding with the Emperor, 217.

Liancourt, (the Duke de la Rochefoucault) informs the King of of the taking of the Baſtille: advice which he gives him, i. 17. Offers to conduct the King to Rouen, to avoid the Jacobins, 244.

Liberum veto, a privilege introduced into the Poliſh Diet under John Caſimer, and which continued till Staniſlaus Auguſtus. Cauſe of the tyrannical influence of foreign powers, iii. 128.

Liege, inſurrection in that city; Expulſion of the Biſhop, ii. 151. Artful conduct of the King of Pruſſia, 152. The inhabitants obliged to ſubmit, recal their Biſhop, and ſend away Rohan whom they had elected, 171. Remarkable ordinance of the Liege government on the occaſion of the great number of Dutch Emigrants, i. 426.

Liſle, the Auſtrians bombard this city, and raiſe the ſiege of it, iii. 17.

Loan, (forced) a revolutionary meaſure, which from that time placed all property at the diſpoſal of government, iii. 68.

Lochem, a town devaſtated by the troops of the Prince of Orange, i. 396.

Lomenie, (the Cardinal de) or M. de Brienne; called to regenerate the finances; he does all in his power to anihilate them, ii. 42. His faults, 43.

Longui, the firſt French town which ſurrenders to the Pruſſians without reſiſtance, ii. 266.

Louis XVI. his character conſidered relatively to the Revolution, ii. 73. Convocation of the States General, 79. Ruinous delay in aſſembling the States, 80. His declaration of the 26th June; conſequences of this ſtep, 82. He diſmiſſes his miniſters, *ib.* His ſituation after the revolution of the 14th July, 88. Repairs to the *Hotel de Ville* of Paris, and puts on the national cockade, *ib.* He reſiſts thoſe who adviſe flight and civil war, 100. Danger of the King at Verſailles on the night of the 5th October on account of the entertainment given by the *Gard-du-Corpſe* to the regiment of Flanders, 101, *et ſeq.* Reconducted by the national guard to Paris, after the dangers and maſſacres of the 6th October, 103. His ſituation before

before his departure from Paris, 127. His evasion; his escape, he is brought back to Paris, 185, *et seq*. He accepts the constitution, 186. He sacrifices his ministers to the Jacobin party, 203. He solicits the disarmament of the Emigrants from foreign powers, 204. He changes ministers, and gives greater strength to the minority, 218. Cause of this weakness, 219. He abandons his ministers for fear of seeing the queen denounced in the Legislative Assembly, *ib.* He declares war against the King of Hungary and Bohemia; effect produced in Europe by this event, and situation of the King at this epoch, 221, *et seq.* Danger he is exposed to by the manifestoes of the courts of Vienna and Berlin, and of the Duke of Brunswick, 235. Obliged on the 20th June, to put on the *bonnet rouge* at the palace of the Tuilleries, 242. He refuses to repair to Compiègne, whither la Fayette wished to conduct him, as well as to accept the asylum at Rouen offered him by Rochefoucault-Liancourt, 245. He abandons his care for his safety and personal defence the 10th August, 252. He seeks an asylum in the body of the Legislative Assembly, 253. It orders him to be shut up in the Tower of the Temple with his family, 255. Said to have written to the King of Prussia in Champagne, that if he penetrated farther into France it would expose his life, 286. His trial; first contest between the Mountain and *la Gironde*, iii. 7. Heads of the accusation against him, 8. Infallible means to have saved him, 9. He appears before the assembly to be interrogated, 11. His defenders, *ib.* Death of the King decided by a majority of five votes; illegality of this decree, 14. The dignity with which he received his sentence; his death and last wishes for France, *ib.*

Luchesini, (the Marquis de) Prussian Minister at Warsaw; his portrait, ii. 36. His address to justify the conduct of the King to the Poles, and provoke their hatred against Russia, 37.

Lukhner, his plan of invading the Netherlands concerted with la Fayette and Rochambeau, ii. 238. He gets possession of Courtray, 241.

Luxembourg,

Luxembourg, (prison of the) Laflotte accuses General Dillon of having begun a conspiracy; almost all the prisoners are, under this pretext, sent to the revolutionary tribunal, and thence to the scaffold, iii. 111.

Luxembourg, taking of that city, after a long blockade: Marshal Bender made prisoner, iii. 223.

Lyons, siege of that city; it's obstinate resistance; the celebrated and unhappy victim of Collot-d'Herbois, iii. 79.

M

MACIEOVITZ, battle where Kosciosko was wounded and made prisoner by the Russians, iii. 159.

Mack, called to the congress of Antwerp to propose plans of conciliation; divided in interest, it's members executed nothing, and each acted separately for himself; this fault saved France, and opened the eyes of Europe to the true intentions of the powers, iii. 76. Sent to London; he is present at a grand council of war held in Flanders; his plans are adopted but not followed, and to him is imputed the bad success of the campaign, 92.

Madalinski, a Pole who first revolts against the tyranny the Russians had exercised at the Diet at Grodno, iii. 145. After having erected the standard of revolt, he defeats the Prussians, traverses the provinces they had conquered, and penetrates into the Palatinate of Cracovia, 149.

Mäestricht, considerable emigration from that city, and all the United Provinces, i. 426.

Magdeburg, a town where Fayette, Mauburg, and Pusay were confined in a subterraneous dungeon, iii. 276.

Malesherbes, defender of Louis XVI. portrait of this worthy magistrate, iii. 11. He protests against the illegality of the decree condemning to death, 14. His stoicism; he lived and died a Socrates, 106.

Mandat, commandant of the National Guard assassinated on the 10th of August by order of the Commune; influence of his death on the events of that day, ii. 251.

Manifestoes,

Manifestoes, of the court of Vienna; it's complaints against France, ii. 234;—of Berlin, 235;—of the Duke of Brunswick, *ib. et seq.*

Mantua, convention made in that city with the Emperor and the ambassadors of England and Prussia, to become mediators between Louis XVI. and the French nation, ii. 182.

Marat, author of the massacres of September, ii. 265. Accused by the Girondists; acquitted by the influence of the Commune, iii. 35. Accuses Dumouriez of treason, 36. Is assassinated; his detestable character, 60.

Marbois, sent to Vienna to induce the powers not to interfere in the affairs of France, and to put an end to the arming of the emigrants, ii. 207.

Maret, sent twice to London to prevent a rupture betwixt the two nations, iii. 27.

Maret and Semonville, arrested on a neutral territory and put in irons by the Austrians, iii. 79.

Marlborough, (the Duke of) the adulation he employed to obtain of the father of Frederic the Great a succour of troops for the service of England, i. 31.

Marriages, (Republican) the irony and atrocious cruelty of Carrier, iii. 81.

Massacres of 2nd of September, part of their authors are announced in a circular notice to the departments, ii. 379.

Mass, (levy in) the revolutionary means which opposed twelve hundred thousand men to the enemy, iii. 72.

Maury, (the Abbé) received a Cardinal's hat for defending the interests of the Pope, who lost Avignon, ii. 181.

Maximum; *Decemviral*, means which produces a general scarcity, iii. 103.

May 31, the celebrated day prepared and conducted by the Mountaineers, the Jacobins, and the Commune; purpose of their insurrection, iii. 45. Arrestation of 22 Girondist deputies, 46. The constitution which was the consequence; the most absurd and favourable to anarchy, 54. Not to be put in action till the country was out of danger, *ib.*

Meaux,

Meaux, the massacres of September make it flow with blood, ii. 271.

Mecklenburg, (the Duke of) He engages to the King of Prussia four bailiwicks, i. 26.

Menou, (General) goes to the *Faubourg* St. Antoine and disarms the seditious who had prevented the execution of the assassins of the deputy *Féraud*, iii. 108. *See Prairial 1st.*

Michelson, stratagem of this Prussian general against the Swedes, ii. 25.

Middelburg, pillages and massacres by the populace in this town, i. 396.

Minden, a great sluice near Amsterdam, which the Patriots wished to oppose to the Duke of Brunswick in order to save that city, i. 244.

Minority, part of the order of *Noblesse* who unite with the Third Estate, ii. 81.

Mirabeau, urges the King to remove the troops from the place of sitting of the States General, ii. 84. Creator of assignats, 123. His character; he connects himself with the court, 125. His death; the regret it inspires, 126.

Moderes, prudent men, confounded by the kings with the Jacobins, and considered as the enemies of their country by the demagogues, ii. 209.

Mollendorff, a Prussian general charged by the King to concur with the Russians in the dismemberment of Poland, under the pretext of dispersing the Jacobins in the neighbourhood of the Prussian dominions, iii. 243.

Monarchy, in Europe saved by revolutionary faults—threatened to be destroyed by the faults of kings, iii. 221, *et seq.*

Monarchists, (constitutional) the party which had for it's object the alliance of the throne with liberty, being an immense majority of the nation, ii. 238.

Mons, panic terror on the attack of that city by General Biron, ii. 239.

Monsieur, the King's brother. He supports the double representation

presentation proposed in favour of the Third Estate in the assembly of the *Notables*, ii. 80.

Montesquieu, his rapid conquest of Savoy, iii. 16. He escapes the scaffold, flying into Switzerland, 44.

Montmorin, his conduct towards the Dutch, i. 93. Project of a quadruple alliance proposed to Louis XVI. ii. 5. Disasters it would have prevented, 6. He quits the administration, 203. Massacred in the days of September, 269. His letter in the name of Louis XVI. to the French ambassadors at foreign courts, announcing the King's free acceptance of the constitution, 331.

Mormale, a forest in which the Austrians entrench themselves after being defeated at Maubeuge, iii. 82.

Monnier, quits the National Assembly after the crimes of the 6th October, ii. 105.

Mountain, (the) name given to the minority in the Convention, iii. 5. Motives of these leaders who wished the execution of the King, 10. It is condemned to exercise a tyrannical power, 16.

Muilman, Munter, and Van-der-goes, recal of these three deputies; deposed for having betrayed to the States the general wish of the city of Amsterdam, i. 199.

Municipality of Paris, (the) its dismission operated by a small number of violent Jacobins, who repair to the *Commune* as deputies of sections; it is the origin of the *Commune* celebrated for its crimes till the fall of Robespierre, ii. 251.

Mystifications, means employed by the *Illuminati* of Prussia to deceive the King, i. 70.

N.

NARBONNE, Minister of War, his character and conduct, ii. 206. Preparations for war, 207. His dismission, 218. Concealed in Paris after the 10th of August, he owes his life to the report spread of his death by his friends, 254.

Nassau, (the Prince of) destroys in the Leman the fleet and army

army of the Captain Pacha, ii. 16. His journey to Vienna, Verfailles, and Madrid; he is charged by the Emprefs of Ruffia to communicate the ambitious views of Pruffia on Poland; plan of alliance to guarantee the integrality of the territory of that republic, 31. He defeats the intrepid Haffan Pacha who ftruggled for fifteen years againft the errors and fall of the Ottoman Empire, 175.

National Guard, it's formation, ii. 86. Proceeds to Verfailles with la Fayette by order of the Commune, and faves the Royal Family, whofe maffacre had been projected in the night of the 5th October, 101. Conducts the King and the National Affembly to Paris, 104.

Neckar, (M.) fucceeds the Cardinal de Loménie; what he was, ii. 44. Advantage which he procured for the Third Eftate, 80. His difmiffion from the miniftry, 82. His buft carried in triumph through Paris, 85. His recal after the 14th of July, 87. His return to Paris, the termination of his triumph and influence, 125. His fecond departure from France, *ib*.

Nerwinde, place where the Auftrians defeated the French commanded by Dumouriez, iii. 32.

Neftor, (Joachim) Leon X. of Brandenburg, i. 19.

Neutrality, (armed) acceffion of Holland to this treaty, i. 128. Caufe of the war declared by England againft the United Provinces, 130.

Neutrality, Convention figned between the minifters of France and Pruffia to eftablifh the neutrality of the North of Germany and to remove the feat of war from the dominions of the King of Pruffia, iii. 215—259.

Neutrality, (line of) the Auftrians break this line, and owe a part of their advantages to this violation, iii. 224. Extent and limits of this line, 260.

Nieverluys, lofs of the Pruffians at the fiege of that place, i. 420.

Noailles, (Mefdames de) their courage on going to execution, iii. 106.

Nobleffe, (order of the) jealoufy of the nobleffe of the provinces

vinces against those of the court one of the causes of the revolution, ii. 77. Their motive for proposing that the deliberations should be by orders, not by voices, 80. The minority of them joins the inferior clergy, 81. Their abolition; sacrifice of their privileges, 93. What they hoped to gain by the disorders spread through France, 200.

Notables, (assembly of the) Difference of the two assemblies which were held under the name of Notables; determination of the latter considered as one of the principal causes of the revolution, ii. 80.

O.

OCTOBER, (day of the 5th) celebrated by the massacres committed at the palace of Versailles, and the dangers to which the Royal Family, particularly the Queen, were exposed, ii. 102. To what it was imputed, 103.

Olmutz, celebrated by the confinement of la Fayette, Maubourg and Puzy in dungeons in that fortress, iii. 278.

Orange, (the Prince of) refuses the title of Count Sovereign of Holland which the people wish to confer on him in their delirium, i. 430.

Orange, (the Princess of) her character, i. 70—83. Arrogant answer which she made to the States General, 84. Pretended affront at Welch Sluys, and her complaints to her brother the King of Prussia, 89. Expressions used to her by Frederic the Great on giving her in marriage to the present Stadtholder, 116. Her departure from Nimeguen for the Hague; she is not allowed to proceed, 391. Her journey to the Hague; pretext for bringing the arms of Prussia against Holland, 401. Her influence on the cabinet of Berlin. How on her retreat at Nimeguen she baffles the measures concerted at Versailles and the Hague, 240. Her proscriptions; her revenge, 482, *et seq.*

Order, (Equestrian) it's prerogatives in Holland, i. 103.

Orleans,

Orleans, (the Duke of) his bust carried in triumph through Paris, ii. 86. Faction which bears the name of that Prince, 98. His character, 99. Suspicions raised with regard to this faction, *ib.* Conduct it observes on the occasion of the banquet given to the regiment of Flanders by the *Gardes-du-corps,* 102. The massacres and day of the 5th October are imputed to it, 105. His journey, or rather exile to England, *ib.* His return to Paris, 119. Imprisoned at Marseilles with his relations, iii. 58. Danton wishes to make him King, 61. Incertitude of Robespierre respecting him; he abandons him to the revolutionary axe, 67.

Osterman, (Count) one of his secretaries betrays the secret of the quadruple alliance projected between France, Russia, Austria and Spain, ii. 7.

Otcantz, Envoy of Spain, the only Minister who after the condemnation of Louis XVI. dared make a noble attempt to prolong his life, iii. 15.

Otchakof, taking of that city, and the horrible massacres, ii. 30.

Oudekirk, loss of the Prussians at the attack of this post, i. 419.

P.

PAPER-MONEY, it's creation the work of Mirabeau, ii. 123.

Paris, general fermentation previous to the 14th of July, ii. 84.

Parker, (Sir Peter) the English Admiral beaten by the Dutch on the coast of Jutland, i. 138.

Parliaments, their defects antecedent to the revolution, ii. 77.

Patents, (right of) prerogative attached to the office of Captain General with which the Stadtholder was invested, i. 109.

Pavia, conferences between Leopold, the agents of the King

King of England and the French Princes to restore Louis XVI. to his liberty, ii. 323, *et seq.*

Paul Jones, his jealousy of the Prince of Nassau, ii. 17.

Paul I. liberates Kosciosko after the death of Catherine II. by whom he had been confined in a dungeon, iii. 159.

Paulus, sent from the United Provinces to France to solicit succours, i. 92. Restorer of the Dutch navy, 135. Employed to concert with M. de Montmorin, means of conciliation with the King of Prussia without the intervention of England, 231. Deprived of his employments at the instigation of that power, 424.

People, their political slavery in feudal times, ii. 59. Their alliance in England with the nobility in favour of liberty against the royal authority: origin of the power of the Commons, and the fall of the feudal power, 62. In France the union of the people with the King diminishes the influence of the nobility and the clergy and augments the royal authority, 63. A terrible instrument in the revolution, 76.

Perignon. After the death of Dugommier, and the capture of Figueires, Perignon and Servan threaten the total ruin of Spain, iii. 205.

Petion, Mayor of Paris, kindles the flames of discord, ii. 200. On the occasion of the Duke of Brunswick's manifesto he demands that Louis the XVIth should be excluded from the throne, 237. Deposed for having in his capacity of Mayor of Paris, favoured the invasion of the gardens and palace of the Tuilleries. His triumph; madness of the people respecting him, 242. He orders the palace to be defended on the 10th of August. Suspended the same day from his functions by the *Commune*, which had just assumed the place of the Municipality, 251.

Philosophers, their influence on the revolution. The honours which they received from foreign courts, ii. 46.

Philosophy, it's influence under the last two King's of France, ii. 70.

ii. 70. Contradictions between the manners and the spirit of the monarchy, 72.

Piastes, (the family of) celebrated in Poland, becomes extinct in the person of Casimir the Great, iii. 126.

Pichegru, he defeats, in conjunction with Hoche, the allies near Haguenau; the redoubts taken at the point of the bayonet. Consequences of this battle, iii. 83. Defeats the English in the Low-Countries and threatens Holland, 96. He attacks the allies at all points from the ocean to the Rhine, and defeats them every where. Picture of this campaign of 1795, in which Holland was subjugated, the enemy repulsed to the Rhine, Biscay and Catalonia taken from the Spaniards, 168, *et seq.* Detail of Provinces and countries taken from the coalition, of battles gained, and captures, 173. He takes possession of Manheim. Defeated near that city, he abandons it to the Austrians, who render themselves masters of the Palatinate and threaten Landau, 224.

Pilnitz, conferences which took place there respecting Louis XVI. What idea ought to be formed of the treaty of Pilnitz, ii. 183. Convention betwixt the King of Prussia and the Emperor, *ib.* Mutual declaration signed betwixt the Emperor and the King of Prussia to act in concert and with other powers, against the French, 329.

Pitt, (Mr.) his policy in the troubles of the revolution, ii. 210. Formerly attached to the Whig party, he changes his opinions when become Minister; expresses his wish for the permanent establishment of liberty in France; prepares to make war against her, after having contributed to destroy the liberty of the Poles, iii. 20. His motives for not declaring war against the French, and his pacific counsels to the King of Prussia, 21. His motives for war after the conquest of Brabant, 22. After the 10th of August he recals the Ambassador, Lord Gower, and refuses to acknowledge Chauvelin, 23. Reasons for not interfering in favour of Louis XVI. *ib.* He wishes to render the war national and popular, by forcing France to take up arms first, 24. Pretexts with which the French and English Jacobins furnished him, 25. He infringes the conditions of the treaty of commerce, and excites Holland against France, 26. On the order given to Chauvelin to depart from England, the Convention fulfil the wish of Pitt by declaring war against England, 27. Absurd decree of that Assembly, which declared him the enemy of the human race, 79. His speech in the House of Commons, in 1790. Wish then expressed by this Minister for liberty and the re-establishment of order in France, 231.

Paix, (the Prince de) his attachment to Louis XVI. he conceals himself in Paris after the 10th of August, and circulates the report of his death, ii. 254.

Poland, her new constitution. The wisdom with which it was framed. Her proclamation, ii. 188, *et seq*. Protestations made against her by the confederates at Targovitz, 191. A concise account of what she was under Casimir the Great, to whom she was indebted for her constitution, which was respected till the death of Sigismund Augustus, iii. 126, *et seq*. Change which she suffered from granting the *liberum veto* to each noble, 128. Division of her forces, after raising the siege of Warsaw by the King of Prussia, against the co-partitioning courts, 153. Partition of that unfortunate country, 162.

Poles, (the) what they have been, ii. 32. What they have been for a century, 34. Their hatred of the Russians, 35. Indignation with which they were inspired by a proposal of alliance with Russia, 36. Wise proposals rejected by the insinuations of Prussia, 37, *et seq*. Brief account of the motives which induced them to make changes in their laws, which were the pretext and the cause of their destruction, iii. 124, *et seq*.

Policy, means of divining it's enigmas, i. 42.

Political guarantee, monstrous examples of, 429.

Poninski, his treachery delivers Poland to the Russians at the moment when Kosciosko triumphed over the enemies which inundated it, iii. 185.

Pope,

Pope, (the) his conduct in regard to France during the revolution. He is deprived of the Comtat Venaifin; calamities of that country, ii. 180.

Pofen, infurrection of the Poles near this place, which forces the King of Pruffia to raife the fiege of Warfaw, iii. 155.

Potemkin, (Prince,) his views on Courland, i. 46. He affembles an army of an hundred thoufand men in the Ukraine and the Krimea, 49. His motives for inducing the Emprefs of Ruffia to make the journey to the Krimea, 51. Artifices which he ufed to deceive her, 53. The deftitute ftate of the Ruffian army when the Turks declared war, ii. 11. His march to Otchakof, 12. Which he befieges and delivers up to pillage and maffacre, 29. Receives the magnificent order of St. George, his mediation offered by England and Pruffia, who had kindled this war, 30. His inconftancy in treaties, 31. His policy to conquer the Krimea; his progrefs in Turkey. Capture of Binder, 135.

Potocki, (Marfhal) he condemns the attacks on property in France, in a fpeech delivered in the Diet, ii. 191. Speech addreffed by him to it, for the purpofe of oppofing the fale of the Starofties. Error which he imputes to the National Affembly of France on the fale of the national effects, 356.

Potocki, Rzewoufky, Branitfky, &c. Polifh confederates at Targovitz for overturning the new Polifh conftitution under the protection of Ruffia, iii. 130.

Potocki, (Felix) he invites Ruffian troops into his country, and in vain flies to Peterfburg to implore the aid of Catherine II. againft the invafion of the Pruffians, with whom fhe was in league, iii. 142.

Prairial, (the day of firft) rifing of the fuburbs of St. Antoine; feditious mob befiege the Convention, kill the Deputy Ferand, and carry about his head in the Tuilleries. This commotion was excited by the decemviral party, whofe object was to refcue fome of their members from tranfportation, iii. 185.

Priefts,

Priests, abjuration of the greater part of them who sat in the Convention. Their scandalous declaration. New deities which they adopt in order to please the decemvirs, iii. 70.

Princes, (French) the forfeiture of their rights, and the sequestration of their property unless they return to France ; reasons and pretexts for disobedience to the King's letter and the decree of recal, ii. 216.

Prisons, the asylum of innocence, virtue, talents and beauty during the decemvirate, iii. 103. Conspiracy in the prisons invented by Robespierre in order to deliver up to the scaffold the victims confined in them, iii. 110, *et seq.*

Proscriptions, (code of) or sequel of the massacres of September, ii. 273.

Provinces, (United) political formation of the States-General, i. 100. Origin of the difference of rights in the towns of the United Provinces, 101. Of how many votes they consisted. The principle of their destruction, 102. Deprived of their powers by William III. become Captain-general, 107. Mode of assessing and paying the troops in Holland, 171. insufficiency of the troops devoted to the Stadtholder. Neutrality of the Swiss regiments, and superiority of the States, 184, *et seq.* Singular situation of the States-General, 188. Serious error in the vote of Utrecht, 189. Defects in their military constitution, 223. Suspension of General Van-Ryssel. Order to disobey the commands of the States of Holland, 373. Danger of an almost general defection, *ib.* and of a total schism, 293. Plan for giving the Patriots a decided superiority in the States General, 293. It is moved in favour of the Province of Holland. Abrogation of the preceding measures, 377. Absurdities and irregularities of the States, 378. Defection of the troops, 379. Zeal and courage of the citizens to supply the deficiency, *ib.* Number of parties into which they were divided in 1787. Error of the Patriotic party, 383. Plan of the States for giving a verbal answer to the complaints of the princess of

Orange,

Orange, and for separating her interests from those of her husband, 404. Proposals made to them to submit the differences which divided the United Provinces to the mediation of France, 412. Division of opinions of the Provinces on this mediation, 414. Prussia and England also offer their's; inconvenience of this offer, 427. Alliance of the Provinces with England and Prussia, 428.

Prussia, (the Duchy of) passes from the Kings of Poland to the house of Brandenburg. People who succeffively inhabit that country. The Poles possess themselves of the cities of Thorn, Dantzic, and a great part of Prussia, i. xxv. Finances; their valuation, 40. Savings of Frederic the Great, *ib.*

Prussian Ministers, bold letter written by them to the King, i. 40.

Prussians, causes which have had an influence on their character, i. xix.

Public opinion, serves as a counterpoise to arbitrary power in France, and ultimately overthrows it, ii. 65. It's influence on the last three centuries, 66.

Pugatscheff, the rebel whose success and rapid march towards Moscow alarms the Empress of Russia, ii. 292.

Q

QUEEN of France, (Maria Antoinette) in danger of being affassinated on the night of the 5th October, ii. 103. Answer which she gave to la Fayette's Aid-du-Camp, 244. The object of calumny, and she is given up to the revolutionary tribunal. Her fortitude in going to death, iii. 67.

Quiberon, descent of the Emigrants on the coast of France; cruelties towards them, of which History furnishes but few examples, iii. 209.

R

RAINNEVAL, sent from France to Holland. His mediation is

is rejected through the influence of the English Minister over the princess of Orange, i. 81.

Ratisbon, (Diet of) receives the complaints of the German Princes, whom the Constituent Assembly had deprived of their rights in Alsace. A pretext with which the Kings disguise their schemes against the independance of France, ii. 169.

Raynal, (the Abbé) endeavours used by the King of Prussia, Frederic William II. in order to retain him at Berlin, i. 24.

Razamowsky, (Count) Russian minister in Sweden, furnishes Gustavus III. a pretext for declaring war against Catherine II. Singularity of this pretext, ii. 21. The disturbances which he was accused of fomenting in Sweden occasions his recal, and Gustavus demands that he be punished, 294, *et seq.*

Reede, the Dutch Minister at the court of Berlin, announces to the States the speedy invasion of Holland, i. 412.

Refractory priests, a term invented by the Legislative Assembly for the purpose of proscribing whole classes of citizens in mass, ii. 202.

Refugees, (French) happy changes which they introduce into Brandenburg. Advantages which resulted from their mixture with the natives of the country, i. xix.

Regents. Artifice of the Stadtholderian regents for annulling all influence of the people, i. 196.

Reichenback, conferences at. Interests which were there discussed, to prevent an approaching rupture betwixt the courts of Vienna and Berlin. Cause of the general peace in order to turn the forces of the powers of Europe against France, ii. 163, *et seq.* Convention signed there, 166. It's inference on the other powers, 167.

Repnin, (Prince) defeats the Grand Vizier Yusuph, ii. 175.

Republican party, discovered itself for the first time on the escape of the King. Weakness and indecision of this party, ii. 128. Fired on at the *Champ de Mars*, 130.

Republicans,

Republicans, at the commencement of the war, weak in number and far from foreseeing their triumphs, ii. 233.

Republic, (French) it's establishment in the first sitting of the Convention, ii. 275.

Requisition, a mean employed under the revolutionary government for the support of the numerous armies of the Republic, iii. 68.

Resumption, a necessary formality to give the force of law to a resolution of the States General, i. 257.

Revolution, (the French) the work of all, and complained of by all, ii. 74. By whom predicted, 75. Facility of predicting disasters, 76. Opinion which prevailed concerning it in France and elsewhere, 90. It's object in 1789 the reform of abuses. The court and the two higher orders the only losers, iii. 49. It's aim in 1792 an equality too absolute. Force and fear it's means; the fall of the throne and the death of the King for it's objects, 50. After the 31st of May the spoliation and the extermination of all proprietors; atrocity and terror for it's means, 52.

Revolutionary clubs and committees, their singular questions to candidates and petitioners, iii. 71.

Revolutionary government, the master piece of the power of Robespierre, Danton, Marat, Collot d'Herbois, Billaud and Cauthon, iii. 53. Intrusted to twelve deputies, 54. It's terrible energy and it's prodigious resources, 56. Deplorable state of France under that government, *ib*. Horrible spoliations, imprisonments, arbitrary judgments, 58. Horrible admiration inspired by it's success, and it's means of terror internally and externally, 66.

Revolutions, their principal causes, i. 70.

Richlieu, (Cardinal) gives the final blow to feudal anarchy, ii. 65.

Rietz, (Madame de) mistress of the King of Prussia, and celebrated for the irregularity of her manners, i. 37. Arrested, after the death of the King of Prussia, by his successor,

cessor as were also those persons who had abused his weakness, iii. 226.

Rivarol, his opinion on the day and the massacres of the 6th of October, ii. 104.

Robespierre, instigation of the massacres of September, ii. 265. His motive for making the King suffer on the scaffold, rather than get rid of him secretly, iii. 4. He compels Danton to retire from the Committee of Public Safety. He is generally considered as the head of the tyranny. His character, 62. Cause of his perfect moral resemblance of the populace, 64. Fear his divinity. It is to avoid being sacrificed, that he sacrifices all those whom he dreads, 65. His tactics, *ib.* He delivers up the Queen of France and the Duke of Orleans to the revolutionary tribunal, 67. He basely betrays his friend Camille Desmoulins, and sends him to execution, 109. He gives up Danton, Fabre d'Eglantine, Chabot, and other bold deputies to the revolutionary tribunal, and from thence to the scaffold, 110. Picture of his tyranny after the pretended assassination, of which Renaud, a young girl, was suspected, iii. 111. His motives for instituting a festival in honour of the Supreme Being, 112. Conspiracy of nine of his colleagues who, to prevent their own destruction, swear to accomplish his, 113. He complains in the tribune of the calumnies spread against him. His violent harangue on the situation of the Republic, 114. Accused in his turn, he is obliged, for the first time to justify himself, 115. The day after the 9th Thermidor, his accusation is decreed, arrested at the Hotel de Ville where he had taken refuge amongst his accomplices, and perishes on the scaffold with that Commune on the 10th of August, 116, *et seq.*

Rochambeau, he complains of the intrigues contrived for the disorganization of the army, and the failure of the plan of it's invasion of the Low Countries, ii. 238. He rallies the fugitives at the attack of Mons, 239. Disgusted with

with the intrigues employed against him, he resigns his command, 240.

Rochefoucault, during the massacres of September is murdered in Normandy, ii. 274.

Rohan, elected Bishop of Liege, ii. 153. Dismissed, 172.

Roland, the Minister sent with Claviere and Servan, ii. 240. The pernicious effect produced by the publication of the letter which he wrote to Louis XVI. 245. The only Frenchman who had the courage to denounce in the Legislative Assembly the massacres of September, 269.

Romantzof, (Marshal) his displeasure with Potemkin, and his complaints to the Empress of Russia, i. 53. His march against Rhotgim. State of his army, ii. 12.

Roone, (Count) warm defender of the Stadtholderian party, i. 210. Address to him by the Grand Pensionary, 211.

Rosenberg, (the Prince de) affected by the virtues of Madame de la Fayette, obtains for her and her daughters an audience of the Emperor, iii. 251.

Rotterdam, revolution in the regency of that city, i. 207.

Royalists, absolute, a faction feeble in number; and whose power was external, ii. 233.

Royalty, it's abolition in one of the pretended sittings of the Convention, ii. 275.

Ryssel, (Van) suspended from his functions of General, prohibition to obey him, i. 273.

Rzewuski, Polish confederate, one of the authors of the ruin of his country. After the combined invasion of the Russians and the Prussians, he is exiled into Gallicia, iii. 142.

S.

SAINTE CROIX, sent to Trèves to induce the powers not to meddle in the affairs of France, and to stop the arming of the emigrants, ii. 207. Vague promises given him by the Elector, 210.

Saint Domingo, cession on the part of Spain to the French Republic

Republic, by the treaty of peace signed at Basle, iii. 218. The English driven from that island, 223.

Sante Menehould, the French camp whence General Dumouriez prevents the enemy from penetrating farther into Champagne, ii. 280. Respective force of the two armies, *ib.*

Saint Priest, (Count) his letter to the Marquis de la Fayette on the affairs of Holland, i. 435.

Salm, (the Rhingrave of) his character, his perfidy towards the French and the Dutch, i. 87. He shamefully abandons the city of Utrecht, 95. His ambition, 246. His duplicity, 248. His treachery, *ib.* His disgrace, 249.

Savoy, conquered by Montesquiou, iii. 17. Requests to be united with France, 18.

Saxony, (the Elector of) his daughter offered the succession to the throne of Stanislaus Augustus which the Poles in Diet had rendered hereditary, ii. 192.

Saxe-Teschen, (the Duke of) refuses passports to la Fayette, Maubourg, and Bureau de Puzy, arrested at an Austrian post, iii. 275.

Schlieffen, letter from this Prussian General to General la Fayette, in order to ascertain whether France has any other intentions respecting the Low Countries but their independence, ii. 309.

Schonfeld, a Prussian General who commands the Brabant insurgents, ii. 151.

Sections, arsenal and magazine for denunciations under Robespierre, iii. 59.

Ségur, (Marshal de) the ineffectual request which he renews to each council for the formation of a camp at Givet, i. 94.

Ségur, French Minister at Petersburg; he signs a treaty of commerce betwixt Russia and France, 148. His representations to the Emperor Joseph on the interest which France takes in the preservation of the Ottoman Empire, 56. He concerts in the Krimea with the Minister Bulgakof and the Austrian internuncio, Herbert, to prevent a rupture
betwixt

betwixt Ruſſia and the Porte, 57. He refuſes the miniſtry, ii. 203. Sent to Berlin to engage the powers not to intermeddle in the internal affairs of France, and to ſtop the arming of the Emigrants, 207. Diſpoſitions of the King of Pruſſia for declaring war, 212. Tranſient ſucceſs of this negociation, 214.

September, (the 2nd and 3rd of) days rendered odious by the maſſacres of Paris. Their inſtigation, ii. 265. Their pretext, 266. Meaſures concerted for ſeizing the victims, 267. Reports circulated in order to ſtifle every ſentiment of pity in the people, 268, *et ſeq.*

Servan, the Committee of Public Safety give him powers to treat with the Spaniſh miniſter on the frontiers of the Pyrenees, iii. 218.

Sevaſtopol, the place where the Ruſſian, Auſtrian and French miniſters concerted meaſures for conciliating the differences between the Ruſſians and the Porte, i. 59.

Sigiſmund, the laſt of the family of the Jagellons, after him was extinguiſhed the conſtitution which Caſimir the Great had given to Poland, iii. 126.

Sigiſmund, (John) Elector of Brandenburg. To his inheritance of Pruſſia he pretended to unite that of Juliers, Cleves, Lamarck, &c. The houſe of Neuburg diſputed this ſucceſſion with him. War on this account, and the blow given by Sigiſmund to his competitor, i. xx.

Siſtovia, city where peace was concluded betwixt the Ruſſians and the Turks, ii. 178.

Sievers, Catherine II. orders him to concert with Bucholz, the Pruſſian miniſter, on the means of regulating the diviſion of Poland, iii. 140. This General ſurrounds the Caſtle of Grodno with artillery, where the Poliſh confederates ſat in deliberation, and thus extorted the conſent of the Diet to the diſmemberment, 141.

Sluices, the States of Holland order the great ſluice of Minden to be opened, in order to ſtop the progreſs of the Duke of Brunſwick, i 244.

Societies, (popular) their eſtabliſhment in the principal towns of the United Provinces. Their zeal, their orators, their deputations, and their political errors, i. 386.

Soignes, (forrest of) Prince Cobourg loses seven thousand men there in attempting to arrest the progress of Jourdan's victorious army, iii. 96.

Sombreuil, (Mademoiselle de) her filial piety, iii. 106.

Spain, is menaced by England: but in consequence of the councils and threatening attitude of France, her ally, she avoids this war, and restores the ships which she had taken, ii. 178. The King in vain sollicits in favour of Louis XVI. He enters into the coalition, iii. 20. Defeated at Saint Jean de Luz, at Figuieres, and at Trun, iii. 97. The injustice which she experiences from England determines her on peace, 101. Apparent motives of that court for continuing war against the Republic. Her true interests in making peace, 204. Threatened with total ruin, 205. The Spanish Ministry found the disposition of the Committee of Public Safety, rapid negociations and conclusion of peace without the knowledge of England, 209. Apprehensions of the court of Madrid on the continuation of war; public prayers throughout all the kingdom, honours conferred on the minister who obtains a peace, 217.

Spengler, expedition of that General against Hattem and Elbourg, i. 175.

Spiegel, (Vander) Grand Pensionary of Zealand; of the Orange party at Middleburg, i. 396.

Spielman, an able Austrian negociator, one of the authors of the dismissal of the minister Hertzberg. He reconciles and unites the courts of Vienna and Berlin, ii. 160.

Sprengporten, Swedish general officer, who had fled into Russia. He raises an army against Gustavus, ii. 27.

Stadtholder, the policy of the Stadtholders to extend their power, i. 105. Their prerogatives, 106. Title of Captain General conferred on him, *ib.* Prerogatives attached to it, *ib.*

Stadtholderate, its abolition and re-establishment principal cause of the troubles, 68. It's interruption and renewal, 112. The

The command of the armed force at the Hague is separated from it. This is the first blow struck against the abuses of that dignity. First cause of the intervention of the cabinet of Berlin in the affairs of Holland, and one of the causes of the civil war, 148, *et seq.* Suppression of other abuses, 154. Another attempt against the abuses of the Stadtholderate, 162. Advantage of the Stadtholderian party and it's adherents, 163.

Stadtholderian, or Northern Gate, privileges, whose abolition brought on the revolution in Holland, i. 76. Remarkable incident which took place in the revolution of 1787, as to passing through this gate, 116.

Stael, baron sent by the Regent of Sweden, in the name of his nephew, to present to the French nation assurances of the friendship which the court of Stockholm entertains towards them, iii. 103.

Stanislaus Augustus, King of Poland. His interview with the Emperor Joseph and the Empress of Russia, i. 49. His character, 39. He allows himself to be opposed to Russia by the reigning spirit of the Diet, ii. 39. Congratulations which he receives from the crowned heads on the constitutions given to Poland, 191. He implores succours from the King of Prussia, and in vain insists on the treaty which should secure them to him, 230. Threatened and deceived by the Empress of Russia, in his turn deceives the hopes of the Poles, who pass under a foreign yoke, 231. His letter to the King of Prussia on the sentiments of justice and amity which the Poles expect from him, 293. He claims the succours stipulated by the King of Prussia in the treaty of alliance of 1790 against the arms of Russia; evasive and dishonest answer of Frederic William, iii. 131. French revolution the indirect cause of the ruin of Poland, 133. He suffers himself to be deceived by the Empress, and thus paralizes the courage of the army, *ib.* He commands it to lay down it's arms. Deceived by Catherine, he merits the misfortunes with which he is afterwards loaded. He accedes to the confederation

deration of Targovitz, and allows the Russians to enter Warsaw, 134. He acquiesces in the dismemberment of Poland at the Diet of Grodno, 142. Delivered from the Russians, whom he had favoured through weakness, he remains after their expulsion from Warsaw without any kind of authority or confidence, 152. Catherine II. commands him to quit Warsaw, and to repair to Grodno, whence he is ordered into Russia, 162. He survives but a short time his fall from his throne and the humiliation of his country. His replies to the notes of the courts of Berlin and Petersburg, *ib*. He declares that he had only acceded to the confederation of Targovitz in order to preserve the integrity of the territory of the Polish republic, 249.

Sudermania, (the Duke of) brother of Gustavus III. Reputation which he acquired in the first sea-fight of this war against the Russians, ii. 26. Become regent of Sweden, he commutes the punishment of death into exile of the assassins of the King, his brother, 226. Motives which induced him to preserve neutrality betwixt France and the coalesced powers, *ib*.

Sulchowsky, privilege which he caused to be granted to the Polish citizens, ii. 188.

Suvarof, (General) takes Ismael by assault; where fifteen thousand men are massacred, ii. 176. His victories in Poland, at Chelm, at Brzesk, at Warsaw. His cruelties in that city, iii. 161.

Sweden. Note of the Charge d'Affaires of Sweden in Russia. This document contains the grievances of Gustavus against that court, and he demands their redress by an affirmative or a negative, ii. 291.

Syeyes, prodigious popularity which he acquired, ii. 81.

Syrakowsky, state of his army for opposing the march of Suvarof into Poland, iii. 157. Compleatly defeated at Brzesk, 170.

Szczekocin, battle at, gained by the King of Prussia in person over General Kosciosko, iii. 194.

TALLIEN,

T.

TALLIEN, one of the deputies, who, on the 9th Thermidor, spoke with the greatest vehemence and success against Robespierre, iii. 113.

Targovitz, city of, where several nobles leagued against the constitution which the Diet had instituted in 1791. Leaders of the confederacy, iii. 130. They, as well as the other Poles, are deceived by the two courts who regulated their plan of partition, 140. They declare their will even to the confederacy, which they accuse of ingratitude and rebellion, *ib.*

Tennis court, became celebrated by the oath of the deputies who took refuge there, ii. 83.

Ternant, (M. de) a French officer who defended the city of Amsterdam against the Duke of Brunswick, i. 96. The defence of Over-yssel is also entrusted to him, 382. Capture of Forte Ommerskans, *ib.* His character and talents. 421. Obstacles which he experiences, *ib.* His escape, *ib.*

Tervere, commotions and massacres at, by the populace in favour of the Prince of Orange, i. 356.

Teschen, Duke of Saxe, defeated by the insurgents in Flanders and Brabant, ii. 142.

Thermidor, (the 9th of) the day on which the conspiracy against Robespierre burst forth and put an end to his tyranny. It's authors, iii. 113. Proposal of Barrere which would have perpetuated the same system of cruelty had it not been rejected, 120.

Third Estate, advantage granted to it. Chief cause of the revolution, ii. 81.

Thulemeyer, demands in the name of the King of Prussia, reparation for the outrage offered to the Princess of Orange, i. 91. His threats and demands on the Dutch, *ib.* He addresses the complaints of the King of Prussia to the States General, 406. conference between that minister and the States General, 407. In answer to their memorial, he announces the march of an army: he communicates it to the French Ambassador. Motives of the court of Berlin

lin, 411. He notifies the intentions of the King of Prussia to the States, with a menace of invading their territory, unless they shall be fulfilled in four days, i. 239.

Toulon, taken by the English. Extraordinary army landed there, iii. 78. Recapture of that city. Burning of the ships and magazines, *ib.* Cruelty of the English almost equal to that of the decemvirs, 79.

Tournay, the French army twice give battle to the coalesced Princes near that place, and obtain the victory, iii. 94.

Treaty of peace betwixt Russia and Sweden, ii. 318. Gustavus III. and Catherine II. forget the motives which had determined them to declare war. By the treaty of Varela, they re-establish all the relations which subsisted betwixt the two powers before the rupture; Gustavus to employ himself in the French revolution, and Catherine to avenge herself on the Poles, *ib. et seq.* Betwixt France and Prussia, iii. 254. Betwixt France and Spain, 264. Betwixt France and the Landgrave of Hesse-Cassel, 271.

Treves, (the Elector of) intreated by Louis XVI. to desist from arming the Emigrants, ii. 207. His evasive answer, advice given him by Leopold, 211.

Trial of the King, crimes of which he is accused, iii. 7, 8. Infallible means of saving him, which were supported by only five deputies, 9. First error of the party which would not vote for his death, *ib.*

Tribunal, (revolutionary) fatal institution of, which covered France with revolutionary committees, revolutionary armies, bastilles and executioners, iii. 58. Victims whom it sacrificed to the tyranny of the decemvirs, 66.

Tronchet, the defender of Louis XVI. iii. 11.

Troppau, able conduct of the Duke of Brunswick in maintaining himself in this port without check, i. 33.

Tuilleries, (the palace of) besieged and taken. Preparation for it's defence and attack, ii. 241. Disposition of minds in the legislative assembly, 243. Dreadful expression of one of the conspirators, 250.

Turkey,

INDEX.   359

Turkey, her preparations for war against the Emperor and
  the Emprefs of Ruffia, i. 50. The Divan confines the
  Ruffian Ambaffador in the prifon of the feven towns, 61.

                           U

UTRECHT, revolution in that city. Petition of the citizens
  against the law of 1674. Another attempt to reform the
  abufes of the Stadtholderate, i. 161. Suppreffion of thirty
  magiftrates, 164. Retreat of the equeftrian order and
  the clergy to Ammersfort. Defective constitution of the
  province of Utrecht, 165. It's preparations for defence
  against the Stadtholder, 247. Abandoned by the treachery
  of the Ringrave of Salm, 248.

                           V

VALENCE, (General) takes Namur, iii. 18. He diftinguifhes
  himfelf, and is wounded at the battle of Nerwinde. He
  is defeated at Liege, and lofes four thoufand men, 32. After the defection of Dumouriez, he takes refuge in a
  neutral country, 40.
Valenciennes, fiege and capture of, iii. 42.
Valmies, (the heights of) where the Duke of Brunfwick attacked the French and was repulfed, ii. 287.
Vandermerfch, leader of the popular faction in the revolution
  in Brabant. His arreft. Troubles refulting from it,
  ii. 145.
Vander-Noot, author of the infurrection of Flanders and
  Brabant, ii. 142.
Van-Eupen, one of the authors of the revolution in Flanders
  and Brabant, ii. 142.
Varela, the city where the preliminaries of peace betwixt
  Guftavus III. and Catherine II. were figned. This treaty
  furprized the Anglo-Pruffian league, and difconcerted it's
  views, ii. 167.
Varennes, the place where Louis XVI. when a fugitive was
  arrefted, ii. 128.
Vendee, (rebels of) fyftem of the coalition in regard to that
                                                    unhappy

unhappy country, iii. 74. Situation of the Royalists. Their number. Their defeats, 89. Why the revolt did not extend to the large cities, 90.

Vendeans, (the) abandoned by England to their own efforts, iii. 209.

Vendemaire, (the 13th of) insurrection of the sections of Paris against the Convention. Cause of this insurrection. What were it's consequences, 202, *et seq*.

Vengeur, (the Ship) foundered fighting against Admiral Lord Howe. The English struck with horror and admiration at hearing the cry of *Vive la Republique!* repeated by the whole crew as they were sinking into the deep, iii. 98.

Verdun, second town in France which yielded to the King of Prussia according to a shameful capitulation, ii. 267.

Vergennes, (the Count de) instructions which he gave to the Ambassadors of France against the interests of the House of Austria, i. 33. One of his most political and important operations, 141.

Verniaud, denounces in the Convention the circular letter of the Commune, tending to provoke murders similar to those of September at Paris, in the departments, ii. 272.

Versailles, the prisoners at Orleans brought to, and murdered in that city by the assassins of the *Commune* of Paris, ii. 273.

Veto, Illusion of this prerogative, ii. 120.

Voss, (Mademoiselle de) sacrifice which she makes to the glory of her lover, the King of Prussia, i. 73.

W.

WALCHEREN, (the isle of) the commotion excited there by the populace of the Orange party, i. 397.

Warsaw, during the combined tyranny of the Russians and Prussians in Poland, a club of four persons formed a conspiracy which extended rapidly over all the country. Kosciosko becomes it's chief, iii. 146. The Russians are defeated

defeated after a battle of forty-eight hours and the loss of six thousand men, 150. Disorders occasioned by the populace who hang several Poles whom they believe attached to Prussia and Russia, 162. Memorable siege of that city. Raising of the siege and retreat of the King of Prussia, *ib.* Illumination of all the streets to celebrate the birth-day of Kosciosko, then a prisoner in Russia, 172. Murderous assault of one of it's suburbs, in which nine thousand Poles perished. Capture of this city by Suvarof, and cruelty of the Russians who destroyed thirty thousand victims, 161.

Wassenaer-Starembourg, a creature of the Stadtholder; sent to Petersburg for the accession of Holland to the armed neutrality, i. 123. Delays and pretexts prescribed by the Stadtholder, 124.

Weissembourg, (lines of) battle where the French lost fifteen thousand men, iii. 57.

Welners, a courtier at Berlin, and one of the sect of the *Illuminati,* i. 38.

Wesel, assembling there of twenty thousand Prussians for the invasion of Holland, i. 412.

Weyman, (the Duke of) of the sect of the *Illuminati,* and a courtier of the King of Prussia, i. 38.

William III. Prince of Orange, deprives three of the United Provinces of the right of election. His usurpations the source of the divisions which have agitated those provinces, i. 68. Other encroachments of power, 107.

William IV. The stadtholderate declared hereditary in his family, with an extension of rights and powers, i. 69, 112.

William V. Prince of Orange, his character, i. 69. His ambition dictates a conduct pernicious to his country, 71. During the American war he is forced, contrary to his inclinations, to unite with the French whom he detested 73. His base and perfidious conduct during that war, 74. Abuses of power the signal for civil war, 78. He rejects the pacific proposals of the States General, 83. He is

declared

declared to have lost the confidence of the States, 90. He recovers all his power, 95. His connivance with the cabinet of St. James's in the American war, 127. Measures adopted to render the fleet useless, and to procure the defeat of the veteran Admiral Zoutman, 137. His regret on the news of the victory, 139. Author of a commotion at the Hague, 145. An event which leads to the first intervention of the court of Berlin, 148. Origin of the troubles and the civil war, ib. Threat to the States of Holland, 148. First blow given to the abused prerogatives of the Stadtholderate, 152. Authority of that Prince in Gueldres, 167. He marches troops against the small towns of Hattem and Elbourg, 169. Ridiculous excuse of this Prince. Provisional suspension of his functions of Captain-General, 177. He renders the sovereignty of the Province of Holland problematical, 187. Obstinate blindness of this Prince, 194. Number of couriers which he dispatches in one day. Orders his troops to march against Utrecht, 216. Public indignation excited by his manifesto, 259. His complaints to the States on the supposed affront offered to the Princess. Measures adopted on this subject, 403. Triumphant entry of the Prince into the Hague. The commotions renewed, 416. The Stadtholder is re-instated, 417. Ironical resolution respecting France, ib. He causes himself to be invested with dictatorial power, but which only renders his fall more rapid. He becomes the object of profound aversion; opposes peace lest he should lose his power. He is compelled to fly with his family to England, iii. 169, *et seq.*

Wilna, recapture of that city from the Russians by Janinsky, the Polish General, iii. 151.

Woerden, prohibition by the sovereign commission of that city against the Princess of Orange, i. 392.

Woiwodes, title given to the nobles of Poland who governed under the supreme power of the King, iii. 126.

Wraclawice, first victory which the Polish insurgents obtain over

over the Russians, under the command of Kosciosko, iii. 160.

Wraschesky, is appointed to the chief command, after the capture of Kosciosko, iii. 166.

Wurtemburg, (the Prince of) of the sect of the Illuminati courtier of the King of Prussia, i. 38.

Y

York, (Duke of) compleatly defeated before Dunkirk, iii. 77. Defeated near Tournay, he owes his safety to the swiftness of his horse, 95. Retreat of his army, destitute of every thing.——He leaves the command to Walmoden, and retires dissatisfied with the Allies and the Dutch, whom he could not defend against Pichegru, 168. The army pursued to Bremen, embarks in order to return to England, 171.

Yranda, (the Marquis d') sent by the court of Madrid to the Pyrenees to treat respecting peace with General Servan, iii. 218.

Yriarte, Spanish Minister for negociating peace with the French Republic, iii. 210. Obliged to depart from Warsaw, where he was Minister, 217. Incident which retards the negociation with which he was charged, 218. He signs the treaty of peace, 219. His death interrupts the treaty of alliance negociated betwixt France and Spain, 220.

Yusuph Pacha, successor of the unfortunate Hasan, defeated by Repnin the Russian General, ii. 173.

Z

ZAMOISKI, obtains for each Noble the right of electing the King of Poland : this becomes the source of oppression and slavery to which the peasants were reduced, iii. 127.

Zayontchik, state of his army for the defence of Galicia against the Austrians and the Russians, iii. 157. Defeated by the latter at Chelm, 160.

Zealand, troubles, pillage and massacres produced by the Orange party there, i. 395.

Zoutman, His heroism, and victory in the sea fight off the Dogger Bank, where the English were defeated, i. 137.

Zutphin, pillage and devastation of that city by the soldiers of the Prince of Orange, i. 394.

END OF THE INDEX.

ERRATA.

Page Line
31, 20, After *of* add *General of the*.
41, 4, After *Spain* add *at Antwerp*.
46, 21, After *deputies*, instead of a comma make a period.
—, 23, After *Mountain*, instead of a period make a comma.
79, 28, For *Marat* read *Maret*.
81, 9, Dele the *were* before *crowded*.
—, 12, After *all* add *these*.
109, 13, For *Les* read *Le*.
132, 5, For *complexion* read *completion*.
177, 7, Dele *and*.

[M. Baldwin and Son, Printers, New Bridge-street, London.]

Check Out More Titles From HardPress Classics Series In this collection we are offering thousands of classic and hard to find books. This series spans a vast array of subjects – so you are bound to find something of interest to enjoy reading and learning about.

Subjects:
Architecture
Art
Biography & Autobiography
Body, Mind &Spirit
Children & Young Adult
Dramas
Education
Fiction
History
Language Arts & Disciplines
Law
Literary Collections
Music
Poetry
Psychology
Science
…and many more.

Visit us at www.hardpress.net

personalised classic books

UNIQUE GIFT

FOR KIDS, PARTNERS AND FRIENDS

"Beautiful gift.. lovely finish. My Niece loves it, so precious!"

Helen R Brumfieldon

★★★★★

Timeless books such as:

Kids

Alice in Wonderland · The Jungle Book · The Wonderful Wizard of Oz
Peter and Wendy · Robin Hood · The Prince and The Pauper
The Railway Children · Treasure Island · A Christmas Carol

Adults

Romeo and Juliet · Dracula

Highly Customizable · **Change** Books Title · **Replace** Characters Names with yours · **Upload** photos for inside pages · **Add** Inscriptions

Visit ImTheStory.com
and order yours today!

CPSIA information can be obtained
at www.ICGtesting.com
Printed in the USA
BVHW091457260819
556817BV00020B/2842/P